THE BEDFORD SERIES IN HISTORY AND CULTURE

France and the Dreyfus Affair

A Documentary History

Michael Burns

Mount Holyoke College

BEDFORD/ST. MARTIN'S   Boston   ♦   New York

For Bedford/St. Martin's

History Editor: Katherine E. Kurzman
Developmental Editor: Louise Townsend
Editorial Assistant: Molly Kalkstein
Production Supervisor: Joe Ford
Marketing Manager: Charles Cavaliere
Project Management: Books By Design, Inc.
Text Design: Claire Seng-Niemoeller
Index: Books By Design, Inc.
Cover Design: Donna Dennison
Cover Photo: Jewish Museum/Art Resource, NY
Composition: ComCom, an R. R. Donnelley & Sons Company
Printing and Binding: Haddon Craftsmen, an R. R. Donnelley & Sons Company

President: Charles H. Christensen
Editorial Director: Joan E. Feinberg
Director of Editing, Design, and Production: Marcia Cohen
Manager, Publishing Services: Emily Berleth

Library of Congress Control Number: 98-86157

Manufactured in the United States of America.

7
f

For information, write: Bedford/St. Martin's, 75 Arlington Street, Boston, MA 02116 (617-399-4000)

ISBN-10: 0-312-11167-3 (paperback)
        0-312-21813-3 (hardcover)
ISBN-13: 978-0-312-11167-0

Photo Credits

Page 23, The Beitler Family Foundation; page 35, Jewish Museum/Art Resource, NY; page 55, Michael Burns Private Collection; page 56, The Beitler Family Foundation; page 58, Jewish Museum/Art Resource, NY; page 63, Copyright: Collection Roger-Viollet; page 69, Used by Courtesy of Simone Perl, Copyright 1998; page 103, The Beitler Family Foundation and Beinecke Rare Book and Manuscript Library, Yale University; page 108, Bibliotheque Nationale de France, Paris; page 109, left, © PHOTOTHEQUE des Musées de laVille de Paris; page 109, right, © PHOTOTHEQUE des Musées de la Ville de Paris; page 143, Copyright: Collection Roger-Viollet; page 166, Michael Burns Private Collection; page 179, Jewish Museum/Art Resource, NY; page 181, The Museum of Modern Art/Film Stills Archive; page 182, AP/Wide World Photos.

IN MEMORIAM

France Reinach Beck

Foreword

The Bedford Series in History and Culture is designed so that readers can study the past as historians do.

The historian's first task is finding the evidence. Documents, letters, memoirs, interviews, pictures, movies, novels, or poems can provide facts and clues. Then the historian questions and compares the sources. There is more to do than in a courtroom, for hearsay evidence is welcome, and the historian is usually looking for answers beyond act and motive. Different views of an event may be as important as a single verdict. How a story is told may yield as much information as what it says.

Along the way the historian seeks help from other historians and perhaps from specialists in other disciplines. Finally, it is time to write, to decide on an interpretation and how to arrange the evidence for readers.

Each book in this series contains an important historical document or group of documents, each document a witness from the past and open to interpretation in different ways. The documents are combined with some element of historical narrative—an introduction or a biographical essay, for example—that provides students with an analysis of the primary source material and important background information about the world in which it was produced.

Each book in the series focuses on a specific topic within a specific historical period. Each provides a basis for lively thought and discussion about several aspects of the topic and the historian's role. Each is short enough (and inexpensive enough) to be a reasonable one-week assignment in a college course. Whether as classroom or personal reading, each book in the series provides firsthand experience of the challenge—and fun—of discovering, recreating, and interpreting the past.

Lynn Hunt
David W. Blight
Bonnie G. Smith
Natalie Zemon Davis
Ernest R. May

Preface

In the summer of 1899, a British journalist scanned the globe and settled on a French Jew, an artillery officer wrongly accused of high treason, as "the most famous man in the world." The reporter was not alone. Captain Alfred Dreyfus had become "a man whose name everyone knows," a French writer remarked, "the most famous name since the death of . . . Napoleon." Newspapers and illustrated magazines, published in unprecedented numbers as the century turned, did the most to create that fame; they fueled passions and exploited tensions. But accounts of Dreyfus's court-martial, public degradation, exile to Devil's Island, and notorious retrial traveled along old networks as well. Peddlers, priests, rabbis, and migrant workers carried the news into villages, farmsteads, and ghettos. And when, after 1900, "the affair" faded from the headlines, the Dreyfus name held its resonance. A Russian poet, articulating the atrocities of the Second World War, looked back to the officer who had become a universal symbol of suffering and survival. "I imagine that I am / Dreyfus," wrote Yevgeny Yevtushenko. "Philistines prosecuting and judging me. / I am behind prison bars, / Trapped, / Harried to exhaustion, / spat upon, / traduced. / And fine ladies with flounces of Brussels lace, / Shrieking, poke their parasols in my face."[1]

This documentary history is designed to introduce the broad outlines and significant legacies of the Dreyfus affair, from the captain's arrest in 1894 to the 1998 centennial of "J'Accuse," Emile Zola's scathing indictment of the French military. "On all great subjects," noted the English historian Thomas Babington Macauley, "much remains to be said." The affair proves the point; its bibliography now surpasses twelve hundred

---

[1]G. W. Steevens, *The Tragedy of Dreyfus* (New York: Harper and Bros., 1899), 42; Charles Péguy, *Notre jeunesse* (Paris: Gallimard, 1993), 285; Yevgeny Yevtushenko, "Babi Yar," in *A Hero for Our Time,* Moshe Decter, ed. (New York: Academic Committee on Soviet Jewry, 1970), 37.

titles, and to the list must be added motion pictures, plays, poems, and an operatic trilogy. Given that vast reservoir of words and images, a brief documentary history places a high premium on selection. This volume, fashioned for a weeklong assignment in a college course, reproduces the affair's most celebrated texts, as well as less familiar, but no less telling, documents. Presented as a chronological narrative, it charts Captain Dreyfus's case as it unfolded in time, and summarizes the major issues and debates that have survived for the past century.

In the history of the Dreyfus affair lies the struggle between the individual and the state; between civilian government and military authority; between the politics of parliamentary institutions and the politics of the mob; between the belief—religious or secular—in a common humanity and the modern calculus of racism. Philosopher Hannah Arendt, examining the origins of totalitarianism and pointing to the emergence of anti-Semitism as a political weapon in late-nineteenth-century France, called the affair "a kind of dress rehearsal for the performance of our time." And more recently, critic George Steiner defined it as that "first moment in which nation, race, religion, receive much of the dynamic impulse they now have."[2]

But history is about more than foregleams and emblems. It is about people rooted in their moment and environment, and from that perspective the Dreyfus affair stands as a central event in the history of France's Third Republic. It also stands as evidence that the civil war unleashed by the Revolution of 1789 remained unresolved in the aftermath of its one hundredth anniversary. Those citizens who engaged the battle for or against Dreyfus fought with equal fervor for a common goal—for the glory of France. They divided not over patriotism, but over conflicting visions of what the nation was and ought to be, and over litmus tests of belonging. For Dreyfusards (as the captain's allies were called), the army and church represented bastions of reaction in a modern, secular state; for anti-Dreyfusards they stood as fortresses of stability in a nation plagued by social upheaval and threatened by enemies from without and within. While Dreyfus's supporters elevated the "duty to question" over the "duty to obey," his opponents revered the established order and defended a military weakened by scandal. Lines were often clearly drawn, but civil wars, even relatively bloodless ones, are never neat, and the

---

[2]Hannah Arendt, *The Origins of Totalitarianism* (New York: Harvest, 1973), 10; George Steiner, "Totem or Taboo," *Salmagundi* 89–90 (Fall 1990–Winter 1991): 385–98.

affair had exceptions to every rule. Not all Catholics, nationalists, and anti-Semites turned against Dreyfus; not all Jews, socialists, and anticlericals rallied to his side. Men and women full of courage, fear, talent, ambition, intolerance, and goodwill populated both camps, and they called on the history of the French Revolution—that sunburst of enlightenment for some, that long night of chaos for others—to justify their crusade.

The affair's catalytic force reached wide and deep. Austrian journalist Theodor Herzl had imagined the rebirth of Israel in the form of an autonomous state before witnessing the captain's public degradation, but crowds shouting "Death to the Jews" in the cradle of the Rights of Man gave sharp immediacy to Herzl's Zionist program. Although many French socialists had accepted the parliamentary system by the early 1890s, the affair broke the dogma of nonparticipation in bourgeois governments and brought the first socialist into a cabinet of the Third Republic. The separation of church and state, on the national agenda since 1789 and a major factor in what Dreyfusards defined as a battle against a reactionary past, finally became law in the affair's immediate wake. And if French intellectuals had long fought for social justice, the Dreyfus case signaled their organization as a political force. Battalions of writers, artists, and professors, down from the ivory tower and armed with petitions, joined the affair's avant-garde.

Finally, the Dreyfus case is inextricably linked with the history of modern journalism, political caricature, and motion pictures. In 1899 the first serial film (and, at fifteen minutes, one of the longest) recreated the case in front of painted backdrops in a Paris studio. From the grotesque cartoons of anti-Semites to the saccharine depictions of Dreyfusard warriors, hundreds of thousands of lithographs, sketches, woodcuts, and paintings put old traditions to modern use. But above all, both sides waged their key battles in print. Sweeping education reforms, instituted a generation earlier, expanded the literate population and provided Dreyfusards and anti-Dreyfusards with a massive audience to inform and mobilize. Scholars debate the extent to which the press is a "maker" rather than a "product of History," but there is little doubt that fin de siècle journalists, perfecting polemic as "the art of attack," helped condemn Dreyfus, and helped save him.[3]

More than one contemporary—the novelist Zola being the most

---

[3]Jean-Pierre Peter, "Dimensions de l'Affaire Dreyfus," *Annales: Economies, Sociétés, Civilisations* 16 (November–December 1961): 1141–67; Richard Griffiths, *The Use of Abuse: The Polemics of the Dreyfus Affair and Its Aftermath* (New York: Berg, 1991), 3.

celebrated among them—compared the Dreyfus case to a marathon play with many acts, countless intermissions, and a final curtain that never fell. Amidst all the intrigue, conflict, and timeless lessons, however, one of the captain's earliest allies captured the most important point of all: Dreyfus "is innocent," he wrote, "and that is something."[4]

ACKNOWLEDGMENTS

For the invitation to revisit the Dreyfus affair as a documentary history, I thank Natalie Zemon Davis, coeditor of the Bedford Series in History and Culture. Of the many colleagues who have been generous with their expertise and time, I am most grateful to Michael R. Marrus, Benjamin F. Martin, and Frances Malino, and to Eugen Weber who introduced me to Captain Dreyfus and the country he honored. Mario Martinus was a superb comrade on the bibliographical front, as were the librarians of Mount Holyoke College, Dartmouth, and the Boston Athenaeum. I thank Lorraine Beitler and members of the Dreyfus family for sharing illustrations and private papers, and the talented team at Bedford/St. Martin's—Katherine Kurzman, Niels Aaboe, Louise Townsend, Emily Berleth, Molly Kalkstein, Frederick T. Courtright, and Nancy Benjamin—for all their help and encouragement. Finally and most especially, I thank my wife, Elizabeth Kennan Burns, for the large and equal measures of insight and patience. This book is dedicated to the memory of France Reinach Beck, granddaughter of two Dreyfusards, Mathieu Dreyfus and Joseph Reinach, and an enthusiastic student of the affair's documentary history.

[4]Bernard Lazare, quoted in Péguy, *Notre jeunesse,* 286.

Contents

APPENDICES

1

The Epoch

Only in the wake of 1914–18, following the unprecedented slaughter of the First World War, did the French look back on the twilight of the nineteenth century and call it *belle*. In part their nostalgia rang true. After France's humiliating defeat in the 1870 Franco-Prussian War, relative peace reigned among the great European powers, and although imperial rivalries threatened new conflicts, the full-scale wars of the fin de siècle erupted in distant lands—on East Asian peninsulas, on Pacific and Caribbean islands, and along the southern tip of Africa. Robust economic development, a hallmark of Napoleon III's Second French Empire at mid-century, continued for at least a dozen years following the proclamation of the Third Republic in 1870; France paid war reparations to Germany with a lightning speed it had lacked on the battlefields of Alsace and Lorraine; and French banks—financing sultans and czars abroad and manufacturers and peasants at home—soon ranked among the world's premier institutions. The Second Empire's golden age of cultural achievement, crowned by the rebuilding of Paris, also endured under the new republic, with the completion of the capital's grand opera house and *grands boulevards*. Academic and avant-garde artists depicted the layers of leisure at racetracks in the Bois de Boulogne, at boating parties along the Seine, and at the World's Fair of 1889, where Gustave Eiffel's controversial tower punctuated the centennial of the great Revolution. Paris earned its reputation as the "capital of the nineteenth century."[1]

And yet, from the birth of the Third Republic to the height of the Dreyfus affair, the nation was at war with itself. In 1870–71, during its

---

[1]The phrase "Paris, capital of the nineteenth century," like "la belle époque," dates from the post–World War I period; see Walter Benjamin, *Reflections: Essays, Aphorisms, Autobiographical Writings,* trans. Edmund Jephcott (New York: Harcourt Brace Jovanovich, 1978), 146–62.

first winter and spring, France's provisional government negotiated with Germans and battled Parisians. Shaped by a volatile mix of proletarian revolution, municipal rebellion, patriotic protest against German occupation, and random thuggery, the popular Parisian uprising known as the Commune—a name that conjured up the Revolution's Reign of Terror—ended in a bloody week of civil war in May 1871. French troops, invading from nearby Versailles, summarily executed at least twenty thousand Parisians and sent nearly double that number into prison and exile. Similar conflicts erupted in provincial cities from Lyons to Bordeaux. But if the Commune failed to realize its vision of an egalitarian republic, it left a powerful legacy: Socialists revered its memory, while conservatives, from monarchists to moderate republicans, feared its return. Aureole and specter, the Commune hovered across the century's end.[2]

By the slim majority of a single vote, the parliament finally embraced the republican constitution in 1875, and two years later pushed back the challenge of a president with royalist sympathies. The crisis of May 16 *(seize mai)* did not seal the fate of monarchism (the Orleanist and Bourbon dynasties continued to claim the throne), but it marked a victory for moderate republicans and signaled the decline of presidential power. Prime ministers and their cabinets, the leaders of government, were increasingly responsible for the design and execution of public policy, and the Chamber of Deputies, the parliament's lower house, became the central arena of French politics. By the 1880s, centrist republicans (dubbed Opportunists) faced more than royalist discontent. Competition from foreign imports, coupled with agricultural crisis, confirmed the unevenness of France's economic progress and brought new waves of popular protest. Socialist ranks swelled, and organized strikes escalated from barely one hundred in 1885 to more than six hundred on the eve of the Dreyfus affair in 1894.

While Opportunist governments came under increasing attack, an ambitious minister of war, General Georges Boulanger, presented himself as a populist savior. Dashing, bearded, and decorated for his military exploits, the general marched out of the cabinet (when the government changed in 1887) and into mass politics. Radicals applauded his defense of striking miners and pledge to democratize the army, while royalists

---

[2]On the Commune's legacy and the epoch that "was as beleaguered as it was *belle,*" see Susanna Barrows, *Distorting Mirrors: Visions of the Crowd in Late Nineteenth Century France* (New Haven: Yale University Press, 1981), 2 and passim.

and Bonapartists, circling for a last assault on the republic they detested, secretly filled his coffers and prayed for a coup d'état. In January 1889, on the night of Boulanger's stunning election to the Chamber of Deputies as a representative from Paris, supporters shouted *"A l'Elysée!"* as they urged *"Général Victoire"* to take the presidential palace. But when he wavered (Boulanger had more respect for the constitution than most of his followers), the government regrouped. Pursued by the courts for plotting to overthrow the state, the general followed his mistress to Belgium, where, after her death in 1891, he shot himself on her grave.

Part tragedy, part comic opera, boulangism, with its colorful parades, rallies, and flood of propaganda, signaled more than the Americanization of French politics. It hastened the political demise of old-style royalism and bonapartism and helped cultivate a new strain of militant nationalism adapted to the age of mass politics. One historian defines it as one of the "crucial mutations" that transformed the French right in the years leading up to the Dreyfus affair; another scholar situates it in the early genealogy of fascism. Competing with socialists for allies among the economically displaced, boulangists and other new nationalists mounted a social platform hostile to international ties and theories of class conflict. Through organizations such as the League of Patriots, a gymnastic society that weighed into politics, they called for the physical and moral regeneration of the fatherland and condemned the republic's bourgeois liberalism as feeble, divisive, and contaminated by enemies from without and within. Fascism may not have been born in the late nineteenth century, but many fascists were, and the epoch that stretched from Boulanger to the Dreyfus affair provided a training ground for their strategies and a hothouse for their prejudices.[3]

Like ships blundering between Scylla and Charybdis, the republic's moderate governments tried to steer a middle course between socialists and nationalists, while also under attack by anarchists, some of whom rallied to Boulanger, but most of whom pursued a freelance crusade for unbridled liberty. Before the 1880s, French anarchists, in contrast to

[3]See René Rémond, *The Right Wing in France from 1815 to de Gaulle,* trans. James M. Laux (Philadelphia: University of Pennsylvania Press, 1965), 205–32; Zeev Sternhell, *La Droite révolutionnaire, 1885–1914: Les Origines françaises du fascisme* (Paris: Seuil, 1978); and Patrick H. Hutton, "Popular Boulangism and the Advent of Mass Politics in France," *Journal of Contemporary History* 11 (1976): 85–106. Hannah Arendt also linked "the mobs" of the late nineteenth century, above all during the Dreyfus affair, to totalitarianism; see *The Origins of Totalitarianism* (New York: Harvest, 1973), 106–20.

their Russian counterparts, had rarely followed violent words with deadly deeds. They pondered the apocalypse in romantic tracts and proclaimed society "rotten," but they remained of little interest to the general public until "the bombs began to explode in a vicious crescendo of repression and revenge" and urban terrorism emerged in the cradle of the belle epoque.[4] During the dozen years following the 1882 trial of anarchists in Lyons, "propagandists of the deed" assaulted government officials, dynamited hotels and restaurants, and hurled a bomb from the gallery of the Chamber of Deputies. Eleven explosions rocked Paris between 1892 and 1894, and in Lyons, in the summer of 1894, a knife-wielding Italian anarchist, out to avenge his fallen French comrades, assassinated the president of the republic, Sadi Carnot. Ignoring protests from its left wing, the parliament finally outlawed the advocacy of anarchism in a series of *lois scélérates* (scoundrelly laws).

The repression worked, as it had in the aftermath of the Commune, but the virulence of political division in France survived in the expanding arenas of the written word and popular caricature—the arenas in which much of the civil war of the Dreyfus affair would be waged. Liberated by the press law of 1881, which rolled back many government restraints, a journalistic revolution swept across the fin de siècle. With literacy rates rising and new print technologies transforming the communications industry, hundreds of daily and weekly broadsheets and newspapers (led by *Le Petit Journal* at more than a million copies a day) reached a wide and eager audience of new readers, many of whom still believed, as they had been taught to believe, what they read. By the 1890s, circulation numbers were growing so rapidly that wholesale paper dealers required an additional one hundred tons of raw stock per day to meet the demand. Priced low, hawked on city streets, and carried into villages and farmsteads, popular newspapers of every political stripe (including anarchist until 1894) published useful advertisements, entertaining serials, and bold front-page articles as sensational as they were skewed. Thriving on the anxieties of the age, they exploited scandals and searched for scapegoats.[5]

And both of these France had in abundance. On the heels of

[4]Eugen Weber, *France, Fin-de-siècle* (Cambridge, Mass.: Belknap, 1986), 115.

[5]For a contemporary account of the avalanche of newspapers and broadsheets, see John Grand-Carteret, *L'Affaire Dreyfus et l'image* (Paris: Flammarion, n.d. [1898?]), 7 and passim.

Boulanger's flight and before Dreyfus's arrest, another "fragrant episode" revealed that political corruption, common under the empire, reached deep into the republic.[6] Throughout the 1880s, the Panama Canal Company tried to repeat the success that its founder, Ferdinand de Lesseps, had enjoyed two decades earlier at Suez. But tropical disease and insufficient capital plagued the project. And while the venerable Lesseps worked to raise funds through (mostly) legitimate means, an army of lobbyists blackmailed politicians and pushed for approval of a lottery loan from the Chamber of Deputies. The loan floated, then failed, bankrupting the company, ruining thousands of small investors, and sparking a hunt for Panama's frock-coated thieves. News reports focused on two company officials accused of bribing more than one hundred deputies and of masterminding a cover-up. But Cornelius Herz and Baron Jacques de Reinach, though surely enmeshed in the web of corruption, served a special purpose in the early 1890s, at a time when the first great depression of the industrializing West struck France simultaneously with the Panama debacle; they fit the roles of enemies within. Reinach's family tree reached to Germany; Herz, though born in France, was a naturalized American; and most important for the purveyors of simple solutions to complex problems, both men were Jews.

In the second half of the nineteenth century, anti-Semites fortified long-standing anti-Jewish prejudices with new accusations adapted to the modern age. One hundred years earlier, two revolutionary edicts of emancipation had abolished all legal restrictions against French Jews. For the first time, full civil liberties were promised to every Jew "who swears the oath of citizenship and fulfills all the duties that the Constitution imposes." In a letter published in the wake of emancipation, one French Jew captured the gratitude that would remain strong through the next century: "France, who first wiped out the disgrace of Judah and broke the shackles of all captives, she is our land of Israel; her mountains—our Zion; her rivers—our Jordan."[7]

New edicts, however, could not sweep away old bigotries, and the belief persisted that Jews constituted a "nation within the nation," a chosen

---

[6]The term is Gordon Wright's; see *France in Modern Times* (New York: W. W. Norton, 1995), 240.

[7]See Paul Mendes-Flohr, and Jehuda Reinharz, eds., *The Jew in the Modern World* (New York: Oxford University Press, 1980), 44–46, 103–8; and Michael Burns, *Dreyfus: A Family Affair, 1789–1945* (New York: HarperCollins, 1991), 10–13.

people hostile to assimilation and unlikely to abandon those "humilating signs," as one observer put it, "which designate them as Jews." By the late nineteenth century, the dogged prejudices of the past had been joined and revived by the new ingredient of racism. Even the word *anti-Semitism* dated from the epoch, and though coined by a German, it was most dramatically popularized by the French. At a time "when racism forged ahead everywhere," notes one historian, "France . . . seemed destined to be the country within which racism might determine national politics."[8]

While Scripture, myth, art, and literature perpetuated images of traitorous Christ killers and grasping moneylenders, contemporary anti-Semites refit those stereotypes to domestic and foreign affairs and to the pseudo-science of race. Pledging allegiance only to the Promised Land of Israel, Jews worshiped, the argument went, only mammon. Ever since Alphonse de Toussenel's mid-century diatribe against the Rothschild family (the Jewish "kings of the epoch"), conventional wisdom had it that "cosmopolitan" Jews controlled the upper reaches of finance—an accusation leveled with equal force from right and left. Later, in the crucible of the Dreyfus affair, the anti-Semitism of the French left would subside. Until then, however, the belief was widespread that Jews—"huckstering" capitalists, as Karl Marx called them; enemies "of the human species," in the words of French socialist Pierre-Joseph Proudhon[9]—had profited from the century's political, industrial, and financial revolutions. In fact, many Jews had profited, but so had many Catholics, a reality anti-Semites ignored in favor of recounting the failure of a Catholic-controlled investment bank, the Union Générale. Economic crisis triggered the bank's collapse in 1882, but the legend spread that Jews had conspired to destroy a Christian rival.

Legends need carriers, and while priests continued the symbolic flogging of Jews during Holy Week services, professional anti-Semites plied their wares in long tomes, short editorials, grotesque cartoons, and election manifestos. Maurice Barrès, novelist, boulangist politician, and enemy of Dreyfus until the end, described the Jewish threat to the soul

---

[8]George L. Mosse, *Toward the Final Solution: A History of European Racism* (New York: Harper and Row, 1978), 150.

[9]Proudhon is quoted in David Cohen, *La Promotion des Juifs en France à l'époque du Second Empire* (Aix-en-Provence: Université de Provence, 1980), 2:653. See also Karl Marx, "On the Jewish Question," in *Karl Marx: Early Writings,* ed. T. B. Bottomore (New York: McGraw-Hill, 1964), 3–40.

and soil of France. His remarks come from an election campaign at the height of the Dreyfus affair, but they repeat a formula contrived throughout the 1880s and 1890s.

MAURICE BARRÈS

Election Campaign Speech
November 1, 1898

Voters, in opposition to a politics which aims only to satisfy hatreds, and whose only motive power is the greed to rule, I come to you again with those *national* and *social* ideas which you have praised before and will not reject today. . . .

At the summits of society as in the depths of the provinces, in the moral order as in the material order, in the commercial, industrial, and agricultural world and on to the building sites where French workers face competition, the foreigner, like a parasite, poisons us.

An essential element of the new French politics should be to protect all citizens against that invasion, and also to guard against that excessively cosmopolitan — or, rather, excessively German — socialism which would weaken the defense of the fatherland.

The Jewish question is linked to the national question. Ranked by the Revolution with authentic Frenchmen, Jews kept their distinctive traits, and after having once been the persecuted, they became tyrants. We support the most complete freedom of conscience; further, we would consider it a grave danger to allow Jews the privilege of appealing to — and that way appearing to defend — the principles of civil liberty promulgated by the Revolution. [They] violate those principles through . . . their habits of monopolizing, of speculation, of cosmopolitanism. Still further, in the army, in judicial offices, in ministries, in all our administration, they far exceed the percentage to which their numbers in the general population may entitle them. They have been appointed prefects, judges, treasurers, officers because they have the money that corrupts. . . . [We] must do away with that dangerous inequality and obtain more respect for our authentic citizens, the children of Gaul and not of Judaea. . . .

For the past twenty years, the opportunist political system has favored

Maurice Barrès, *Scènes et doctrines du nationalisme* (Paris: Félix Juven, 1902), 432–34.

Note: Translations by Michael Burns, unless otherwise noted.

the Jew, the foreigner, the cosmopolitan. Those who commit this criminal error explain themselves by saying that exotic foreigners bring energetic elements to France. Some fine elements . . . which have corrupted us rotten! Here is the full truth: The energetic elements that French society really needs it will find in itself, in promoting the rise of the poorest, the most downtrodden, in raising them up to the greatest well-being, to the greatest professional training.

One sees how nationalism necessarily gives rise to socialism. We define socialism as "the material and moral improvement of the most numerous and poorest class."

After centuries the French nation has reached the point of giving its people political security. Now it must protect them against the economic insecurity they suffer at every step.

Another standard-bearer of France's new nationalism, Edouard Drumont, emerged as the most powerful anti-Semite of the European fin de siècle. Through his popular newspaper, *La Libre Parole* (Free Speech), launched in 1892 with "France for the French" emblazoned under its title, he attacked the "Jewish conspiracy" behind Panama and helped chase Cornelius Herz out of France and Baron Jacques de Reinach to suicide. Six years earlier, Drumont had penned one of the bestsellers of the era. *La France Juive* (Jewish France), reaching one hundred thousand copies in the first year and two hundred editions by the turn of the century, stood next to the Bible on the bookshelves of the most modest homes. Richly detailed, vividly written, and ecumenical in its hatred, its two volumes railed against every foreign menace, from Prussian junkers and British shopkeepers to Italian workers who crossed the Alps to steal the jobs of good Frenchmen. (Italians, more than any other group in France, suffered violent physical attacks throughout the fin de siècle, and journalists helped fuel the rage.) But Drumont leveled his sights on the Jewish ruination of France since "the dawn of history."

Charting the conflict of "Aryans and Semites," he moved his narrative to the contemporary scene. Emancipated by the Revolution and empowered by industrial capitalism, Jews held the republic in their grasp. The "hooknosed tribes" of Eastern and central Europe—the mostly Orthodox Jews who sought refuge in France following the pogroms of 1880–81—infected the nation, Drumont wrote, like microbes on a host. And France's established Jewish families, though cloaked under a refined veneer, were no different from those "Galician kikes with their curly forelocks, who, come together for some ritual murder, laugh with one another while, from the open wound of the victim there runs pure and crimson the Christian blood for the sweet bread of Purim *[sic]*."[10]

To intensify the Jewish threat, Drumont and his followers designed their own demography. They knew, as one scholar has observed, that in the marketplace of xenophobia, "fiction is almost always of greater importance than fact."[11] On the eve of the Dreyfus affair, when the Jewish population of France numbered barely eighty thousand, or less than two-tenths of 1 percent of the total population, *La France Juive* put the figure at more than half a million (one Drumont acolyte soon raised it to six hundred thousand). And while most Jews in the cities and small towns of eastern France and in the quarters of central Paris were poor or on the margins of the middle class, anti-Semites stressed the all-encompassing power of Jewish financiers and politicians.

Equally effective were the perverse interpretations of accurate facts, especially when most readers had few ways to verify evidence or little desire to do so. Since the revolutionary and Napoleonic wars, Jews had served with distinction in the French military; they had graduated from the nation's most prestigious institutions—from Saint-Cyr and the Ecole Polytechnique (which counted young Alfred Dreyfus among its alumni in 1880); and through the late nineteenth century, the percentage of Jews among regular army officers was superior to the proportion of Jews in the general population. Many of those men traced their origins to the eastern province of Alsace and, like Dreyfus, joined the military to avenge the defeat of 1870 and return their homeland to France. Anti-Semites, however, twisted that manifest proof of patriotism into evidence of infiltration. Jews penetrated the army, they warned, as part of a cabalistic campaign of treason.

If the French Revolution, in its early, humanitarian phase, had turned intolerance into a taboo, Drumont and his followers, professed enemies of that Revolution, turned it into a totem, a mystical emblem of kinship

[10]Such language runs throughout Drumont's work; see, above all, *La France Juive: Essai d'histoire contemporaine,* 2 vols. (Paris: Marpon et Flammarion, 1886). The description of "Galician kikes" is quoted in David S. Landes, "Two Cheers for Emancipation," in *The Jews in Modern France,* ed. Frances Malino and Bernard Wasserstein (Hanover, N.H.: University Press of New England, 1985), 298. Drumont should have alluded to the bread of Passover, not Purim, but the confusion did not cloud his point.

[11]Robert Byrnes, *Antisemitism in Modern France* (New Brunswick, N.J.: Rutgers University Press, 1950), 93.

for all those who believed in "France for the French." Free to operate under the liberal press law, they chased their prey like hounds off the leash. Although many French men and women remained hostile or indifferent to their campaigns, many did not, especially when anti-Semites shifted their focus to the sacred ground of the French army, the only temporal hierarchy, as one scholar tells us, in which many citizens still had faith. As France entered the third decade of its cold war with Germany, newspapers throughout the country ran reports of German espionage and French agents in the pay of the enemy. And not all the stories were fabricated. *La Libre Parole,* its circulation faltering in the aftermath of Panama, sought to boost sales by capitalizing on what one historian has called a French plague of "espionnitis."[12] The paper seized the moment to rekindle fears with an article titled "Jews in the Army."

[12]See Maurice Baumont, *Au coeur de l'Affaire Dreyfus* (Paris: Del Duca, 1976), chap. 1; Weber, *France, Fin-de-siècle,* 121; Allan Mitchell, "The Xenophobic Style: French Counterespionage and the Emergence of the Dreyfus Affair," *Journal of Modern History* 52 (1980): 414–25; and D. W. Brogan, *The Development of Modern France, 1870–1939* (Gloucester, Mass.: Peter Smith, 1970), 1:310, 343.

LA LIBRE PAROLE

Jews in the Army

May 23, 1892

Longer than the rest of contemporary society, the army has avoided Jewish influence. This immunity is due to the army's traditional esprit and to the very nature of its mission.

What would the kikes do in its ranks? . . . Why wear oneself out, why rough it, why always have empty pockets, when it is so easy, on the stock market or through shady business dealings, to make a fortune without hardship and without deprivation?

If Jews cared little about entering the army, the army cared even less about having them. Beyond all religious consideration, there exists among the vast majority of military men a feeling of instinctive repulsion against the sons of Israel. One sees in them the usurer who completes the ruination of the indebted officer, the tradesman who speculates on the soldier's hunger, the spy who traffics without shame in the secrets of national defense. Everywhere and always, in peace as in war, the army has seen the Jew stand against it—against its duties, against its well-being, against its honor.

Since 1870 and the adoption of compulsory military service, the situation has altered. Israelites are no longer allowed to exempt themselves, for an average of two thousand francs, from all duty toward the fatherland. . . .

They had barely placed a foot in the army when they searched, by every means, to gain influence. They understand the opportunity there for the spread of power; already lords of finance and administration, already dictating judgments to the courts, they will definitely be masters of France on the day they command the army. Rothschild will deliver the mobilization plans—and one can imagine toward what end!

Happily, we are not there yet. The semitic invasion is like the breeding of microbes: When the environment is not favorable, the growth process suffers. Though there have been some hints of weakness, the army has joined the combat with a remarkable strength of resistance. In undertaking this series of articles, we want to encourage the army in this holy struggle. At the same time, we want to uncover the criminal deeds that would have the immediate effect of endangering the country's interests.

Before 1870 the greatest proportion of Jews were found in the technical branches and above all in the Corps of Engineers. Many entered the Ecole Polytechnique with the ambition of becoming engineers, but when their graduation results did not allow them to secure a civilian career, they settled for the artillery or military engineering as a makeshift compromise. Quite often, they quickly resigned after finding employment in private industry or business. . . .

The tendency to avoid the army, which was widespread before 1870, has abated since then in a very notable way. But there remains a considerable proportion of Jews who, unable to find careers with the state, turn to positions offered by private industry, commerce, or banking.

Those Jews who have entered the army have found a way of setting themselves up in the most agreeable posts . . . in the choicest situations. With each opening that attracts twenty qualified candidates, it is the Jew who climbs over his nineteen Christian competitors. . . .

Are these statistics not striking testimony to the favoritism enjoyed by the sons of Israel?

And yet one of them, Reinach (Joseph), had the audacity a few years ago to condemn . . . the composition of certain cavalry regiments, and to pretend that all its favorable positions were assigned to reactionaries! Military publications, statistics at the ready, have demonstrated that those accusations were absolutely false. . . .

If anyone has the right to complain about ministerial nepotism, it is certainly not the Jews: Indeed, we have just proved how they have been clever enough to grab a large part of the pie.

That attack on France's Jewish officers, old in stereotypes but new in scope and virulence, sparked an immediate reaction. On May 29, 1892, *La Libre Parole* published on its front page a letter addressed to Drumont by a Jewish captain in the Eighth Dragoon Regiment. "By insulting the three hundred French officers on active service who belong to the Jewish faith," wrote André Crémieu-Foa, "you insult me personally. I call upon you to cease this odious campaign, and I warn that if you do not act on this letter, I will demand recourse to a duel." Provoked by the challenge and delighted with the publicity, Drumont responded, "If Jewish officers are wounded by our articles, let them choose delegates and we will oppose them with an equal number of French swords."[13]

Pistols at twenty-five paces took the place of swords, and Crémieu-Foa chose as his second Commandant Ferdinand Walsin-Esterhazy, a French Catholic officer of Hungarian ancestry and dubious allegiance who would soon emerge as a central figure in the Dreyfus affair. Like the majority of duels throughout the fin de siècle (more than two hundred a year by one count), the confrontation between Drumont and Crémieu-Foa ended with only slight injuries to both parties. Three weeks later, however, another anti-Semite, the marquis de Morès, struck a fatal blow to another Jewish captain, Armand Mayer.[14] One report described the marquis armed with a battle sword that exceeded the customary weight for such affairs of honor, which was not surprising for an adventurer who had made a career of pushing anti-Semitism to the limit—in the American West, where he accused Jews of forcing him out of the cattle business, and in France, where he aimed "to chase every last one of them from our midst."[15] A colleague of Drumont's, Morès shared all of that writer's vitriol but none of his political savvy, and when he killed Captain Mayer, a "greatly esteemed" professor at the Ecole Polytechnique, his act unleashed a flood of sympathy, not only for the victim but for the entire community of patriotic and assimilated French Jews.

Barely two years before Dreyfus's arrest, the confrontation between the defenders of Mayer and Morès provided a foreshadowing of the affair. "In one single day," declared the newspaper *Le Matin*, "anti-Semites

---

[13]*La Libre Parole,* May 29, 1892; see also Ernest Crémieu-Foa, *La Campagne antisemitique: Les duels. Les responsabilités* (Paris: Alcan-Lévy, 1892).

[14]Jean Garriques, "Mourir pour Dreyfus," *L'Histoire,* Jan. 1994, 52–53. In the same issue, see Pierre Birnbaum, "L'Armée française est-elle antisémite?" 22–27.

[15]Quoted in L'Archivisite (pseud.) *Drumont et Dreyfus* (Paris: P.V. Stock, 1898).

have made Jews more sympathetic than they had made them antipa-
thetic across four or five years of daily attack and slander." *Le Siècle* condemned Morès and Drumont for the "anti-patriotic campaigns" that "re-
vive the wars of religion," and *La Nation* announced that anti-Semites
spilled the blood of an officer "who had devoted his life to the service of
France. . . . May this blood put an end to a wretched war which is shameful for our country and our time." In the Chamber of Deputies, Camille
Dreyfus (unrelated to Alfred Dreyfus) had survived his own duel with
Morès two years earlier. Asking the minister of war, Charles Freycinet,
if there were "two kinds of swords in the army," the deputy received a
response that echoed the ideals of the French Revolution and reasserted
the state's historic pledge of protection.[16]

[16]Patrice Boussel, *L'Affaire Dreyfus et la presse* (Paris: Armand Colin, 1960), 19–23. See
also *New York Times,* June 24–27, 1892.

CAMILLE DREYFUS AND CHARLES FREYCINET

Exchange in the Chamber of Deputies

June 25, 1892

M. CAMILLE DREYFUS: Sirs. . . . Israelite by birth, proudly claiming, in these
times of abuse, solidarity of descent with the men who have been the coreligionists of my ancestors . . . I would have preferred that someone else
had come here to demand the explanations that seem to me so necessary.
However, it appears that this duty must be fulfilled. *(Very good! Very good!)*
  I will not dwell on religious questions, I will not even dwell for a moment on the end of that horrible duel which gave rise to a unanimous feeling of emotion and compassion in Paris and in the Chamber. *(Applause.)*
I address the minister of war, and ask if it is possible to let pass without
protest those words . . . which have been at the source of this entire deplorable event.
  It has been written—I do not want to cite the text itself, you know it—
that French swords would stand against Jewish swords. *(Various stirrings.)*
  Well! I come to ask you, Minister of War, if there are two kinds of
swords in the army: the sword carried by our comrades in the regular

army, and the sword we will carry with pride on the day the fatherland calls us. And is the latter French or something else?

I have nothing to add. I await your response with confidence. *(Applause on the left.)*

M. DE FREYCINET, minister of war: Sirs, the emotion that the honorable M. Camille Dreyfus has just expressed is felt by us all. It is felt particularly by the minister of war who sees vanish, in the prime of life, an officer who gave great hope to the military. . . .

Sirs, in the army we know neither Israelites nor Protestants nor Catholics *(Applause);* we know only French officers, without regard of birth. *(Renewed applause.)*

We know only soldiers devoted to their military duty and ready for all the sacrifices that the fatherland can expect of them. *(Very good! Very good!)*

I will say, therefore, to those officers who have felt injured by the polemics we profoundly condemn *(Applause),* by those appeals to the passions of another age *(Very good! Very good!),* to the prejudices which the French Revolution refuted long ago, I will say to them: You cannot be harmed by these collective insults, which touch neither your military bravery nor your personal decency; rise above these attacks, because you are supported by the government, by the chambers, by public opinion in its entirety . . . maintain your calm in the face of these abuses; the minister of war will see to them, and if new incidents occur, be certain that he will take all appropriate measures to put them to an end. We will not tolerate, we cannot tolerate these provocations that attempt to sow division in the army's ranks. *(Very good! Very good!)*

To inflame citizens one against the other is always an evil thing, but to create division between officers is a national crime. *(Lively applause.)*

On the day of Captain Mayer's funeral, a company of Ecole Polytechnique cadets, in full-dress uniform, led a procession of mourners that numbered in the tens of thousands. Military bands played, government officials and other notables joined the cortege, and the crowd shouted "Long live the army!"

One year earlier, French Jews had commemorated the centennial of the revolutionary edict that made France the first nation to promise full and equal rights to its Jewish citizens.[17] Freycinet alluded to the spirit of that law in the Chamber of Deputies, and at Mayer's graveside the grand rabbi of France reaffirmed the strength of its legacy.

[17]For the September 28, 1791, resolution of the National Assembly and related documents, see Paul Mendes-Flohr and Jehuda Reinarz, eds., *The Jew in the Modern World: A Documentary History* (New York: Oxford University Press, 1995), 118.

RABBI ZADOC KAHN

Funeral Oration

June 26, 1892

In the midst of our indescribable grief, there remains at least one consolation. . . . The entire soul of France has just revealed itself, with its native generosity, its passion for justice, its tender pity for the stricken, and its ardent love for members of the army—the army . . . which is its strength, honor, hope. All hearts, without exception, have trembled with emotion; the same cry of anguish has issued from all lips. Never has the national conscience asserted itself with such force. Never has the holy concord of the fatherland manifested itself with more brilliance.

These funeral ceremonies have their own eloquence, for they are, as it were, conducted by France herself. And then, there is a voice that emerges from this coffin, just as it emerges from all the tombs that surround us. In this solemn field of final rest, all divisions give way, all hatreds abate, all violence is gone. . . . Take, then, into the world of work, into all your daily relations, some of this spirit of tolerance, of mutual respect, of benevolence, which is the grand lesson that death gives to life.

Ah! . . . I only express a wish, and in making it I am sure that I am the faithful interpreter of Captain Mayer himself: that his wisdom from beyond the grave bears fruit; that all those who have the honor to take pen in hand and affect public opinion consider it their sacred duty to unite and not divide, and to proclaim it a crime against the fatherland to stir hatreds and to sow mistrust among citizens who love the country with equal passion; that thoughtful people, public men, and above all religious ministers . . . use their influence to make all the children of France, in imitation of France's army, a single family with a single passion in their soul: to secure the glory and grandeur of the fatherland and to watch over its good name.

In that way we will honor the memory of this young martyr, who was a stranger to every narrow and intolerant idea, to every hateful feeling, and who, like all those who carry the sword of France, devoted himself completely to the cult of duty and honor. The sacrifice of his life will not have been in vain for the causes that were dear to him, if it serves to dispel fatal misunderstandings, and if it lets shine forth, through the veil of mourning that covers it today, the flag of France, that glorious and immortal symbol of justice, concord, and fraternity.

Zadoc Kahn, *Souvenirs et regrets: Receuil d'oraisons funèbres prononcées dans la communauté israélite de Paris, 1868–1898* (Paris: Durlacher, 1898), 330–31.

Other observers shared Rabbi Kahn's belief that Mayer had not died in vain. From the provinces, the *Journal de Rouen* declared that Drumont and his disciples "had killed anti-Semitism in France."[18] In Paris, while the editors of *Univers israélite* warned that "the enemy had not yet disarmed," the Central Consistory, the government-sponsored board of France's established Jewish community, expressed its hope that "the attacks which have been made against us will give way to more healthy and more equitable opinions."[19] Examining the Consistory's decision to refrain from confrontation with anti-Semitic journalists, one scholar has noted how that mistake "soon became apparent."[20] But in the early 1890s, memories of Jewish emancipation during the French Revolution, strengthened by the government's recent pledge to protect citizens of all faiths, convinced the majority of Jews that anti-Semitism was an aberration in a land that still held promise.

Alfred Dreyfus, an infantry captain about to join the General Staff at the dawn of the decade, did not need convincing. No one honored French justice and pledged allegiance to the fatherland with more intensity. Grandson of a peddler and kosher butcher, son of a prosperous textile manufacturer in the eastern French city of Mulhouse, Dreyfus was ten years old in 1870 when Prussian troops marched past his Alsatian home. Later, he would point to that "first sorrow" as the defining moment of his patriotism, of his resolve to join the military. But no less important for young Dreyfus was the atmosphere of his native Mulhouse, "the most French city of Alsace," where Protestants and Jews dominated the manufacturing elite. As descendants of the persecuted peoples of "two diasporas," those families shared a common gratitude for the liberties granted by the French Revolution. Throughout the nineteenth century, they developed French markets as the source of their wealth and cultivated the French language as both a practical tool and a sign of allegiance. Dreyfus's parents, observant Jews and fervent patriots, personified the marriage of God and country, and their religious leaders in Alsace encouraged their assimilation into what contemporaries called "the great French family."[21]

Treaty provisions following the Franco-Prussian War enabled Alsa-

---

[18]Boussel, *L'Affaire Dreyfus et la presse,* 21.
[19]Quoted in Michael R. Marrus, *The Politics of Assimilation: The French Jewish Community at the Time of the Dreyfus Affair* (Oxford: Oxford University Press, 1980), 199–200.
[20]Ibid., 200–201.
[21]On the history of the Dreyfus family, see Burns, *Dreyfus: A Family Affair.*

tians to opt for French citizenship. While the eldest Dreyfus son remained behind to manage the family's factories in German-occupied
Mulhouse and in the neighboring French territory of Belfort, Alfred, the
youngest of seven siblings, attended boarding schools in Paris. A diligent student with a gift for languages, mathematics, and science, he
passed the rigorous entrance examination required by the Ecole Polytechnique, and after graduation in 1880 followed the customary routine
of military service in provincial garrisons. By the end of the decade, he
had risen to the rank of artillery captain, and in 1890 he married twenty-
year-old Lucie Hadamard, ten years his junior and the daughter of a leading diamond merchant in Paris. Grand Rabbi Kahn presided at the wed-
ding in the principal synagogue of France. Only two generations had
passed since Dreyfus's ancestors had peddled trinkets along the back
roads of Alsace.

The captain's next step took him to the Ecole Supérieure de Guerre,
established in the wake of the Franco-Prussian War as part of the young
republic's attempt to streamline the old empire's military bureaucracy.
Drawing lessons from the German system and attracting France's most
gifted officers, the school trained an elite corps, with top graduates
bound for the General Staff. Dreyfus's military record *(Feuillet du personnel)*, compiled by a succession of superior officers, shows the trajec-
tory of his career and the qualities that led to his success at the Ecole de
Guerre. With "very good" constituting a high mark, it was a solid record,
almost stellar, and it would elicit from Dreyfus's colleagues a mixture of
admiration and hostility.

Military Personnel Record of Alfred Dreyfus
1882–1892

1882 Health and constitution good—slightly nearsighted—physique
good—will make a good officer. . . .
1883 Dreyfus is an intelligent officer and extremely willing. He
has . . . shown a zeal for service . . . but still has a great deal of military in-

Archives Nationales, BB/19, Feuillet du personnel.

struction to complete. The sound of his voice is, above all, very poor; nevertheless, if his work remains consistent, he will become a good officer.

1884 Zealous and conscientious . . . well trained and intelligent, very spirited. . . .

1886 A very hearty officer, a fearless horseman, well educated, intelligent, manages the riding lessons of the new recruits with the greatest competence. Unfortunately, has a deplorable voice.

1887 Very intelligent, very skillful, leads well despite his bad voice. A good battery lieutenant despite some lack of punctuality and precision.

1888 The best lieutenant in the division. Knows a great deal and is always learning. Endowed with an excellent memory and very lively intellect. . . .

1889 Still an excellent lieutenant . . . very good teacher . . . has been able to slightly improve the sound of his voice. . . . Dreyfus has been promoted to captain in the Twenty-first Artillery Regiment.

1890 Performs his duties well. Has been admitted to the Ecole de Guerre.

1891–92 Marks from the Ecole Supérieure de Guerre—physique and health fairly good; nearsighted . . . ; education good; broad intellect; very good conduct and appearance; widely informed; knowledge of military theory, practice, and administration very good; fine command of German; fine horseman; works well. Admitted to the Ecole sixty-seventh of eighty-one, graduated ninth of eighty-one; obtained General Staff certificate with the mark of very good. Fine officer, lively spirit. . . . Very well suited for service on the General Staff.

Dreyfus's official record reveals nothing, however, about the complaint lodged in 1892 by a member of the Ecole de Guerre examination jury. At the moment that *La Libre Parole* was attacking Jews in the military, General Pierre de Bonnefond announced that he did not "want a Jew on the General Staff." Attempting to lower the overall marks of Captain Dreyfus and another Jewish officer, he submitted critical reports on their "personal character." In November 1892, after Dreyfus learned of his high score (despite Bonnefond's critique) and assignment to the General Staff, he demanded a meeting with the commanding officer of the Ecole de Guerre. Only a few months had passed since Crémieu-Foa had challenged Drumont, and Dreyfus's interview captured the same pride, the same refusal to remain silent in the face of prejudice. Protesting "in the name of Israelite officers," Dreyfus posed a single question to General Lebelin de Dionne: "Is a Jewish officer not capable of serving his country as well as any other soldier?" Dionne, echoing the remarks of his minister of war, assured Dreyfus that the army made no distinctions based on religious faith. Jewish officers, he confirmed, were "valued as highly as any others." Dreyfus, now satisfied, believed that Bonnefond had been an exception to the army's rule of justice.[22]

Having cleared every hurdle placed before him, the captain prepared for service on the General Staff and settled into the comfortable life of a bourgeois officer with a growing family and a formidable private income. "A brilliant and easy career opened before me," he later recalled; "the future appeared full of promise. After my days of work, I found the rest and charm of family life. . . . We were perfectly happy, and our first child, a son, brought cheer to our home; I had no material cares, and felt the deep affection of my family and my wife's family. Everything in life seemed to smile on me."[23]

In the summer of the following year, Dreyfus experienced a high point of his career when he accompanied the army's new chief of staff, General Raoul François Charles Le Mouton de Boisdeffre, on a fact-finding mission to eastern France. Impressed by Dreyfus's intelligent grasp of detail and suggestions concerning artillery modernization, Boisdeffre invited the captain for an hour-long walk along the banks of the Moselle River. Unlike most of his colleagues, Dreyfus had never benefited from the protection of a patron within the military. Shy as a child, reserved as an adult, he made few friends in society and even fewer in the high reaches of the army, where, as more than one historian has demonstrated, officers of mostly Catholic and aristocratic background rarely embraced outsiders. But the meeting with Boisdeffre, former ambassador to St. Petersburg and one of the principal architects of the recent Franco-Russian Alliance, fueled Dreyfus's hope that the high command valued his talents.[24]

At the same time, however, personnel reports filed by the captain's immediate superiors revealed a prejudice that blended anti-Semitism with the military's "tie of caste." In the coterie of the General Staff, Dreyfus was an arriviste, a new man of new wealth who had risen quickly and lived comfortably; income from his investments alone surpassed the annual salary of a full captain. Moreover, he suffered no fools. Aware of the

[22]Joseph Reinach, *Histoire de l'affaire Dreyfus* (Paris: La Revue Blanche, 1901–11), 1:168; Jean Denis Bredin, *The Affair: The Case of Alfred Dreyfus,* trans. Jeffrey Mehlman (New York: George Braziller, 1986), 22; and Burns, *Dreyfus: A Family Affair,* 91.

[23]Alfred Dreyfus, *Cinq années de ma vie* (Paris: La Découverte, 1994), 50.

[24]Douglas Johnson, *France and the Dreyfus Affair* (London: Blandford, 1966), 42–43. See also Burns, *Dreyfus: A Family Affair,* 106–7.

envy and bigotry that surrounded him (much of it couched in code words and cold shoulders), he seems to have treated many comrades with silent disdain. Not the first Jew assigned to the General Staff, but the only Jew serving in that sanctum sanctorum in the wake of Drumont's campaign, Dreyfus provided a ready target for staff officers on whose desks were stacked copies of *La Libre Parole*.[25]

Late in 1893, after a dozen years of nearly unanimous praise, one of the captain's superiors, Colonel Pierre Fabre, filed a report describing him as "an incomplete officer.... Very intelligent and gifted, but pretentious and not fulfilling—from the point of view of character, integrity, and manner of service—the conditions necessary for employment with the General Staff of the Army." A few months later, another officer noted that Dreyfus "is perhaps a bit too sure of himself." The next report, filed in the fall of 1894, was the last of Alfred Dreyfus's career for half a decade. It ran to only one line: Dreyfus "is the object of court-martial proceedings for the crime of high treason."[26]

[25]Eugen Weber, "Reflections on the Jews in France," in *The Jews in Modern France,* ed. Frances Malino and Bernard Wasserstein (Hanover, N.H.: University Press of New England, 1985), 22. On the army's "tie of caste," see Hannah Arendt, "From the Dreyfus Affair to France Today," *Jewish Social Studies,* 4 (July 1942): 210.

[26]Archives Nationales, BB/19, Feuillet du personnel.

2

The Arrest

A sheet of thin, almost transparent, paper with a message left unsigned and undated, launched the military case that would lead to the Dreyfus affair. From the beginning, mystery shrouded the memorandum *(bordereau)*.[1] The Statistical Section of the General Staff—the nebulous name given to the espionage and counterespionage office established following the Franco-Prussian War—seems to have received the document through one of its "ordinary channels," most likely by way of a concierge assigned to the German embassy in Paris. On the payroll of French intelligence since the mid-1880s, Madame Bastian, known as "agent Auguste," picked through wastebaskets, mailboxes, and cloakrooms in search of suspicious documents. She carried her booty into the dim recesses of Saint-Clothilde and other Paris churches, and most often into the rough but practiced hands of Commandant Hubert-Joseph Henry, a peasant's son who had turned to the harvest of spies, double agents, informants, forged letters, and stolen documents for the General Staff.

Torn into six pieces and found among the papers of Maximilien von Schwartzkoppen, the German military attaché, the bordereau was delivered to Henry in late September 1894. Pasted together, it revealed the work of a traitor within the French military.

---

[1]Jean-Denis Bredin examines the debates surrounding the bordereau and its provenance in *The Affair: The Case of Alfred Dreyfus,* trans. Jeffrey Mehlman (New York: George Braziller, 1986), 58–65.

The Bordereau
1894

Having received no news that you wish to see me, I am nevertheless sending, sir, some interesting information:

1. A note on the hydraulic brake of the 120 [millimeter field gun] and the way the part has worked
2. A note on covering troops (some modification will be made by the new plan)
3. A note on a modification of artillery formations
4. A note concerning Madagascar
5. The draft of the firing manual for field artillery (March 14, 1894)

This last document is extremely difficult to procure, and I am able to have it at my disposal for only a very few days. The War Ministry has sent a fixed number of copies to the regiment, and the regiment is responsible for them. Each officer holding a copy must return it after maneuvers. If, therefore, you take from it what interests you and then keep it at my disposal, I will call for it. Unless you would like me to have it copied in extenso and send you the copy.

I am off on maneuvers.

Espionage and the scent of treason, though part of the daily routine for the Statistical Section's five staff officers, still made the pulse race. Commandant Henry immediately showed the bordereau to two colleagues and then to his superior, Colonel Jean Conrad Sandherr. From there the circle widened. Sandherr alerted other high-ranking officers, including the minister of war, General Auguste Mercier, recent successor to Charles Freycinet. Photographs of the bordereau went out to department heads, and in the first week of October Lieutenant Colonel d'Abboville, another staff officer, did his part to ferret out the traitor. Since the memorandum covered a wide range of military topics, it must have been drafted, d'Abboville maintained, by a *stagiaire,* a recently commissioned officer of the General Staff whose apprenticeship included six months of duty in each of the staff's four sections. Only a few men fit that

---

Reprinted in Bernard Lazare, *Une Erreur judiciaire: L'affaire Dreyfus* (Paris: P.V. Stock, 1897), 253.

Figure 1. The foundation document of the Dreyfus case, this one-page military memorandum (bordereau) was discovered by a secret agent in the German embassy in Paris and delivered to the intelligence section of the French General Staff in the late summer of 1894. Following comparisons with Alfred Dreyfus's handwriting, it was used as "proof" of the captain's treason.

Le Bordereau

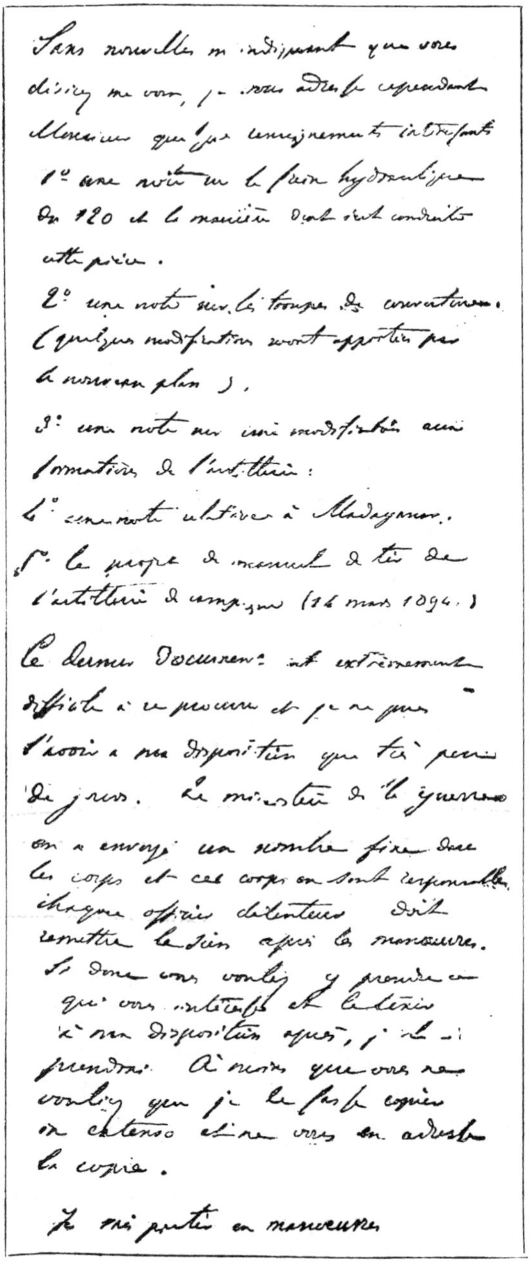
Sans nouvelles m'indiquant que vous désirez me voir, je vous adresse cependant Monsieur quelques renseignements intéressants

1° une note sur le frein hydraulique du 120 et la manière dont s'est conduite cette pièce.

2° une note sur les troupes de couverture. (quelques modifications seront apportées par le nouveau plan).

3° une note sur une modification aux formations de l'artillerie:

4° une note relative à Madagascar.

5° le projet de manuel de tir de l'artillerie de campagne (14 mars 1894.)

Ce dernier document est extrêmement difficile à se procurer et je ne puis l'avoir à ma disposition que très peu de jours. Le ministère de la guerre en a envoyé un nombre fixe dans les corps et ces corps en sont responsables. Chaque officier détenteur doit remettre le sien après les manœuvres. Si donc vous voulez y prendre ce qui vous intéresse et le tenir à ma disposition après, je le prendrai. À moins que vous ne vouliez que je le fasse copier in extenso et ne vous en adresse la copie.

Je vais partir en manœuvres

profile, and only one had recently received negative marks in his personnel dossier. The most damning of those marks had been submitted by Colonel Pierre Fabre, and it was Fabre who suggested that the bordereau be compared to documents penned by the recent *stagiaire,* Captain Alfred Dreyfus.

At first glance Dreyfus's handwriting, with its particular slant and tight form, bore a resemblance to the bordereau, though hardly a striking one, as his accusers would insist. For many staff officers, however, the captain fit the part. According to more than one account, Colonel Sandherr, an Alsatian reared to suspect the Jews in his midst, reacted to the handwriting comparison with the exclamation, "I should have realized!"[2] Chief of staff General Boisdeffre, impressed by Dreyfus only a few months before, now wondered if the captain's keen knowledge of artillery matters had been the intelligence of a traitor. Obsessed with leaks and proceeding with caution, Boisdeffre called on a relative, Commandant Armand Mercier du Paty de Clam, to analyze the evidence. One of the General Staff's many aristocratic officers, du Paty, with his monocle, handlebar mustache, and flamboyant bearing, was a man of considerable talents and many hobbies. Second in his class at Saint-Cyr and a graduate of the Ecole de Guerre, he pursued amateur graphology when not preoccupied with the transvestism of his private hours. Noting only a few disparities in the handwriting samples, he confirmed his colleagues' suspicions that Dreyfus had written the bordereau.

Minister of War Mercier pushed the investigation on. Convinced of the captain's guilt but anxious to honor the legal formalities, he briefed the president of the republic, the prime minister, and other high government officials on the broad outlines of the inquiry, though not on the identity of the accused. A few colleagues advised Mercier to drop the entire matter; they worried about the slim evidence and potential blow to the reputation of the French military if a wolf turned up within its fold. Mercier, however, ignored most of his comrades and paid only fleeting attention to the minister of foreign affairs, Gabriel Hanotaux. A formal accusation built on an unsigned document stolen from a foreign embassy was not only of dubious legality, Hanotaux argued, but it could

---

[2]Theodore Reinach, *Histoire sommaire de l'affaire Dreyfus* (Paris: Ligue des droits de l'homme, 1924), 23; and Eric Cahm, *L'Affaire Dreyfus: Histoire, politique et société* (Paris: Le Livre de Poche, 1994), 23.

spark an international incident. He made Mercier promise to halt the investigation if no hard proof emerged, and over the coming weeks and months, the General Staff would take note of the warning and fashion a dossier brimming with evidence.

For now, however, the bordereau stood alone, and the amateur insights of Commandant du Paty would not suffice. The General Staff called in a handwriting expert from the Bank of France, but when he reported "numerous and important disparities" between the documents (prompting some officers to wonder whether the man was in league with Jewish bankers), Mercier turned to Alphonse Bertillion, a part-time graphologist with the Judicial Police. Renowned for his work in criminal anthropometry and fingerprint analysis, Bertillion was also a professed anti-Semite who would soon be described by the president of the republic as a "compulsively rational madman . . . completely insane." But he won Mercier's praise when he declared that the handwriting samples matched.[3]

Still, the decision to arrest Dreyfus did not come from pseudoscientists and anti-Semites, or at least not from them alone. It involved the entire military hierarchy, the majority of which played by the rules and believed in the captain's guilt. General Boisdeffre, influenced perhaps by his summer meeting with Dreyfus, never relished the chase after the Jewish officer and seemed saddened by it all, though never enough to doubt the accusation. As for Mercier, though he may not have been the diabolical criminal depicted by Dreyfus's supporters, he was consumed by prejudice, ambition, and fear. He had been feeling the wrath of critics on his right flank, and especially the diatribes of Henri Rochefort, editor of *L'Intransigeant,* and Edouard Drumont, who suspected the minister of anticlericalism and condemned him for allowing Jews to infiltrate the army. During the early phase of the Dreyfus case, before the anti-Semitic right crowned him as their hero, Mercier was a bureaucrat under siege. Embarrassed by the discovery of a Jewish spy on his watch, he aimed to silence his critics, prove his patriotism, and hold his job.

But to settle on Dreyfus as the traitor within, the General Staff had to deal with a mountain of evidence in the captain's favor. His family had opted for French citizenship when they could have prospered as sub-

[3]Quoted in Bredin, *The Affair,* 68, 74.

jects of the German Reich; Dreyfus had sacrificed the easy life of a ren-
tier, a man of independent means, for the rigors of military training and
service; and at a time when Germans paid French spies meager sums
that would not keep Dreyfus in cigars, the captain had nothing to gain
from the petty commerce of treason. Even the bordereau posed a problem. Its final line announced that the author was to leave on maneuvers,
but Dreyfus had been posted in Paris for more than a year. With some
imagination, however, the General Staff could argue that "maneuvers"
referred to the captain's summer fact-finding trip to eastern France. Furthermore, Dreyfus's visits to German-occupied Mulhouse (technically
prohibited but the habit of countless French citizens with families in Alsace) could be interpreted as the sojourns of a spy. His knowledge of
German was defined as a key tool of his trade, and if his betrayal of
France earned him less than Judas's thirty pieces of silver, it satisfied the
treasonous impulse that, according to his accusers, contaminated all
members of the Jewish race.

Not a whit of this mattered, however, without the bordereau, and in
that regard blind chance, along with anti-Semitism and the animosity of
competitive colleagues, played a role in Dreyfus's fate. Had his penmanship curled in a different direction, he would never have been targeted—
unless, of course, the bordereau had been forged to incriminate Dreyfus
and rid the army of an unwanted Jew, a theory that would emerge later
and take a long time to die. But there were easier ways to frame the captain, and if the memorandum had been made to order, its topics, timing,
and handwriting would have fit Dreyfus with greater precision. In fact,
another officer, undiscovered until 1897, wrote the document in a hand
that, by chance, resembled the penmanship of the Jewish captain. The
weight of evidence suggests that the framing of Alfred Dreyfus—elaborate, criminal, haphazard, and desperate—postdated the discovery of
the bordereau and the early suspicions of the captain's treachery.

The summons to appear at the War Ministry on Monday morning,
October 15, 1894, puzzled Dreyfus but did not upset him. Called for an
inspection of staff officers, he wondered about the time, 9:00 A.M., an
early hour for a "general inspection." Equally unusual, the order speci-
fied "civilian dress." The entire scenario, as Dreyfus would later learn,
had been choreographed by Commandant du Paty, the General Staff's
choice to stage the arrest and manage the interrogation. Early on the
morning of October 15, an officer armed with an order drafted the pre-

vious night informed the director of Paris's Cherche-Midi Prison that Captain Dreyfus, about to be arrested for the crime of high treason, would be delivered to solitary confinement. With all players sworn to secrecy, the General Staff confronted Alfred Dreyfus.

ALFRED DREYFUS

Arrest and Interrogation

October 15, 1894

The morning was beautiful and cool; the sun rose on the horizon, dispersing the thin, light fog; everything pointed to a superb day. Arriving a bit early at the ministry, I strolled for a few minutes outside and then went up. Upon entering, I was received by Commandant Picquart, who seemed to have been waiting for me and who immediately brought me into the office. I was surprised that none of my comrades were there, since general inspections always assemble officers as a group. After a few minutes of banal conversation, Commandant Picquart led me into the office of the chief of the General Staff. I was greatly astonished; instead of finding myself in the presence of the chief of the General Staff, I was received by Commandant du Paty de Clam in uniform. Three people in civilian dress, all unknown to me, also were there. . . .

Commandant du Paty de Clam approached and said in a choking voice, "The general is coming. While we wait, I have a letter to write, and since my finger is sore, would you write it for me?" It was such a strange request under the circumstances that I quickly agreed. I sat down at a small table, already prepared, and the commandant sat close beside me, watching my hand. After having me fill out an inspection form, he dictated a letter. . . . During the dictation, the commandant broke in sharply, saying, "You tremble." . . . That vehement remark, as well as Commandant du Paty's hostile attitude, surprised me greatly. . . . My fingers were cold, for the temperature outside was cool and I had only just arrived in the heated room. . . .

As I continued to write without any problem, Commandant du Paty de Clam interrupted again and said violently, "Pay attention; this is serious!" Though I was surprised by that behavior, as rude as it was unusual, I said nothing and simply applied myself to writing better. . . .

Alfred Dreyfus, *Cinq années de ma vie* (Paris: La Découverte, 1994), 52–54.

As soon as the dictation ended, Commandant du Paty stood up and, putting his hand on me, shouted out in a thundering voice, "In the name of the law, I arrest you; you are accused of the crime of high treason." A lightning bolt at my feet would not have produced a more violent emotion. I spoke in disconnected sentences, protesting the infamous accusation that nothing in my life could justify.

Then [the men in civilian dress] charged forward and searched me. I put up not the least resistance and shouted, "Take my keys; open everything in my home; I am innocent!" I added, "Show me the least proof of this infamy you pretend I have committed." The charges are overwhelming, they responded, without specifying those charges.

I was then taken to Cherche-Midi Prison by Commandant Henry, accompanied by an agent of the criminal investigation department. . . .

On my arrival in prison, I was locked in a cell with a window looking out on the convicts' courtyard. I was kept in solitary confinement, all communication with my family prohibited. I had no paper, pen, ink, or pencil. Through the first days I was treated as a condemned convict, then that illegal measure was annulled.

The men who brought food were always accompanied by the sergeant on guard and the chief guard, who had the only key to my cell. It was forbidden to speak to me.

When I found myself in that dismal cell, still shaken by the atrocious scene I had just experienced and by the monstrous accusation directed against me, when I thought of all those I had left, in joy and happiness, only a few hours earlier, I suffered a terrible nervous collapse and shouted in anguish.

I paced the cell, beating my head against its walls. The prison commandant, accompanied by the chief guard, was able to calm me for a few minutes.

Commandant Ferdinand Forzinetti, director of Cherche-Midi Prison, became the first Dreyfusard, long before that term entered the French lexicon. More renowned names would be linked to the affair, but no one rallied to Dreyfus at an earlier hour. He heard the prisoner's nightmares and the cry, "My only crime is to have been born a Jew!" Ordered to deny Dreyfus's requests to contact his family (the General Staff worried about news reaching "upper Jewdom"), Forzinetti tried to calm the accused.[4] When du Paty planned to enter the cell at night, shine a power-

[4]Forzinetti recalled the events in *Le Figaro*, Nov. 21, 1897.

ful projection lamp in the prisoner's face, and take him off guard, Forzinetti refused to allow it, but he could not stop the interrogator's other tactics: the angry threats followed by the quiet promise of leniency if Dreyfus confessed; the incessant bouts of dictation, with the prisoner ordered to write left-handed, right-handed, seated, lying down, and standing. For two weeks, in violation of the law requiring authorities to inform prisoners of the charges brought against them, du Paty ignored Dreyfus's demands for information.

Meanwhile, Forzinetti, convinced of the prisoner's innocence and fearful that he would not survive his ordeal, alerted the minister of war and military governor of Paris. "Captain Dreyfus, imprisoned by your order and placed in solitary confinement," Forzinetti wrote on October 27, "is in an indescribable mental state. . . . He cries then laughs and never stops saying that he feels he is losing his mind. He constantly protests his innocence and shouts that he will go mad before that innocence is recognized. At all times, he asks for his wife and children. There is reason to fear that he will commit some desperate act, despite all the precautions taken, or that madness will come."[5]

The official transcript of Dreyfus's interrogation charts the strategies of his questioners and the prisoner's efforts to respond with clarity and control, despite the use of sedatives and the threat of nervous collapse. Leaning on every cliché associated with traitors and treason, du Paty and the judge advocate of the first court-martial, Commandant Bexon d'Ormescheville, accused Dreyfus of amorous ties with foreign women and double agents of the demimonde, and of massive gambling debts at casinos and racetracks. And while the interrogators went about their work, a former police agent hired by the Statistical Section probed the captain's secret life. Most findings were erroneous or useless, and the rare accurate discoveries—of Dreyfus's racetrack visits, Alsatian contacts, and liaisons with women—could never be tied to treachery. The captain's private income, ten times the sum of his military salary, amply covered his modest gambling ventures, and his rakish life as a young officer in Paris and the provinces had come to a quiet end, as he admitted, after his marriage to Lucie Hadamard.

[5] Archives Nationales, BB/19 75, Oct. 27, 1894.

Interrogation of Alfred Dreyfus
October 18–November 29, 1894

QUESTION: You believe that you are the victim of a plot. Could the vengeance of some woman lay behind it?

ANSWER: I have no basis for that. I can only say one thing, that a woman, with whom I had no intimate relations, wrote a final letter to me in July or August, which closed with these words: "in life and in death."

Q: Have you had relations with a person residing at 1 rue Bizet, and what do you know about this person?

A: I never had intimate relations with her. I have visited her home two or three times and have not returned since the end of 1893. . . .

Q: How did you know Madame Cron at the horse races?

A: By speaking to her at the horse races. . . .

Q: Do you know other women besides the two mentioned above?

A: No. . . .

Q: How do you explain that a letter announcing the delivery of secret documents to a foreign power—documents that only an officer of the army General Staff could obtain—is recognized as having been written in your hand?

A: I deny, as I have from the first day, that I have ever written any agent of a foreign power. I know no such agent and have never spoken to one. I can only imagine one thing, that someone has copied my handwriting. . . .

Q: Here is a photograph of a letter that is attributed to you [the bordereau]. This picture was taken abroad, by means of a pocket-size camera, and we have the negative. Do you recognize this letter as being in your handwriting?

A: First I declare that I never wrote that infamous letter. A certain number of words resemble my handwriting, but it is not mine. The letter as a whole bears no resemblance to my handwriting. They have not even tried to imitate it. As for its content: (1) It would be impossible for me to furnish any precise information on the subject of the hydraulic brake of the 120-millimeter gun, for I have not even seen it since my time at the Ecole de Guerre; (2) I did know, through my work with the General Staff, about covering troops; (3) as for "a note on the modification of artillery formations," I do not know what it means; if it concerns the new artillery organization, then yes, I would have been familiar with that; (4) a note about Madagascar—I have never had my hands on a document dealing with that subject and never dealt with the question . . . ; (5) I have never heard a word about this preliminary Firing Manual of Field Artillery. . . .

Archives Nationales, BB/19 128, Cour de Cassation, 1905; reprint of 1894 interrogation.

Q: During your last interrogation, you asked to be heard by the minister of war, in order to propose that you be sent somewhere, anywhere, for a year under police surveillance, while a thorough investigation is conducted by the War Ministry?

A: Yes. . . .

Q: The minister is ready to receive you if you want to consider a confession.

A: I tell you again, I am innocent and have nothing to confess. It is impossible for me, within the four walls of a prison, to understand this horrible mystery. Put me with the chief of criminal investigations, and my entire fortune, my entire life will be devoted to explaining this affair. . . .

Q: The first time that you spoke of a woman named Déry you said she received spies. Is that correct?

A: I never said that. Perhaps after my arrest, in a moment of rage, I may have said about her: Has that filthy spy played a trick on me?

Q: Is Déry a courtesan?

A: Yes, I believe so; I am even quite sure of it.

Q: Why did you stop your relations with Déry?

A: I love my wife, and I was afraid that she would not understand that. . . .

Q: Do you write in German to one or more persons?

A: No, but I have added a few words, once or twice, to a letter my wife has written to my father for New Year's Day.

Q: Does Madame Dreyfus speak and write German?

A: She speaks German very well. I know she writes it, because she wrote to my father a number of times before his death.

Q: How do you explain the fragments of phrases written in German on blotting paper found in your home?

A: As part of my work, I often translated German at home. Words that I needed to look up in the dictionary, I would put on a scrap of paper, in order to learn them. . . .

Q: Are you affiliated with the Washington Club? Who were your sponsors?

A: I am affiliated with no club.

Q: Are you affiliated with the Betting Club of Paris? Who were your sponsors?

A: No. . . .

Q: Are you a gambler, and have you lost money gambling?

A: Never. I am not a gambler.

Q: But we have turned up in your account book for 1893 an expenditure dated July 1, with the note, "supplement Alfred, 150 francs" (with . . . fifty francs lost gambling). What do you have to say?

A: I frequently visit the home of my in-laws and my uncle's family, where some game probably took place one evening. I have never gambled outside the family. . . .

Q: Yesterday, at the end of your interrogation, you declared that you would give one hundred thousand francs to your lawyer, indeed even your entire fortune, to discover the author of the incriminating letter, that if you were set free you would succeed in finding him. How would you achieve that? You added that the incriminating letter was the work of a forger. You have just been able to give it another good look; on what basis do you reach this opinion?

A: I have built a thousand hypotheses on the origin of that letter. Certainly, I cannot unravel this affair all alone. . . . But, to be sure, I would gladly devote all my fortune and life to discover the miserable wretch. . . . Is it a forger or someone else? I am not the one who can resolve that enigma. . . .

Q: Do you still have something to say?

A: For more than six weeks, I have been in solitary confinement, six weeks during which I have suffered the most horrific martyrdom that an innocent man can tolerate. Alsatian, from a family that protested the German occupation, I left my situation in Alsace to come and serve my country with devotion. Today, as yesterday, I am worthy of leading my soldiers under fire.

Six weeks earlier, on the afternoon of the captain's arrest, Commandant du Paty had appeared with a police agent at the Dreyfus apartment on the avenue du Trocadéro. Frightened, at first, that her husband had suffered an accident, Lucie Dreyfus learned only that he had been arrested. Refusing to divulge the prison or the charges brought against him, du Paty threatened the captain's wife: "One word, a single word uttered by you, could mean war," and your husband "will be ruined. The only way to save him is through silence." Confiscating Dreyfus's army notebooks, private letters, and household accounts, du Paty and his partner moved on to rifle the home of Dreyfus's in-laws, the Hadamards. During a two-week period, Lucie Dreyfus received only one note from her husband, approved by du Paty: "I assure you of my honor and my affection."[6]

From the discovery of the bordereau through the first two weeks of Dreyfus's interrogation, the General Staff kept the case from the public eye. In the closing days of October, however, the leaks began. According to one theory, Commandant Henry, in a secret letter to *La Libre Parole,* announced Dreyfus's arrest and warned that "All Israel is in a state of agitation." But whatever the source and however hyperbolic, the news

---

[6]Michael Burns, *Dreyfus: A Family Affair, 1789–1945* (New York: HarperCollins, 1991), 113.

was out. The Havas Press Agency picked up the story of "a French army officer suspected of contact with a foreign power," and *Le Soir* was the first to come forward with Dreyfus's name.[7] On November 1, directly under its motto "France for the French," *La Libre Parole* ran the dramatic headline "High Treason: Arrest of the Jewish Officer A. Dreyfus."

[7]Patrice Boussel, *L'Affaire Dreyfus et la presse* (Paris: Armand Colin, 1960), 35–36; Bredin, *The Affair,* 76.

LA LIBRE PAROLE

High Treason

November 1, 1894

Is it true that an extremely important arrest has recently been made by order of the military authorities?

The arrested individual, it seems, has been accused of espionage. If the news is accurate, why are military authorities guarding it in such absolute secrecy?

An answer is essential!

Such was the question we posed on Monday, the 29th of this month, and to which the War Ministry refused to respond.

We have been aware of this arrest since Sunday. But being told the seriousness of the accusations, the name and rank of the criminal, we wanted—and one will understand our caution—to wait for the results of the inquiry.

Today we no longer have the same reasons to wait. In fact, here is what our colleague, *L'Eclair,* has said on the subject. . . .

"An officer—not, however, a superior officer—is at this moment in Cherche-Midi Prison.

"He has committed the most abominable crime that an officer can commit. He has, for venal ends, betrayed his fatherland.

"The secret investigation is concluded, the dossier established, the proof positively secured. . . ."

Therefore, there are no longer reasons for us to maintain our strict reserve.

The officer who is vile enough to sell the secrets of our national defense, who is miserable enough to have committed this crime of treason against the fatherland, is Captain Dreyfus (Alfred), of the 14th Artillery Regiment. . . .

Last night we received new confirmation of this extraordinary crime.

"Arrested fifteen days ago, he has confessed everything, and *absolute proof* is in hand that he sold our secrets to Germany.

"Whatever one says, he is in Cherche-Midi Prison, *but not under his name;* some want to shelter him in Mulhouse, where his family resides."

We went to the officer's home. . . .

On a table in the smoking room lay a schedule for the Eastern Railroad. Everything is in order, and one senses that the police have passed through. There is not a single paper on the captain's desk.

We do not push our investigation, for we understand the delicacy of our mission. Moving on to a dimly lighted anteroom, we notice in the corner a baby's little balloon; it is a heart-rending sight.

Last night I was with our friend Gauthier de Clagny, deputy from the Seine-et-Oise.

"It will not be possible," said the deputy, "given all the Codes and all the laws, to condemn that miserable wretch to death, and I regret that the Chamber has not yet acted on the law I proposed long ago concerning that subject. . . ."

But however painful that revelation may be . . . we have the one consolation of knowing that it is not a true Frenchman who committed such a crime!

With her husband's name now in public, Lucie Dreyfus broke du Paty's order of silence and, by contacting Alfred's family in Alsace, drew the first circle of defense. For the next half-decade, Alfred's brother, Mathieu Dreyfus, two years older and a protector since childhood, would orchestrate the Dreyfusard campaign. He shared the captain's fervent patriotism but had little of his aloof and rigid bearing. More diplomatic and with greater charm, he had the qualities to deal with the strong personalities who would rally to the cause, and with their conflicting philosophies. As one historian has remarked, Mathieu's "courage and selflessness contributed, to a great degree, in cementing the Dreyfusard camp." His role was essential, "for without him the affair would not have existed."[8] Even his enemies, while vilifying his leadership of the "Jewish

---

[8]Alain Pagès, *Emile Zola: Un intellectual dans l'affaire Dreyfus* (Paris: Seguier, 1991), 202–7. See also Michael Burns, "L'Honneur incarné: Mathieu Dreyfus et l'affaire," *Les Cahiers Naturalistes* 69 (1995): 292–301.

2ᵉ Année. — Nᵒ 70   Paris et Départements, le Numéro CINQ Centimes   Samedi 10 Novembre 1894

LA LIBRE PAROLE
ILLUSTRÉE
La France aux Français!

RÉDACTION
14, Boulevard Montmartre

Directeur : ÉDOUARD DRUMONT

ADMINISTRATION
14, Boulevard Montmartre

A propos de Judas Dreyfus

— Français, voilà huit années que je vous le répète chaque jour !!!

Figure 2. Edouard Drumont, director of *La Libre Parole* ("Free Speech") and fierce critic of Jews in the army, announces: "Frenchmen, for eight years I've been telling you about this every day!!!" Appearing on November 10, 1894, nine days after the announcement of Dreyfus's arrest, the illustration draws on familiar stereotypes; cowering and hook-nosed, the "Judas Dreyfus" wears the spiked helmet of the German enemy.

35

Syndicate," would respect the integrity, energy, and devotion of the "admirable brother."

Still, he had critics, and not only among anti-Semites. Radical members of his own camp would struggle to shake his respect for government authority, order, and the rule of law. But Mathieu, like his brother, believed in the liberal traditions of the modern French state and in the transcendent power of French justice. Though uninterested in Judaism, he adhered to what Rabbi Zadoc Kahn called a "religious respect for the law."[9] All this would frustrate the socialists and anarchists who aimed to turn the affair into a revolution of epic dimensions, and it would drive a wedge between Mathieu and the Zionists and Jewish nationalists who helped fight for his brother's release.

But those conflicts would come later, many of them much later, when the allies rallied and the Dreyfusard movement took form. In the closing weeks of 1894 and throughout the months that followed, "a deadly silence hovered around" the family. Arriving in Paris from his base in Mulhouse, Mathieu heard newspaper hawkers call out the headlines of his brother's arrest. Meeting with Commandant du Paty, he learned only that "devastating" charges had been brought against the captain. Refused access to the prisoner and shocked by du Paty's rambling description of the accused as a womanizing "monster . . . with a double life," Mathieu came away convinced that the army's chief interrogator was insane: "I was frightened knowing that my brother was in the hands of that man."[10]

Ready to commit their fortunes to securing the captain's release and reestablishing the family's honor, the Dreyfuses and Hadamards searched for a lawyer. Their first choice, René Waldeck-Rousseau, a future prime minister of France, accepted only civil cases but recommended Edgar Demange, a criminal lawyer with a high profile and, for a Jewish client accused of treason, a peculiar track record. Defender of the marquis de Morès following the duel with Captain Mayer, Demange was a devout Catholic and strong supporter of the French military. But he was also a consummate professional without a trace of anti-Semitism. He agreed to take the Dreyfus case with a caveat: If, after studying the court-martial dossier, he doubted the captain's innocence, he would

---

[9] Quoted in Michael R. Marrus, *The Politics of Assimilation: The French Jewish Community at the Time of the Dreyfus Affair* (Oxford: Oxford University Press, 1980), 145.

[10] Mathieu Dreyfus, *L'Affaire telle que je l'ai vécue* (Paris: Grasset, 1978), 22–24, 47.

refuse to defend him. Then, he warned, "the public . . . will conclude that [the prisoner] is guilty, and he will be irredeemably lost."[11] Mathieu agreed to the conditions.

On December 3, 1894, the judge advocate d'Ormescheville submitted his interrogation report, and on the following day military authorities announced that Captain Dreyfus's court-martial would begin on December 19. Edgar Demange could now meet his client for the first time and gain access to the army's dossier. He learned that along with the handwriting analyses submitted by Bertillion and Alfred Gobert, an expert with the Bank of France, three other experts had filed assessments that were far from uniform or categorical. But Demange was shocked by more than the topic of graphology. Immediately after studying the dossier, he described its contents to the prisoner's wife and brother.

[11]Ibid., 25.

MATHIEU DREYFUS

Account of the Court-Martial Dossier

December 1894

In the evening my sister-in-law and I went to Demange's home. After six weeks of anguish, of suffering, of wondering about this dossier that supposedly held state secrets, we went to finally learn about the overwhelming charges mentioned by General Mercier. . . .

Demange, politeness itself, did not even greet us when he entered his study. With great emotion he said, "If Captain Dreyfus was not a Jew, he would not be in Cherche-Midi Prison.

"The basis of the accusation," he continued, "is a covering letter, written on copying paper, unsigned, undated, and listing the dispatch of five documents. The indictment gives no indication of the letter's origin.

"It asserts that this piece had been addressed to a foreign power and that it reached its destination, but there is no mention of how the document was recovered. . . .

"Five experts have analyzed the piece: two . . . declaring that it is not written by your brother, the three others . . . asserting that it is."

Mathieu Dreyfus, *L'Affaire telle que je l'ai vécue* (Paris: Grasset, 1978), 31–32.

"There is no other charge of substance.

"Witnesses for the prosecution have submitted depositions on your brother's character without furnishing any fact to support the accusation.

"It is abominable; I have never seen such a dossier. If there is justice, your brother will be acquitted."

"Our hope," Mathieu Dreyfus wrote, "now rested with the court-martial." Optimistic that "seven loyal, honest officers" would not condemn a comrade on the basis of a suspicious document, Mathieu set out to conduct his own investigation and gather character witnesses for the defense. But only a few Alsatian friends and a handful of Captain Dreyfus's colleagues from the Ecole Polytechnique and Ecole de Guerre agreed to testify. The majority of officers refused.[12]

Nearly seven weeks after his arrest, Alfred Dreyfus received permission to contact his wife. "I will not describe all that I have suffered," he wrote on December 5. "Still today, I feel that I am the object of some horrible nightmare." But, he added, "I put my trust in God and in justice that truth will finally prevail."[13] Later, on the eve of his court-martial, he repeated those professions of faith and tried to calm the fears of his young wife and children.

[12]Ibid., 34–35.
[13]Alfred Dreyfus, *Lettres d'un innocent* (Paris: Stock, 1898), 20–21.

ALFRED DREYFUS

Letter to Lucie Dreyfus
December 18, 1894

My Dearest One: I finally come to the end of my suffering, to the end of my martyrdom. Tomorrow I will appear before my judges, my head high, my soul at peace.

The ordeal I have just undergone, terrible as it has been, has cleansed my soul. I will return to you better than I was. All the life that is left to me, I want to devote to you, my children, our dear families. . . .

Alfred Dreyfus, *Lettres d'un innocent* (Paris: Stock, 1898), 33.

I am ready to stand before soldiers, as a soldier who is beyond reproach. They will see on my face, they will read in my soul, they will be convinced of my innocence, as are all those who know me.

Devoted to my country, to which I have dedicated all my energy, all my ability, I have nothing to fear.

Sleep peacefully, my dear, and have no worry. Think only of the joy we will soon find in each other's arms. . . .

A thousand kisses as we await that happy moment.

If Dreyfus had nothing to fear from his country, he had much to fear from its servants, and as the court-martial approached, the Statistical Section turned its thin dossier into a thick portfolio of treason. Led by Sandherr and Henry, staff officers poured over every paper scrap stolen from foreign embassies and submitted by double agents. Assisted by a former police agent, they lifted sentences from the letters of the Spanish military attaché in Paris, a regular informant who warned the General Staff (without proof) about treacherous "wolves in your sheep pen"; they shifted the dates of documents to fit the timing of the bordereau; and they cobbled passages from the rich correspondence of the German attaché, Schwartzkoppen, and his Italian counterpart, Alessandro Panizzardi. Not surprisingly, both men had a stable of French informants, and their letters often alluded to agents of espionage. One missive, later to become a notorious document of the affair, described French fortification plans delivered to Panizzardi by "that scoundrel D. . . . " Though the diplomat was probably referring to a civilian cartographer named Dubois, the Statistical Section seized on the initial. Not yet desperate enough to insert the prisoner's name or to fabricate documents out of whole cloth, staff officers relied on the imaginations of the court-martial judges to fill in the blanks. And crucial to their case, they aimed to keep the secret dossier from Dreyfus's defenders, on the grounds of national security.[14]

---

[14]Douglas Johnson presents the full text of the *"canaille de D"* (scoundrel D) letter, followed by an English translation, in *France and the Dreyfus Affair* (London: Blandford, 1966), 228. See also Louis L. Snyder, *The Dreyfus Case: A Documentary History* (New Brunswick, N.J.: Rutgers University Press, 1973), 83–87.

3

Trial and Exile

From prison cell to courtroom, Captain Dreyfus had only a few yards to travel. Taken across the rainswept rue du Cherche-Midi before dawn on Wednesday, December 19, he never saw the crowds gathered at daylight along the narrow street or the onlookers perched in windows rented by enterprising landlords. At noon, in the high-ceilinged hall of the former Convent of the Good Shepherd, Dreyfus faced his judges. Six infantry officers and a cavalry major would decide the fate of an artillery captain arrested on the basis of a document that dealt largely with artillery topics. But expertise mattered less than the quick dispatch of the case. And above the tribunal, on the wall directly in front of the accused, hung a crucifix. Religious images had been removed from civil courtrooms in the 1880s, but until the legal separation of church and state in 1905 (largely as a result of the Dreyfus affair), France's chambers of military justice guarded Catholic tradition.

Immediately prior to the trial, Dreyfus's lawyer, recognizing the dangers of a closed session, had appealed through political contacts to the president of the republic. But Jean Casimir-Périer refused to meddle in military affairs. At the same time, newspapers in Paris and the provinces debated the question, with some journalists calling for a closed session to preserve "the peace of Europe" and others favoring a public trial. The *Archives Israélites* wanted "full light [shed] on this sad affair"; the anti-Semitic press wanted the air cleared of treason's stench.[1]

Dreyfus's judges settled the debate on the trial's first morning. When Edgar Demange announced before the full court that the charges brought against his client rested "on a single piece of evidence," the presiding judge ordered the lawyer to file his comments without reading

[1] *L'Eclair,* Dec. 13, 1894; Patrice Boussel, *L'Affaire Dreyfus et la presse* (Paris: Armard Colin, 1960), 58–60; and Jean-Denis Bredin, *The Affair: The Case of Alfred Dreyfus,* trans. Jeffrey Mehlman (New York: George Braziller, 1986), 92.

them. But when Demange declared that "for seven weeks the honor of a French officer has been exposed without defense to every outrageous polemic," the judges cut him off, withdrew, and voted for a closed session.

During the three-day trial, more than two dozen witnesses from nearly every office of the General Staff testified against Dreyfus, while less than half that number—and not a single representative from the high command—appeared in his defense. Still, the opening sessions worried Commandant Georges Picquart, the officer chosen by Mercier and Boisdeffre to observe the trial and submit periodic reports. Even prosecution witnesses, under oath, had to acknowledge Dreyfus's qualities (one classmate from the Ecole de Guerre believed him "incapable of treason"), and it became obvious that the case rested only on the fragile pillar of the bordereau. Furthermore, the handwriting expert Alphonse Bertillion confounded the court with a new and byzantine theory. Displaying enlarged photographs of the bordereau and a maze of diagrams, he argued that Dreyfus had used elements of his own handwriting, blended with specimens from his wife and brother, as part of an "auto-forgery." And he had encoded his payment for treason (the staggering sum of five hundred thousand francs) within the memorandum's orthography.

In his memoirs Dreyfus alludes to Bertillion's fantasies and to the most dramatic moment of the trial, the testimony of Commandant Henry.

ALFRED DREYFUS

Witnesses for the Prosecution
December 1894

I listened to the false and hateful deposition of Commandant du Paty de Clam, and to the deceitful deposition of Commandant Henry. . . . Energetically, but calmly, I refuted them both. Still, Henry returned to the witness stand a second time and, in a solemn tone, declared that he had it from an "absolutely honorable" person that an officer from the Second Bureau of the War Ministry had committed treason. At the time he received that in-

Alfred Dreyfus, *Cinq années de ma vie* (Paris: La Découverte, 1994), 60–61.

formation . . . I was attached to the Second Bureau. Indignant, I stood up and demanded in the strongest terms that the person alluded to be called before the court. Then, striking his breast with a theatrical flair, Henry added, "When an officer has a secret in his head, he does not even confide it to his military cap." Turning toward me, he added, "And the traitor, there he is!" Despite my violent protests, I was unable to make him explain his words and could not therefore demonstrate their falsity.

I listened to the experts' contradictory reports: two testifying in my favor, two testifying against me, and all verifying the numerous discrepancies between my handwriting and that of the bordereau. I attached absolutely no importance to Bertillion's deposition, which seemed to me like the work of a madman.

During those sessions, all additional accusations were disproved. No motive could be found to explain such an abominable crime.

In the fourth and last session, the prosecutor abandoned every minor charge and kept, as evidence, only the bordereau. He seized that paper, held it up, and cried out:

"If I have given you no motive for this crime, the most serious that can be committed, if I have no other proof, this letter remains as a crushing blow to the accused. Take up your magnifying glasses; you will be convinced that Dreyfus wrote it. And if he did, he is guilty of the most infamous treason."

The lawyer Demange, in his eloquent argument, refuted the experts . . . and closed by demanding how such an accusation could be made without providing any motive whatsoever.

To me, acquittal seemed certain.

Dreyfus's memoir omits Commandant Henry's most grandiloquent gesture. Asked by the presiding judge to affirm on his honor that the prisoner had betrayed France, he lifted his hand to the crucifix and cried out, "I swear it!" The message was clear: The case had been distilled into a matter of faith in the sacred spirit of the French military, in the reputation of the high command.[2]

On the third day, when deliberations began, Commandant du Paty, on behalf of General Mercier, delivered to the judges the secret dossier in a sealed envelope. Not a single member of the civilian government knew of its existence, and in gross violation of military and civil law, it was kept from the defense. It is possible, even probable, as more than

[2]For accounts of the Henry testimony, see Joseph Reinach, *Histoire de l'affaire Dreyfus* (Paris: La Revue Blanche, 1901–11), 1:417–20; and Armand Charpentier, *Les Côtés mystérieux de l'affaire Dreyfus* (Paris: Rieder, 1930), 70.

one historian suggests, that Dreyfus would have been convicted without the Italian attaché's "scoundrel D . . . " letter and the other documents compiled by the Statistical Section. After all, the presiding judge later admitted that he had hardly given them a glance; his "mind was made up."[3]

On December 22, in keeping with military law, the prisoner did not appear for the verdict. But minutes later, in a courtroom annex, Captain Dreyfus stood at attention while the prosecutor read the judgment by candlelight.

[3]Quoted in Bredin, *The Affair,* 96.

The Verdict
December 22, 1894

Today, the 22nd of December 1894, the First Council of War of Paris, hearing the requisitions and conclusions of the government's judge advocate, declares Dreyfus, Alfred, captain of the 14th artillery regiment, probationer of the army's General Staff, *guilty by unanimous decision* of having delivered to a foreign power or its agents, in Paris in 1894, a certain number of secret or confidential documents concerning national defense, in order to procure for that power the means of committing hostilities toward, or undertaking war against, France.

Accordingly, the said Court, *by unanimous decision, sentences the aforementioned Dreyfus to the sentence of deportation in a fortified prison and to military degradation,* conforming to the [codes] of military justice. . . . The Court orders Dreyfus, Alfred, to repay trial expenses to the public treasury, from his current and future assets . . . the sum total of expenses . . . amounts to 1,615 francs, 70 centimes.

From all sections of the Chamber of Deputies to the editorial offices of newspapers on the left, right, and center came a collective declaration of relief and good riddance. "Justice has not only been done," announced *Le Temps,* "it has been done well."[4] The court-martial had protected na-

[4]*Le Temps,* Dec. 24, 1894.

Archives Nationales, BB/19 95, Dec. 22, 1894 (emphasis in original).

tional security without igniting a European war. Doubts about Mercier's leadership turned into praise for his wise blend of caution and firmness, and the feeling of triumph reached to the Quai d'Orsay, home of the Ministry of Foreign Affairs. On the morning after the verdict, Maurice Paléologue, a diplomat with close connections to the General Staff, recorded the joyous reactions in his diary. Like most observers, Paléologue, swept up in the moment, exaggerated the public's engagement. Indifference to the case, or ignorance of it, was common.[5] But through many quarters of Paris and provincial cities, in government offices and backstreet cafés, news of the judgment resounded.

[5]On the impact throughout France of the Dreyfus trial and the affair that followed, see Nancy Fitch, "Mass Culture, Mass Parliamentary Politics, and Modern Anti-Semitism: The Dreyfus Affair in Rural France," *American Historical Review* 97, no. 1 (Feb. 1992): 55–95; and Michael Burns, *Rural Society and French Politics: Boulangism and the Dreyfus Affair, 1886–1900* (Princeton: Princeton University Press, 1984).

MAURICE PALÉOLOGUE

My Secret Diary of the Dreyfus Case

December 23, 1894

There is only one note in the comment on the verdict this morning throughout the whole of the Paris press, from the extreme right to the extreme left, from the clerical and monarchist journals to the organs of the most extreme Socialism: approval, relief, satisfaction, joy — a triumphant, vindictive, ferocious joy.

Being curious to know what the provincial newspapers said, late this afternoon I went to the Quai d'Orsay, where I asked for the telegraphic summary of the departmental Press. It struck the same note, a fierce, tumultuous joy, as if we had just escaped from a great national danger. . . .

There is no doubt about it; the French conscience has been profoundly stirred.

Maurice Paléologue, "Sunday, December 23rd, 1894" (excerpt) from *My Secret Diary of the Dreyfus Case,* translated by Eric Mosbacher (London: Secker and Warburg, 1957), 34–35. Reprinted with the permission of Librarie Plon and Random House UK, Ltd.

But Dreyfus's conviction has surprised no-one; it can even be said that in everyone's eyes he was convicted by the mere fact of having been accused. One of the most violent of the nationalist swashbucklers acutely foresaw this mentality of the crowd when at the beginning of the preliminary investigation he wrote: "If it is proved that the Minister of War has cast opprobrium on the army without irrefutable proofs; in a word, if Captain Dreyfus is acquitted, it is General Mercier who becomes the traitor." Thus the conviction came to look like a mere procedural detail, the consequence implicit in the charge.

But what was unexpected, what even the ranters of the *Libre Parole* had not dared to hope for, was a unanimous verdict.

Thus the most scrupulous were able to rejoice without fear, for seven officers would not have convicted a comrade, a brother-in-arms, even if he were a Jew, without striking proof of his guilt.

In any case, the commotion into which the country has been plunged can be explained easily enough. The monstrousness of the crime, France's love of her army, the stain cast on the flag, the social rank of the accused, the melodramatic circumstances, the secret manœuvres of Jewry to save the traitor, the threatening attitude of Germany, the terrible secret which hovered over the Kaiser's personal role—less than all this would have sufficed to exalt people's imaginations and fill them with fanaticism.

The cascade of hatred for "Iscariot II," as one provincial paper dubbed Dreyfus, did not flow from the anti-Semitic press alone. Many journalists and deputies lamented the 1848 law prohibiting the death penalty for "political crimes." In *La Justice* Georges Clemenceau, one of France's leading radical politicians, stripped Dreyfus of his humanity: "He has no relatives, no wife, no children, no love of anything, no human or animal ties, nothing but a filthy soul and abject heart." In the Chamber, the socialist Jean Jaurès accepted the verdict while condemning the system that did little more than slap the wrist of a bourgeois traitor. "Captain Dreyfus, convicted of treason by unanimous decision, has not been condemned to death," announced Jaurès. "In contrast, the country sees that simple soldiers, guilty of the most minor error or violent act, are shot without pardon and without pity." A loud round of applause came from the Chamber's extreme left.[6]

---

[6]*La Justice,* Dec. 25, 1895. Jaurès is quoted in Boussel, *L'Affaire Dreyfus,* 67–69.

While socialists used the Dreyfus case to attack the class-bound evils of French justice, commentators from across the Channel pointed to the power of anti-Semitism in France and to the Gallic penchant for secrecy. At this point, foreign reactions, including British reactions, focused on judicial procedures and cultural differences, and not on the question of guilt or innocence. Abroad, as at home, the vast majority of observers accepted the judges' decision.

THE TIMES OF LONDON

December 24, 1894

A profound sensation has been created in Paris, and, indeed, throughout France, by the trial, before a Court-martial, of Captain Alfred Dreyfus, an officer of artillery attached to the General Staff of the War Office, on a charge of "having procured for a foreign Power a certain number of secret documents connected with the national defence." On Saturday night the Court, after sitting for four days with closed doors, returned the unanimous verdict that the accused was guilty of the offence of which he was charged....

We have no wish to criticize the susceptibility of the French people in the case of offences which involve not only the security of a great military Power, but the sanctity of the obligations which are specially binding upon soldiers. Yet we must point out that, the more odious and unpopular a crime is, the more necessary is it that its proof and its punishment should be surrounded by all the safeguards of public justice. Of these the most indispensable is publicity. It would be impossible, in this country, to allow any body of officers to decide with closed doors on a charge involving degrading penalties almost more crushing to a man of honour than death itself. Indeed, if the precedent, borrowed from the worst days of the Revolution and of the Napoleonic despotism, is to prevail, there is no reason why capital sentences should not be determined upon, in the same way, with closed doors and on the pretext, of which the Court itself remains the sole judge, that publicity is "dangerous to order." It is intelligible that important military documents, such as that alleged to have been abstracted by Captain Dreyfus, may be of a nature justifying the War Office authorities in declining to permit the public discussion of their contents. But it is

Times (London), Dec. 24, 1894.

quite possible for any tribunal to identify such documents, and to deal with the question of their unlawful abstraction or possession, without permitting their tenour to be divulged. The objectionable part of the procedure on the trial of Captain Dreyfus was not the suppression of the contents of the papers alleged to have been stolen, but the conviction of the prisoner without the proof, in open Court and on sworn testimony, of his having stolen them. No doubt the members of the Court-martial were honourable men, whose desire it was to do justice. At the same time, we cannot forget that the very character of the charge against Captain Dreyfus was calculated to create a prejudice against him in the military as well as the popular mind, and that publicity given to the arguments for the defence and to the cross-examination of witnesses is the only effective security against such a bias. It is to be feared also that the Anti-Semitic propaganda in France increased the hostility to Captain Dreyfus, who is a member of a well-known Jewish family, and for whom his namesake, the Chief Rabbi of [Paris], was cited as a witness to character. The presumption is, of course, that the verdict of the Court-martial was justified by evidence communicated to that tribunal only, but the conditions of secrecy unfortunately imposed engender doubts which, in the case of so grave an accusation, involving penalties both degrading and severe, ought not to be left undispelled. It may be important for the French people to preserve the secrets of their War Department, but it is of infinitely greater importance for them to guard their public justice against even the suspicion of unfairness or of subjection to the gusts of popular passion.

. . . If Captain Dreyfus was guilty of purloining confidential documents to sell them to a foreign Power . . . his crime was, undoubtedly, one of the blackest of which a soldier can be found guilty. We can hardly be surprised at the agitation in the streets and the popular outcry against the misplaced tenderness of the law. The French populace must not be expected to look behind the verdict of the Court-martial. It is true Captain Dreyfus has a right of appeal, of which he has given notice that he will avail himself, and, till that appeal has been disposed of, it would be improper to regard his guilt as conclusively proved; but the verdict against him reverses the presumption of his innocence.

Nevertheless, when we come to consider the circumstances of the trial, we cannot refrain from expressing our astonishment at the positive manner in which not only the populace, but the Press, of Paris appear to have taken for granted the criminality of the accused. We are told that public opinion and the newspapers unanimously approve the finding of the Court-martial. But, as we have said, the trial was conducted with closed doors, and the Parisian public cannot, therefore, have founded their approval on any knowledge whatever of the facts upon which the conviction was based. At the opening of the proceedings last week the prosecutor, on behalf of the Government, claimed that the inquiry should be secret. The general

rule governing Court-martial in France is that their proceedings are null
and void unless conducted in public, but in case publicity is held by the
Court to be dangerous to order or morality, secrecy can be enjoined. It was
so decided in the case of Captain Dreyfus. His counsel, Maître Demange,
entered a protest, and attempted to argue the point, but was summarily cut
short by the presiding officer when he ventured to touch even indirectly
on the facts, by referring to the "single document" on which he was understood to assert that the charge really rested. What this is, and why it was
deemed necessary to conceal its character and its origin, are questions
which have been left by the decision of the Court-martial at the mercy of
public conjecture. It has been reported that the document or documents
abstracted by Captain Dreyfus had passed into the hands of the German
Embassy and that it, or they, had been won back from its archives by a
process of a similar kind. But, though the proceedings of the Court-martial
have been secret, the names of the witnesses for the prosecution and for
the defence have been published. It is evident that no persons connected
either with the German Embassy or with any foreign Legation whatever
have been cited on the one side or the other.

The captain "will be acquitted tonight," Demange had told Mathieu
Dreyfus on the trial's last morning, unless the judges receive "an order
to convict him."[7] Barred from the closed session, the Dreyfus family had
learned of the verdict by telephone. Assured that the prison director,
Forzinetti, would guard against a suicide attempt, Mathieu met with Demange that night and learned of the lawyer's suspicion that something,
unknown to the defense, had transpired in the deliberation hall. Agree-
ing that his brother should lodge an immediate appeal, Mathieu returned to Lucie Dreyfus and promised to remain in Paris until the truth
was out.

On New Year's Eve, Commandant du Paty informed the prisoner that
his appeal had been rejected. He intimated, however, that a bargain
might be struck: a lighter sentence, perhaps, in exchange for full disclo-
sure of the documents passed to Germany. When Dreyfus protested, du
Paty grew angry and suggested that the traitor's wife was also implicated
in the conspiracy. "Enough!" the prisoner shouted. "I am innocent and
your duty is to pursue your investigation," to which du Paty responded,

---

[7]Mathieu Dreyfus, *L'Affaire telle que je l'ai vécue* (Paris: Grasset, 1978), 43.

"If you are innocent, you are the greatest martyr of all the centuries." On the same night, Dreyfus wrote to Mercier, "I have received, by your order, a visit from Commandant du Paty de Clam, to whom I have again declared my innocence. . . . I have been convicted. . . . But in the name of my honor, which I hope will be returned one day, I implore you to continue your investigation. After I have left, keep up the search, it is the only mercy I ask."[8]

On January 2, 1895, Dreyfus saw his wife for the first time in seven weeks. Two iron grilles separated the couple in the prison's frigid basement. Letters written immediately after the meeting describe the conditions, the frustrations, and the mutual call for courage.

[8]Alfred Dreyfus, *Cinq années de ma vie* (Paris: La Découverte, 1994), 68. See also, Bredin, *The Affair,* 99–100.

LUCIE DREYFUS

Letter to Alfred Dreyfus

January 2, 1895

MY DEAREST ONE, Finally, we have had the meeting we so desired. . . . What boundless joy I felt when I saw your kind eyes again, when I heard your voice, but how horrible to be so close and yet separated by those hideous bars. I had a dreadful feeling . . . ; I was so overjoyed, I wanted to say so many things, I wanted to give you courage, to comfort you, but I no longer had the strength to tell you what I felt, I could not even find the words to express the admiration that I have for you, for your immense sacrifice. It is you who give me courage; you are the one whose feelings are the most sublime.

After leaving you, I went to the office of General Tyssère [Forzinetti's superior] and asked permission . . . to be able to speak to you away from witnesses, away from those bars. I only hope that he is humane. . . .

Adieu, my dear, I embrace you, as I love you, with all my strength.

Quoted in Alfred Dreyfus, *Souvenirs et correspondance* (Paris: Grasset, 1936), 54–55.

ALFRED DREYFUS

Letter to Lucie Dreyfus

January 2, 1895

My Dear, I need to write to you again, a few words for you to find when you awaken tomorrow morning.

Our talk, even through prison bars, has done me good. My legs trembled as I walked down to our meeting; I held myself rigid to avoid collapsing with emotion. Even now, my hand is still not steady; that meeting has so shaken me. If I did not insist that you stay longer, it was because I was exhausted, and I needed to hide my tears. Don't imagine that my spirit is any less strong . . . only that my body has been weakened by three months in prison. . . .

What has done me the most good is to feel your courage and strength, so full of affection. Let us continue, my dear wife, through our bearing and our courage, to compel the respect of the world. As for me, you must have felt that I am determined in every way; I want my honor, and I will have it; no barrier will stop me.

Send thanks to everyone; thank Demange for all he has done for an innocent man. . . . Tell him that I count on him in this struggle for my honor.

Two days later, in letters to his family and lawyer, Dreyfus pledged to face his public degradation "with head held high." Originally scheduled for Friday, January 4, the "execution parade" was moved, without explanation, to the following morning at 9:00 A.M., a shift some observers found appropriate: The traitor would be punished on the Jewish Sabbath. Held in the Cour Morland, the main courtyard of the Ecole Militaire, under the chisled inscription "Ecole Supérieure de Guerre," the degradation took place on the grounds where Captain Dreyfus had trained as a young officer. Military authorities ordered every regiment of the Paris garrison to send two detachments, and nearly four thousand troops, silent and at attention, lined the square's periphery. An immense crowd (estimated by a correspondent from the *New York Herald* at "not less than 20,000 persons") pressed against the iron rails separating the

---

Alfred Dreyfus, *Cinq années de ma vie* (Paris: La Découverte, 1994), 70.

Cour Morland from the Place de Fontenoy, while farther on, other spectators climbed the golden dome of the Invalides and scaled the roof of the Galerie des Machines. A rainstorm had just passed, and pools of mud lay on either side of the courtyard's narrow cobblestone pathway, where General Paul Darras, on horseback, drew his sword and called out, "Present arms!"[9]

Recounted in newspaper reports, diaries, memoirs, and illustrations, as well as in a handful of rare photographs, Dreyfus's public degradation, punctuated by shouts of "Death to the Jew!" became a touchstone of memory for many of those who witnessed or read about the ten-minute ritual of humiliation. Maurice Barrès dubbed it "the parade of Judas," a spectacle "more exciting than the guillotine."[10] For journalist Léon Daudet, it marked an orgy of revenge against a "wretched" Jew. Laced with hatred and crafted with skill, Daudet's account, composed for *Le Figaro* and titled "The Punishment," stands as one of the affair's most notorious monuments.

[9]For the full text of the *New York Herald* report, see Louis L. Snyder, *The Dreyfus Case: A Documentary History* (New Brunswick, N.J.: Rutgers University Press, 1973), 38–40.
[10]Maurice Barrès, *Scènes et doctrines du nationalisme* (Paris: Félix Juven, 1902), 134.

LÉON DAUDET

The Punishment

January 6, 1895

Behind the high iron gate, in the vast, square, and solemn Morland Courtyard, troops begin to assemble. Companies march past. I hear that singular step, formed of hundreds of steps, the rattling of rifles, leather belts and sabers. . . .

The hour strikes nine. The general pulls his sword. The drums roll, their dull rumble translating the shudders felt by the entire silent gathering. The fatal door opens on the hideous cortege: four artillerymen and, between them, the criminal; close by, the executioner, a sergeant major of the Republican Guard. That small and mournful group crosses the diago-

Le Figaro, Jan. 6, 1895 (emphasis in original).

nal at a military step and stops a few meters in front of the general. Every heart trembles. A riotous silence reigns. Clouds give way to a ray of sunshine, brief and bloody, pouring a bit of life on this death worse than death.

The military clerk comes forward. He reads the verdict. But his voice, like that of the general, is lost in the vast space. Quickly, the executioner, a sort of helmeted giant, approaches the condemned man, a rigid and dark silhouette on which all attention is focused. Without an instant of hesitation, the executioner goes for the military cap; he tears off the insignia, the fine gold braids, the ornaments of the jacket and sleeves. The dumb puppet prepares himself for the atrocious work; he even lifts his arms. He shouts a few words—"Innocent! . . . Innocent! . . . Long live France! . . . "—which hardly carry through the heavy, anguish-filled atmosphere.

In the public square beyond the courtyard . . . the crowd grows restless and clamorous. It howls. It hisses. It is a strident and intersecting storm of outrage. Anger prevails over dejection and stupor.

But nothing stirs among the soldiers who witness and judge. I take up my opera glass. It dances in my hands, and through a kind of steam, I find myself close to this symbolic act of stripping away, to the fall of buttons and epaulets. . . . I catch a glimpse of the condemned man's wan and weasel-like face, raised up in final defiance. But I am engrossed by his body, that run-down body of a liar, from which is skinned away, piece by piece, everything that gave it social value. . . .

The giant takes the sword of the man who had been a captain and, with a final, sharp, lightning blow, breaks it over his knee. The vestiges are on the ground, pitiful rags, punished for the wretch who wore them, dead in his place, and dishonored with him.

What more can one do with this little automaton, completely black and stripped of everything, with this hideous beast of treason who remains upright on his rigid limbs, survivor of his own catastrophe . . . ? He will be exposed to the contempt of those who were his comrades, and for whom he prepared defeat, all those brave officers, all those humble soldiers, motionless and terrified. Within them rage struggles with disgust and the remains of pity that exist in noble souls, even in the presence of the worst crimes. He will march in front of those honorable men, in front of rectitude, discipline, duty, in front of that empire of heroism, all the sentiments that mean nothing to him, the traitor. . . .

He approaches, between his guards, a walking corpse, with the step of a zombie on parade, thin in appearance, but magnified by infamy. . . . Close to us he finds again the strength to shout "Innocent!" in a voice without tone. There is he before me, at the instant of passing, the cold eye, the look lost in the past, no doubt, since his future is dead with his honor. He no longer has age. He no longer has a name. He no longer has a complexion. He is the color of *treason*. His face is ashen . . . without appearance of remorse, surely foreign, a wreck of the ghetto. . . .

The shouts of the crowd have stopped. The ray of sunlight has disappeared. Our strength has been sapped. It is time for the drama to end. The degradation and parade have lasted only ten minutes, but our emotions have been stirred, it seems, for twenty-four hours. The sinister march ends down there, at the black carriage of the prison guard, on the backstreet where the corpse, lifted up by gendarmes, is finally put in its oven *(s'enfourne)*. We are relieved at its presence.

Life resumes. The troops disband. Beat the drums! Sound the fanfare! Cast your proud and sonorous mantle over this obscene burial. . . . The soldiers march ahead firmly, the spectacle fixed forever in their eyes. For the idea of the fatherland is so deep-seated and so proud that it can be strengthened by its antithesis, by the assaults directed against it. On the wreckage of so many beliefs, a single faith remains genuine and sincere: that which safeguards our race, our language, the blood of our blood, and which brings us together in solidarity. The closed ranks are our ranks. The wretch was not French. We knew it by his actions, his demeanor, his face. He plotted our disaster, but his crime has exalted us. And as I leave this cursed spectacle, in the midst of the tumult, the words of command, the martial processions, I see standing before me the proud and simple column raised "to the memory of the officers and soldiers of the land and sea forces who have fallen on the field of honor in defense of the fatherland."

Another journalist reported on the degradation for the Austrian newspaper *Neue Freie Presse.* Only a few months later, Theodor Herzl, a Viennese Jew on assignment in Paris since 1891, would complete the first draft of *Der Judenstaat* (The Jewish State), and at decade's end he would declare that "the Dreyfus case made me a Zionist." As one scholar has written, Herzl saw "the bitter irony embedded" in the fact that a vicious anti-Semitism, directed at an assimilated patriot, flourished in the cradle of the European Enlightenment. If Jews were in danger in the nation of the Rights of Man, they were in danger everywhere. But the "terrible and significant" lessons Herzl learned from the Dreyfus case seemed to have crystallized over the months following the degradation.[11] On the morning of the event, the founder of modern Zionism, like the majority of his contemporaries, made no declaration of belief in the prisoner's innocence.

[11]David Vital, "A Prince of the Jews," *Times Literary Supplement,* June 7, 1996, 6–7. See also Alain Dieckhoff, "Le Jour où Theodor Herzl devint sioniste," *L'Histoire* 173 (January 1994): 106–11.

THEODOR HERZL

Account of the Dreyfus Degradation

January 6, 1895

The degradation of Captain Dreyfus on this dreary morning drew a crowd of curious onlookers to the neighborhood of the War College, located just behind the terrain of the 1889 World's Fair. There were numerous officers, some with their ladies. Only officers and a few journalists were admitted to the inner courtyard of the Ecole Militaire. Gathered outside was the usual mob of gaping busybodies who make it a point to attend every execution. A large contingent of police had been deployed. By 9 A.M. the huge yard was filled with troops forming an open square, in the center of which sat a general on horseback. A few minutes later, Dreyfus was led out wearing the uniform of a captain. Four soldiers brought him before the general, who declared: "Alfred Dreyfus, you are unworthy to bear arms. I hereby degrade you in the name of the French people. Let the judgment be executed." Thereupon Dreyfus raised his right hand and shouted: "I swear and declare that you are degrading an innocent man. Vive la France." With that, the drums began to roll, and the military bailiff tore the already loosened buttons and straps from the uniform. Dreyfus maintained his proud bearing, and the procedure was completed within a few minutes.

Now began the ordeal of filing past the troops. Dreyfus marched like a man convinced of his innocence. As he passed a group of officers who yelled "Judas! Traitor!" he shouted back: "I forbid you to insult me." By 9:20, Dreyfus had made the rounds. He was thereupon shackled and turned over to the gendarmes, who will from now on treat him as a civilian prisoner. The troops filed out, but the mob lingered in front of the gate waiting for the prisoner's departure. Bloodthirsty cries filled the air, such as "If they bring him out now, he'll be ripped to pieces." But they waited in vain. Those, however, who had actually witnessed the degradation ceremony left in a curious state of agitation. The strangely resolute

Neue Freie Presse account of Dreyfus degradation, January 5, 1895, as printed in Ernst Pawel, *The Labyrinth of Exile: A Life of Theodor Herzl* (New York: Farrar, Straus & Giroux, 1989), 206–7. Copyright © 1989 by Ernst Pawel. Reprinted with the permission of Farrar, Straus & Giroux, Inc. and Russell & Volkening, Inc.

Right: **Figure 3.** A rare photograph of Dreyfus's military degradation in the courtyard of the Ecole Militaire on January 5, 1898, taken at the precise moment when the captain's saber is being broken. (Dreyfus stands at attention, sixth from the left.) Seconds later the crowd will erupt with shouts of "Death to the Jew! Long live the army!"

Dégradation du Capitaine Dreyfus, le 5 Janvier 1895.

Grille Côté de l'avenue Bosquet

Beau à la Grandière

Canonniers escorte du Général

Officiers d'ordonnance

G.al Darras

le greffier Valle calle

appuient de la Garde républicaine Bonnin adjudant de Gendre ?

Capt Dreyfus

adjudant Vabricole

Côté sur l'Ecole Supérieure de Guerre
Avenue La Mothe Piquet

55

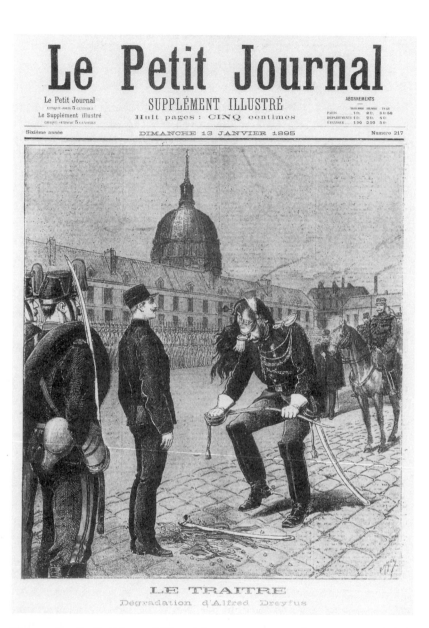

Figure 4. *Le Petit Journal Illustré,* January 13, 1895. Though an anti-Semitic and anti-Dreyfusard publication, the newspaper presents an accurate rendering of the degradation ritual.

attitude of the degraded captain had made a deep impression on many eyewitnesses.

The visual images of the degradation—the quick sketches and elaborate lithographs aimed at a wide audience in Paris and provincial towns— often repeated the same inaccuracies found in newspaper reports and editorials. Whereas *L'Illustration* and *Le Petit Journal* published faithful depictions of Dreyfus standing at attention in the Cour Morland, *Le Quotidien illustré* carried a portrait of the "traitor" with head bowed and body stooped in defeat. Soon to become an icon of the affair, it depicted a moment that never happened. And a photograph, taken from a distant window of the Ecole Militaire, proved the point. While "the executioner," a ghostlike blur, breaks Dreyfus's sword, the captain (sixth from the left on the cobblestone path) stands straight, his head held high.

In the days following the degradation, a rumor spread that Dreyfus had confessed to an officer of the Republican Guard. While waiting to appear in the Ecole Militaire courtyard, the story went, he told Captain Lebrun-Renault of du Paty's insistence that documents had been transmitted to Germany. Although the day's official report noted nothing unusual, the guard later elaborated on the conversation for partygoers at the Moulin Rouge. Enthused by his celebrity and full of drink, Lebrun-Renault proclaimed that Dreyfus had admitted to selling documents "in order to procure others of more importance." With journalists scouring Parisian nightclubs for sensational items, it is not surprising that morning editions ran the bold headline "Dreyfus Has Confessed!" Within a few days Lebrun-Renault had been called to the Elysée Palace and chastised by the president of the republic. Casimir-Périer wanted the Dreyfus case closed, the prisoner exiled, and tensions with Germany (drawn tight since the court-martial) defused. The rumors of a confession ebbed, but anti-Dreyfusards would later resurrect the Lebrun-Renault legend.[12]

From the moment of the captain's arrest and through the years that followed, the words *calvary* and *martyrdom* appeared frequently in Dreyfus's correspondence and diary entries. Even Lucie Dreyfus, an observant Jew of deep faith, called on a Christian vocabulary to articulate her husband's tragedy. Now, between January and March 1895, the first stages

[12]See Reinach, *Histoire de l'affaire Dreyfus,* 1:494ff; and Snyder, *The Dreyfus Case,* 43–44.

Figure 5. Dreyfus's police identification photograph, taken after the public degradation. His brass buttons, insignia, and gold epaulets have been stripped away. Thirty-five years old, he awaits deportation.

of Dreyfus's exile conjured up a *via dolorosa,* a long and agonizing journey that took him from the civilian Santé Prison to the fortress of Ile de Ré off France's west coast, and on to the Iles du Salut, almost seven miles from the French Guiana mainland of South America. Shackled in a wire-mesh cell and exposed to the wind aboard the steamship *Ville de Saint Nazare,* the prisoner was thrown old cans of food by guards ordered to remain silent. On March 12 the ship anchored off the main island of the Iles du Salut, and one month later the prisoner was transported to the nearby Devil's Island, a former leper colony recently "purged of its vermin."[13] During the next four years, only a few architectural details would change: A new hut would be constructed to house the island's solitary prisoner, and a high wall would block his view of the sea beyond.

[13]Marie-Antoinette Menier, "La Détention du capitaine Dreyfus à l'île du Diable, d'après les archives de l'Administration pénitentiaire," *Revue française d'histoire d'Outre-Mer* 44, no. 237 (1977): 460–63.

ALFRED DREYFUS

Devil's Island Diary

April 14, 1895

MY DIARY   (to be given to my wife)
Today I begin the diary of my sad and frightening life. Indeed, only today do I have paper at my disposal, paper that has been numbered and initialed so that I cannot substract a single sheet. I am responsible for its use. But what would I do with it? What use would it have for me? To whom would I give it? What secret do I have to confide to paper? So many questions, so many enigmas!

Until now, I worshiped reason; I believed in the logic of things and events; I believed, finally, in human justice! Everything strange, extravagant, could hardly penetrate my mind. Alas! how all my sound reason, all my beliefs, have collapsed.

What horrible months I have just passed; how many sad months still await me?

I had decided to kill myself after my unjust conviction. To be condemned for the most infamous crime, on the basis of a suspicious document with handwriting that imitated or resembled mine, certainly that is enough to drive to despair a man who places honor above all. During that crisis of confusion, my dear wife, so devoted, so courageous, made me understand that I, being innocent, did not have the right to abandon her, or to willfully desert my post. I knew that she was right, that my duty was there. But, on the other

---

Alfred Dreyfus, *Cinq années de ma vie* (Paris: La Découverte, 1994), 103–5.

hand, I was afraid—yes, afraid—of the atrocious mental suffering I would have to endure. Physically, I felt strong; a clean, pure conscience gave me superhuman strength. But the mental and physical tortures have been worse than even I expected, and today I am broken in body and spirit.

Still, I have yielded to my wife's requests, and therefore have the courage to live! . . . My conscience sustains me; every day my reason tells me: Truth will finally triumph; in a century like ours, the light cannot be hidden long. But alas! every day brings a new disappointment. Not only does the light remain concealed, but everything has been done to block it from shining forth.

I was, and I am still, in the most absolute solitary confinement. Everywhere my correspondence is read; it is examined by the Ministry and often left unmailed. I am prohibited from writing to my wife about the investigations I want her to pursue. It is impossible to defend myself.

Once in exile, I thought I would find, if not rest—I will never know that until my honor is restored—at least a certain tranquillity of spirit and life that would help me wait for the day of rehabilitation. What new and bitter disappointment!

After an ocean voyage of fifteen days in a cage, and after the ship anchored off the Iles du Salut, I remained on board for four days, kept below in a torrid heat. . . . When I disembarked, I was locked in a prison room, the shutters closed, the order given that I speak to no one. Alone with my thoughts, I followed the regime of a convict. . . .

I stayed that way for a month, closed up in my room. . . . Several times I was at the point of going mad; . . . my horror of life was such that I thought I would stop caring for myself, and that way the martyrdom would be over. It would be a liberation, an end to all this pain, for I would not have perjured myself, my death being natural.

The memory of my wife, my duty to my children, gave me the strength to resist. I did not want to belie her efforts, to abandon her in her mission of searching out the truth, of finding the guilty man. For that reason, despite my fierce aversion to any new face, I asked to see the doctor.

Finally, after thirty days of confinement, they transported me to Devil's Island, where I will have a semblance of freedom. Indeed, during the day I will be able to walk in a space of a few hundred square meters, followed by a guard, step for step. At nightfall (between six and half past six), I will be locked in a hut of four square meters, with a door made of iron rails, in front of which the guards will change shifts all night long.

A chief and five guards have been appointed to watch over me. My ration is a half-loaf of bread per day, three hundred grams of meat three times a week, and, on the other days, canned stew or pork. I drink water.

For a man who places honor above everything else in the world, how horrible it is to be under constant watch and continual suspicion!

4

Treasons and Strategems

Within days after Alfred Dreyfus's prison wagon galloped from the Ecole Militaire, his case faded from the headlines. Captain Lebrun-Renault's account of the prisoner's "confession" caused a brief sensation, and Edouard Drumont, Henri Rochefort, and others whose emotions were mixed when their target departed published articles on Dreyfus's journey into exile, including reports of a near riot when the prisoner reached the coast town of La Rochelle. But the inflammatory articles kindled little interest. Over the previous half-dozen years, six French citizens had been convicted of spying for Germany, and though the case of the Jewish captain had sparked more high drama than all the others combined, it had ended on a similar note. Dreyfus was gone and soon forgotten by all but his family, a handful of friends, and a detachment of colonial functionaries.

And so it would go for nearly two years, until new revelations came to public light and new evidence pointed to the real traitor. In the interim the Dreyfus case remained a largely private affair for the prisoner's circle of allies, who tried desperately to make it public again, and for the General Staff, embroiled in a secret civil war within its ranks. During this middle phase, Colonel Sandherr, chief of the Statistical Section, suffered the first attacks of a general paralysis. In July 1895 he was replaced, not by his key deputy, the loyal Commandant Henry, but by forty-one-year-old Georges Picquart, graduate of Saint-Cyr, veteran of African and Southeast Asian campaigns, and the officer who had reported on the court-martial for General Mercier. Sandherr trusted Picquart, a fellow Alsatian and fellow anti-Semite, and tutored him on the usefulness of the secret dossier. If the Dreyfus case ever reared its head again, the new intelligence chief could call on the special file. Sandherr died before he could regret his confidence in Picquart, whose devotion to justice would prove more potent than his loyalty to the military caste and his hatred of Jews. Almost simultaneously with Mathieu Dreyfus, though along a separate track and without pre-meditation, Picquart would discover the author of the bordereau.

The Statistical Section, its new chief soon learned, needed cleaning up. Discipline had deteriorated, and no rational system separated important intelligence papers from the waste hauled out of embassies or dropped on General Staff desks by Parisian informants. Picquart, who appreciated Henry's sleuthing but not his office management, announced that he would personally examine all incoming documents. In early March 1896 Madame Bastian, still on the job as "agent Auguste," delivered a new load of papers from the German embassy, including shreds of a small letter-telegram, written in French on thin blue paper. Barely a year after Dreyfus's deportation, the brief and enigmatic *petit bleu* suggested the presence of yet another traitor within the French military. Like the bordereau, it had come from the basket of the German attaché.

The Petit Bleu

1896

Sir, I await above all a more detailed explanation of the matter in question than the one you gave me the other day. Consequently, please be good enough to give it to me in writing, so that I may determine if I am able to continue my relations with the firm of R. or not. C.

From Joseph Reinach's multivolume account of the Dreyfus affair to the most recent scholarship, historians have tried to unravel the mysteries of the *petit bleu*. Though signed with Maximilien von Schwartzkoppen's code (C.), it was not in his handwriting (nor in that of his mistress, as some theories had it), and though the attaché later admitted to dealings with French agents, he denied ever disposing of the letter-telegram. The document—like another, with a similar text, found in the attaché's basket and delivered to the Statistical Section the same day—raises more

---

Reprinted in Douglas Johnson, *France and the Dreyfus Affair* (London: Blandford, 1966), 229.

Figure 6. Ferdinand Walsin-Esterhazy, officer, journalist, and traitor, described by Mathieu Dreyfus and others as a "great bird of prey."

questions than it answers. But the addressee, clearly indicated, has never been in doubt: The German embassy's *petit bleu* was destined for "Monsieur le Commandant Esterhazy, 27 rue de la Bienfaisance—Paris."

At this point, Picquart made no connection with the Dreyfus case, except to avoid its early leaks and embarrassments. Launching a secret investigation, he shared his suspicions with only a few officers, including Henry, who had worked briefly with Esterhazy in the intelligence bureau nearly two decades before. Picquart's agents had little trouble uncovering information on the notorious commandant. Descendant of a noble Hungarian family (through an illegitimate line), Marie Charles Ferdinand Walsin-Esterhazy had been born in Paris with no title and no wealth. An indifferent student but with a good command of the German language, he joined the French army and fought his way through the 1870 war with Prussia and campaigns in Tunisia. Gambling and womanizing forced him to scramble for cash from every source he could tap. He volunteered as a second for Jewish officers who dueled with anti-Semites (he accompanied Captain Crémieu-Foa in 1892), and then, in return for his services, coaxed money out of prominent Jews, including Baron Edmond de Rothschild. At the same time, he drew a stipend from Drumont's *La Libre Parole,* for which he became an anonymous editor in 1895. Given the commandant's perverse résumé, the selling of secrets was hardly a surprise.

A few years later, the journalist Séverine, on the staff of *La Fronde,* France's first feminist daily newspaper, provided one of the most striking descriptions of Esterhazy.

SÉVERINE (CAROLINE RÉMY)

Memories of Esterhazy

January 1898

A strange physiognomy, not ugly, perhaps worse, the face of a Florentine mercenary. An animal of prey, to be sure: a birdlike head; a huge beaked nose; short, straight hair combed forward; a jutting, skeletal frame—eyes deep in their sockets, under a thatch of thick eyebrows.

They are not large, these eyes, and they are without brightness and expression, but there is a liveliness of movement that is absolutely bizarre. They dart about, ferreting around without stop, on the watch under drooping eyelids, or as if lurking behind eyelashes, uneasy, in the nervous sense of the word.

And all this fits precisely enough with the broken, minced voice, with modulations that are both persuasive—and unexpected!

For neither the glance nor the accent corresponds to the exterior look.

Séverine (Caroline Rémy), *Vers la lumière: Impressions vécue* (Paris: Stock, 1900), 7–9.

Between them all, something explodes, something disconcerts. One expects bluntness, almost brutality . . . and yet one encounters only a peculiar elegance, a blank anger, a cold indignation. . . .

Meanwhile, does one imagine that the man is violent? . . . I find a living puzzle; I study it. That is all.

Thin as a rake, a mustache too black for the rest of his coloring, two huge rings on his right hand, M. Esterhazy certainly looks like a foreigner, of a race that has naturalized a notorious and hereditary bravery; not disagreeable, but coming from farther than Florence; . . . from the Orient of scimitars . . . and of wretched coffee.

And with that, an intelligence perhaps even greater than one imagines; accustomed to trouble; delighted by complications; very supple and very shrewd—a dagger blade in the sheath of a sword!

Picquart's agents uncovered a mass of negative information on Esterhazy but found no hard evidence of treason, and during the summer of 1896 the investigation stalled. Chief of Staff Boisdeffre and Minister of War Jean-Baptiste Billot (Mercier's successor after a change of government) learned of the inquiry and approved its continuation, but only with caution. They did not want, as they put it, "a new Dreyfus Affair."[1]

In a case within a case, full of curious turns and inexplicable delays, Georges Picquart's long wait to examine Esterhazy's handwriting ranks near the top of unanswered questions. Perhaps, as one historian notes, superior officers rejected Picquart's requests to open Esterhazy's mail and military file, or perhaps the intelligence chief considered graphology less pressing than other avenues of inquiry. Whatever the explanation, a full six months passed from Picquart's first suspicions until late August 1896, when he studied two letters by Esterhazy and sensed something familiar, something strange. Reaching into a drawer where he kept a facsimile of the bordereau, Picquart compared the handwriting specimens and grew "terrified," as he later described his discovery. Esterhazy had written the document that had sent Dreyfus to Devil's Island.[2]

[1]Joseph Reinach, *Histoire de l'affaire Dreyfus* (Paris: La Revue Blanche, 1901–11), 2:286.

[2]On Picquart's research and discoveries, see ibid., 241–290 and passim; and Jean-Denis Bredin, *The Affair: The Case of Alfred Dreyfus,* trans. Jeffrey Mehlman (New York: George Braziller, 1986), 140–52, 161–69.

For the first time, Picquart called for the secret file from the 1894 court-martial. Squirreled away by Henry, it was covered with dust and filled with nonsense. Examining the Italian attaché's "scoundrel D . . ." letter and other documents, Picquart realized that the dossier held nothing concrete and reported those findings to Boisdeffre (who was shocked that the file had not been burned) and to the deputy chief of staff, General Charles Gonse (who ordered the intelligence chief to "keep the two affairs separate"). Picquart wanted to lay a trap for Esterhazy, or even move forward with an arrest, but could move neither superiors nor subalterns, including Henry and du Paty. He could not fathom why. He held no brief for Dreyfus; in fact he continued to warn comrades about the dangers of the "Jewish Syndicate." Later, the German attaché summarized his adversaries' dilemma. "If Picquart proved Dreyfus's innocence and Esterhazy's guilt," Schwartzkoppen wrote, it would be "all over" for Gonse, Boisdeffre, and the minister of war, as well as "for the prestige of the army and the reputation of France. Therefore Picquart's investigation had to be rendered impossible and Dreyfus's guilt reestablished."[3]

To that end, the General Staff ordered Picquart out of Paris in the late fall of 1896. Too independent of spirit and too heavily armed with information that could embarrass the army, he was sent on missions far from the epicenter of the Dreyfus and Esterhazy affairs—first to the eastern frontier, then to the Alps, and finally on to Algeria and Tunisia. And Picquart's exile would soon lead to Henry's arrival at the helm of French intelligence.

Starting in September 1896, a few weeks prior to Picquart's departure, a series of newspaper articles increased the panic of the General Staff and revived the hopes of the Dreyfus family. Having faced hostility and indifference for nearly two years, Mathieu Dreyfus took a desperate step. With the help of an English journalist, Clifford Millage of the *London Daily Chronicle,* he fashioned a scheme to shock the public and resuscitate the Dreyfus case. On the evening of September 3, 1896, the Havas Press Agency in Paris picked up the story from its English source.

[3] Maximilien von Schwartzkoppen, *Les Carnets de Schwartzkoppen: La verité sur Dreyfus* (Paris: Rieder, 1930), 150.

HAVAS PRESS AGENCY

Dreyfus Escapes!

September 3, 1896

The *Daily Chronicle* says that the journal *South Wales Argus* prints a report that a naval captain has made a statement that Captain Dreyfus has escaped from the Salvation Islands on board an American ship.

The *South Wales Argus,* which gave the details, is a journal published in Newport in Monmouthshire. That report is based on declarations made by Captain Hunter of the steamer *Non-Pareil* which had just arrived in Newport.

While taking on a cargo of phosphates at Connétable Island [off the coast of Guiana], Captain Hunter heard that Dreyfus had escaped from Devil's Island. The account is a long one, but it says in substance that the escape was arranged by Mme. Dreyfus immediately after the departure of the French dispatch boat, which, according to the account, visited the Salvation Islands only rarely.

The American schooner, whose name is not mentioned in the report of the *South Wales Argus,* is supposed to have taken on board not only Dreyfus but also his warders.

After a flurry of telegrams went out to French Guiana, government officials exposed the press release as fiction. But Mathieu Dreyfus had achieved his goal. Paris newspapers of every political stripe revisited the Dreyfus case, and from *La Libre Parole* and *L'Intransigeant* came new warnings of an "Escape Syndicate" financed by Jewish gold.[4] On Devil's Island, however, the prisoner paid for his brother's ploy. Shortly after the *Daily Chronicle* story appeared, the minister of colonies increased the number of guards, suspended Dreyfus's letter-writing privileges, ordered a high fence built around the island hut, confined the prisoner to his cabin, and had him shackled. On a reconstructed hospital bed, an

---

[4]Theodore Reinach, *Histoire sommaire de l'affaire Dreyfus* (Paris: Ligue des droits de l'homme, 1924), 51.

From *L'Angence Havas* (September 3, 1896), translated and reprinted in Louis L. Snyder, *The Dreyfus Case: A Documentary History* (New Brunswick: Rutgers University Press, 1973), 71. Copyright © 1973 by Rutgers University. Reprinted with the permission of Rutgers University Press.

iron "bar of justice," similar to a wooden pillory, was clamped down over the inmate's legs for more than forty nights.[5]

Of all the Dreyfus-related articles that appeared in the late summer and fall of 1896, "The Traitor," published in *L'Eclair* on September 15, caused the greatest stir and had the most lasting significance. Hostile to the prisoner, the anonymous report presented a long summary of his case, including reference for the first time in public to documents contained in the secret dossier. Acknowledging that the file had been shown to the court-martial judges "out of the presence even of the defense attorney," for reasons of national security, *L'Eclair* printed a dramatic revision of the Italian attaché's letter ("that scoundrel D . . . ") but used the wrong adjective and filled in the blanks: "Decidedly that animal Dreyfus," went the newspaper's version, "is becoming much too demanding." The article's source of information has never been confirmed, but the details presented—of the arrest, trial, and secret file—point to the General Staff, and undoubtedly to Henry. Worried that Picquart and the press were about to reopen the case, the army wanted it known that hard evidence had convicted Dreyfus.

When the government remained silent on *L'Eclair*'s revelations, Edgar Demange drafted a petition signed by Lucie Dreyfus, the legal guardian of her husband's interests, and addressed to the president of the Chamber of Deputies.

[5]Alfred Dreyfus, *Cinq années de ma vie* (Paris: La Découverte, 1994), 162–65.

LUCIE DREYFUS

Petition to the Chamber of Deputies
September 18, 1896

The newspaper *L'Eclair,* in its edition of September 15, appearing Monday morning, made public, in defiance of every denial, that there was irrefutable, material proof of my husband's guilt, that that proof was in the hands of the War Ministry, which communicated it confidentially, during

Reprinted in Mathieu Dreyfus, *L'Affaire telle que je l'ai vécue* (Paris: Grasset, 1978), 83.

Figure 7.   Lucie Hadamard Dreyfus, with son Pierre, born in 1891. Twenty-five years old at the time of her husband's arrest, Lucie Dreyfus cared for their two children, petitioned government officials, sent scores of letters to Devil's Island, and gave the prisoner "the strength to resist."

the deliberations, to the court-martial judges, [and] that it helped form the conviction, without the accused or his attorney having had knowledge of it.

I refused to acknowledge such a fact, and I awaited the denial that the semiofficial Havas Press Agency issues in response to all spurious news, even of the least importance.

The denial has not come. It is, therefore, true that after debates shrouded in the most complete secrecy, given the closed session, a French officer has been convicted by a court-martial on the basis of a charge about which he had no knowledge, and that, by consequence, neither he nor his counsel were able to examine.

This is a denial of all justice.

Subjected for nearly two years to the most cruel martyrdom, like the martyrdom felt by the man in whose innocence I have absolute faith, I held myself in silence despite all the odious and absurd slander propagated in public and in the press.

Today it is my duty to break that silence, and without commentary, without recrimination, I address myself to you, Gentlemen of the Chamber of Deputies, the only power to whom I have recourse, and I demand justice.

The Chamber would reject Lucie Dreyfus's petition in November, but Commandant Henry, to be safe, hammered an extra nail in the prisoner's coffin. Probably on his own initiative, though perhaps prompted by Deputy Chief Gonse, he gathered papers from Madame Bastian and pasted together excerpts of recent letters addressed to Schwartzkoppen by Panizzardi. On graph paper similar to that used by the Italian diplomat, Henry forged the attaché's handwriting, added words that incriminated Dreyfus, and inserted his work into a final product held together by transparent tape. Since most of Bastian's deliveries came in pieces, the reconstructed letter had an air of authenticity. It also had a road map of imperfections that any close examination would reveal (the graph squares did not match, nor did the blue color of the lines). But few of Henry's superiors ever leveled a magnifying glass on the Dreyfus case, and by fattening the secret file, the forgery was designed to put those superiors at ease. Presented as a genuine discovery on November 2, 1896, the new "evidence," soon to be supplemented by other products from Henry's "fake-factory,"[6] delighted General Boisdeffre and Minister of War Billot. And for good reason: The "traitor" was named.

---

[6]The term is Hannah Arendt's in "From the Dreyfus Affair to France Today," *Journal of Social Studies* 4 (July 1942): 211.

The Henry Forgery
October 1896

I have read that a deputy will put a question to the government regarding Dreyfus. If Rome is asked for new explanations, I will say that I have never had relations with that Jew. That is understood. If they ask you, say the same thing, for no one must ever know what has occurred with him.

While the General Staff, armed with the Panizzardi letter and about to be rid of Picquart, enjoyed a moment of relief, Mathieu Dreyfus worked to expose the secret dossier. He had known about the file since a curious interview in the port town of Le Havre in the early weeks of 1895. Through an in-law, Mathieu had met a local physician, Dr. Gibert, with an international reputation in mental pathology. Most important, Gibert believed in Alfred Dreyfus's innocence and counted among his close friends the president of the republic, Félix Faure. The doctor, having come to the case through the world of clairvoyance, invited Mathieu to meet his most illustrious "patient," Léonie, a stout Norman peasant noted for her ability to see beyond the physical world.

Desperation alone did not prompt Mathieu's turn to the occult. Though a religious skeptic, he believed, with his brother, in a transcendent power, and his keen interest in metaphysics and all aspects of modern science extended to the possibility of the paranormal. In that curiosity he joined distinguished company. The peasant clairvoyant Léonie also attracted the attention of London's highly respectable Society for Psychical Research, which included among its followers Prime Minister William Gladstone; Poet Laureate Alfred, Lord Tennyson; and author Arthur Conan Doyle. Of course, charlatans, crackpots, and confidence tricksters also staged séances and levitations, but they populated politics and organized religion as well, and from Mathieu's point of view, Dr. Gibert and Léonie were both more stable and more sympathetic than the officers who had engineered his brother's conviction. Furthermore, just prior to the Le Havre visit, Mathieu had received highly emotional

---

Reprinted in Douglas Johnson, *France and the Dreyfus Affair* (London: Blandford, 1966), 229–30.

letters sent by his brother on the eve of his deportation. "Our two souls are sisters," Alfred Dreyfus had written, "and I feel all that you suffer." Urging Mathieu to search for the truth with "courage and energy," he begged him to "try everything, even the impossible."[7]

The hypnotic sessions with Léonie—soon to be continued in Paris, where the Dreyfus family would lodge the peasant for nearly two years—led to startling revelations corroborated by worldly evidence.

[7]Bibliothèque Nationale, N.A.F. 17387, letters from Alfred Dreyfus, Dec. 26, 1894, and Jan. 12, 1895.

MATHIEU DREYFUS

The Clairvoyant and the President

February 1895

Upon arriving at Dr. Gibert's, I was brought into a room where Léonie was waiting.

I saw a peasant seated on a couch, her eyes closed, appearing to be in her fifties, with classical features and wearing a Norman bonnet.

The doctor asked me to sit in front of her.

She took my fingers, felt them all over, scratched them; then, searching for words, pausing . . . she said slowly, "You are his brother; your wife is with you; you have two children . . . who are with their grandmother. Your brother is down there, he suffers a great deal." Then she let go of my hands and began to speak as if she were in my brother's presence: "Why are you wearing eyeglasses? Who gave you those glasses?" But, I said to her, my brother never wears eyeglasses. He always wears pince-nez. Aren't you confusing the two? "No, no," Léonie shouted in anger. "I know what I am saying. . . . They are eyeglasses. You will go farther away and farther still . . . but you will return, it is certain. I do not know how long it will be— the likes of us are unfamiliar with time—but surely, surely, you will return."

Léonie announced that she was tired and asked to rest. The doctor said, "Sleep." She grew drowsy, and the séance was over.

I was struck by her comments: about my visit to Paris with my wife, about the goal I pursued, about my children staying with their grandmother. . . .

Mathieu Dreyfus, *L'Affaire telle que je l'ai vécue* (Paris: Grasset, 1978), 49–52.

But these facts were known to my relative [in Le Havre]; they could have been told to the doctor. Had he alluded to them in front of Léonie?

As for the eyeglasses she mentioned, I knew that my brother never wore them. And I would be able to confirm that fact with my sister-in-law, who was about to leave for the Ile de Ré fortress [in western France, where Dreyfus was held prior to Devil's Island] in two or three days.

Upon her return, she told me that her husband had been wearing eyeglasses. He was very nearsighted, his pince-nez were always falling off, and he had asked the prison director for a pair of glasses.

That fact, which none of us had known and then found to be accurate, came as a great shock.

I went to Le Havre many times. Dr. Gibert let me know when Léonie was ready. At times she told us things that were inscrutable or improbable, above all when she was urged on too quickly. . . .

During another séance at the beginning of February, Léonie said spontaneously, "What are those papers that are being shown to the judges in secret? Don't do that; it's not right. If Mr. Alfred and Demange see them, their effect will be ruined."

What do you mean, I asked, by those papers?

"Papers you do not know," she said, "that have been shown to the judges. You will see later."

I did not push it.

Those words were explained to me on February 21, 1895. . . .

The doctor was very close to Félix Faure, the president of the republic, and had been his physician in Le Havre. He took it as his duty to approach the president and ask him to delay my brother's departure for Devil's Island for as long as possible. . . .

A meeting was set for February 21 at seven o'clock in the morning. . . .

Dr. Gibert returned from the Elysée Palace profoundly shaken. The president had told him, "Dreyfus was not convicted on the basis of the bordereau, nor on what transpired during the court session. He was convicted on the basis of documents communicated to the judges in the deliberation room, documents that could not be shown to the accused, or to his lawyer, for reasons of state."

The doctor strongly protested that violation of the rights of the defense. He declared to the president that Dreyfus was innocent and that his absolute certainty was based on a combination of facts: the family, the attitude of the condemned man during his degradation, his protests of innocence, and, finally, the absence of motive.

"No motive, no crime," the doctor added.

Dr. Gibert insisted on all of this. He had the president read a letter from my brother to his wife following the degradation, a letter which seemed to move Félix Faure, and then he took control.

"Do not associate yourself with this crime," the doctor said. "Take care, my dear president, that this crime does not fall on you."

The president remained inflexible. Dr. Gibert added, "The brother, my friend Mathieu Dreyfus, knows that I have approached you. Do you permit me to tell him about our conversation?"

"Yes," the president responded.

Thus we knew that the words uttered by Léonie, words we had not understood ("What are those papers that are being shown to the judges?") referred to the communication, made to the judges in the deliberation room, of documents unknown to the accused and his lawyer.

The closed session had been a farce.

Mathieu Dreyfus, never given to exaggeration, maintained until the end of his life that Léonie had been the first to inform him of the secret dossier and that her discovery had been confirmed, unwittingly, by the president of the republic. Still, a peasant clairvoyant was hardly a convincing witness, and President Faure would surely deny any compromising statements made to Dr. Gibert. The Dreyfus family now knew of the military's criminal action (Demange also learned of the secret file from other sources) but had to convince others. Under the constant fear that his brother would die on Devil's Island, Mathieu continued, as he put it, "to undertake, without tiring and without being discouraged by anything, a personal campaign of propaganda in every milieu I could penetrate; to make recruits and to ask them and all our friends to help . . . find the criminal."[8]

One of the most brilliant and unlikely recruits needed convincing. Bernard Lazare, a young anarchist fighting capitalism on the barricades of the literary avant-garde, had written, late in 1894, two articles condemning the anti-Semitism of the Dreyfus case. At that point, however, Lazare's commitment to social justice did not extend to the prisoner himself, to that affluent bourgeois officer in trouble. Nor did it reach to his less fortunate coreligionists. An assimilated and nonobservant Jew, Lazare condemned the invading "hordes" of Orthodox Jews, those "coarse and dirty, pillaging Tartars," as he wrote in 1890, "who come to feed upon a country which does not belong to them." Understanding the hatred directed at that flood of immigrants, Lazare insisted that the full acceptance of French Jews (whom he called *israélites* in contrast to foreign *juifs*) would follow only from their total disappearance into "the mass of the nation."[9]

---

[8]Mathieu Dreyfus, *L'Affaire telle que je l'ai vécue* (Paris: Grasset, 1978), 47.

[9]Lazare is quoted in Michael R. Marrus, *The Politics of Assimilation: The French Jewish Community at the Time of the Dreyfus Affair* (Oxford: Oxford University Press, 1980), 170–71.

Although Mathieu Dreyfus abhored Lazare's anarchism, he admired his literary talent and readiness to confront the scourge of anti-Semitism. Besides, the Dreyfus family was in no position to critique the politics of potential allies. In February 1895 Mathieu arranged a meeting with Lazare, described the details of the case, and invited the writer to draft a pamphlet exposing the "judicial error." His key source would be the judge advocate d'Ormescheville's original indictment, which Alfred Dreyfus had secretly annotated in his Cherche-Midi cell, and which, at great risk, Ferdinand Forzinetti had passed on to the prisoner's family.

Completing his pamphlet in the summer of 1895, Lazare pushed for immediate publication. But Mathieu Dreyfus and Edgar Demange hesitated; they wanted to strike at a more "favorable moment." In the interim, and largely in reaction to his cautious colleagues, Lazare began a journey that took him from his old advocacy of assimilation to a new and passionate call for Jewish nationalism—not as a religious resurgence (he remained a nonbeliever), nor as a quest for a Jewish state (he also remained an anarchist), but as a social and political commitment to "Jewish preservation." Lazare's "re-education into Jewishness" following 1895 grew out of frustrations with the Dreyfus family and all those French Jews who were, he believed, paralyzed by anti-Semitism. Simultaneously with Theodor Herzl's campaign for a Jewish state, Lazare, who would soon criticize the "bourgeois" Herzl as too removed from "our impoverished, miserable proletarian people," encouraged Jews to assert their nationhood within France. And he attacked on two fronts: While condemning Jews who played "dead so as not to attract the lightning," he also confronted anti-Semites in print and on the dueling ground. A confrontation with Edouard Drumont in June 1896 ended with shots fired but no injuries.[10]

Mathieu Dreyfus and Bernard Lazare agreed that without the element of "an atrocious and shameful anti-Semitism" (in Mathieu's words), the captain "would never have been sent to Devil's Island."[11] But they disagreed over the most effective strategy to win the prisoner's release and over the wisdom of turning the case into a struggle between Jews and anti-Semites. Whereas Mathieu and his brother believed in the benevolent

[10]Nelly Wilson, *Bernard Lazare: Antisemitism and the Problem of Jewish Identity in Late Nineteenth Century France* (Cambridge: Cambridge University Press, 1978); and Marrus, *Politics of Assimilation,* 164, 182. On Lazare and Herzl, see David Vital, "A Prince of the Jews," *Times Literary Supplement,* June 7, 1996, 7; and on their differences, see Pierre Vidal-Naquet, *Les Juifs, la mémoire et le présent* (Paris: La Découverte, 1991), 1:89–91.

[11]Bibliothèque Nationale, N.A.F. 14382, letter from Mathieu Dreyfus to Dr. Dumas, Mar. 7, 1901. Lazare is quoted in Marrus, *Politics of Assimilation,* 183.

power of French justice and looked back to the Revolution's edict of emancipation with gratitude, Lazare, who once shared their faith, felt betrayed. His new reverence was for a nationalism that rejected the conformity of assimilation and honored diversity. "Nothing seems more necessary for humanity," he wrote, "than variety."[12] In broad terms, those conflicting views mirrored a schism within the Jewish community that the Dreyfus case would deepen, widen, and leave as a legacy to the twentieth century.

Still, Lazare never lost sight of the man on Devil's Island, and as a loyal lieutenant, he waited for Mathieu's signal to act. It came, finally, after the *L'Eclair* article and others had returned the case to the public arena in the fall of 1896. Printed at the Dreyfus family's expense in Brussels (to avoid legal action in France), thirty-five hundred copies of Lazare's pamphlet went out in early November to a select audience of journalists, judges, deputies, senators, and other influential notables. Its sixty-four pages presented a "luminous demonstration" of Dreyfus's innocence,[13] at least for readers with open minds.

[12]Quoted in Marrus, *Politics of Assimilation,* 191.
[13]Philippe Oriel, "Bernard Lazare," in *L'Affaire Dreyfus de A à Z,* ed. Michel Drouin (Paris: Flammarion, 1994), 222.

BERNARD LAZARE

A Judicial Error

November 1896

One day Captain Dreyfus was arrested, then accused, tried, convicted, without it being known on what grounds he was arrested, what accusation had been leveled against him, how he was tried, and why he was convicted. Despite all that, public opinion, without hesitation, acknowledged his guilt and heaped anger and execration upon him. Not even the instinct of self-interest prompted his fellow countrymen to rise up and shout, "If they arrest, try, and convict in this way, it affects the liberty of everyone." No one said, "I do not know the crime this man is accused of; I do not know the indictments brought forward, the way he is charged, the way he

Bernard Lazare, *Une erreur judiciare: L'affaire Dreyfus* (Paris: Stock, 1897), 8–9.

defends himself. I do not accept his guilt, because I cannot impose a judgment on my reason without having a way to verify that judgment."

If that protest had been lodged, it would surely have been met with the response, "You are a poor citizen, for you are not at all bearing in mind the excellence of the tribunal that pronounced the sentence. Is that tribunal not a military court, and is it for you to say that its seven officers could be mistaken?" There, in effect, is the ultimate argument, the bizarre argument, because those who maintain with such tenacity that a military court cannot be mistaken, also concede that a soldier can betray his country, and while it is a crime to charge the corps with an error, it is lawful to accuse one of its members of treason. The army, when it judges, must be infallible. . . .

If [Dreyfus] found no one to take his side, even though he was only a suspect, should we look for the reason in the siegelike fever that was stirred up at the moment of his trial, that fever which inflames all nations living in a system of armed peace? That would not suffice to explain the incredible fury with which he was attacked. What, then, is the principal reason for that attitude? Did I not say that Captain Dreyfus belonged to a class of pariahs? He is a soldier, but he is a Jew, and it is as a Jew that he was prosecuted. Because he was a Jew, he was arrested; because he was a Jew, he was tried; because he was a Jew, he was convicted; because he was a Jew, the voice of justice and truth could not be heard in his favor, and the responsibility for the condemnation of that innocent man falls entirely on those who provoked it by their vile excitations, lies, and slander. Because of those men, such a trial was possible; because of them, the light could not penetrate. They needed their own Jewish traitor to replace the classic Judas; a Jewish traitor whom one could recall to mind unceasingly, every day, in order to cover an entire race with shame; a Jewish traitor who could be used to give license to a long campaign of which the Dreyfus affair has been the last act.

Fast in the wake of Lazare's manifesto, *Le Matin* published a facsimile of the bordereau, which the newspaper had secretly purchased from a graphologist consulted by the General Staff. Certain of Dreyfus's guilt, *Le Matin*'s editors printed the document in order to be "finished" with the case. But Mathieu Dreyfus recognized "an event of the highest importance." With the bordereau in the public eye for the first time, he commissioned posters that displayed his brother's handwriting alongside the facsimile and had them distributed throughout Paris. The streets and the opinions that ran along them were becoming as important to the Dreyfus case as the halls of parliament and the offices of the high command.

Maximilien von Schwartzkoppen, picking up his copy of *Le Matin,* recognized his agent's handwriting. As of November 10, 1896, the German military attaché "had in his hands the proof of Dreyfus's innocence," notes Jean-Denis Bredin, "and the proof of Esterhazy's treason. He held their fates in the balance." But the attaché was, after all, the enemy, and Germany could only profit from the French army's preoccupation with a case it had gotten all wrong. Schwartzkoppen said nothing, except to his superiors. Calling the affair "mysterious," he confirmed to Berlin that the embassy in Paris "never had relations with [Dreyfus], directly or through an intermediary," and that the French government alone must assume "the heavy responsibility for this judicial murder."[14]

Events moved quickly in the Dreyfus camp, but membership remained minuscule outside family and friends. By 1896 the alliance included a military prison director ostracized by his army comrades, a criminal attorney who had defended anti-Semites, a clairvoyant peasant and her doctor, an anarchist writer advocating Jewish nationalism, and a celebrated member of the Chamber of Deputies, Joseph Reinach, with a name anti-Semites loved to hate. Cousin and in-law of the baron of Panama fame, Reinach had doubted Alfred Dreyfus's guilt from the beginning. He would soon develop a close friendship with Mathieu Dreyfus, and he worked shoulder to shoulder with Bernard Lazare, despite an abhorrence of anarchism and Zionism. Former aide to Léon Gambetta, one of the founders of the Third Republic, Reinach had emerged as a leading figure of the Chamber's centrist, or Opportunist, wing. And he brought to the Dreyfus campaign the much-needed ingredient of political influence.

Through the winter of 1896–97, however, Reinach made little progress. Only in the search for handwriting experts did the Dreyfus camp succeed. Acting as Mathieu's emissary, Lazare hired independent graphologists, including Gabriel Monod, who refused a fee. Monod, a medieval scholar and a former professor of Lazare's, would soon rank among the most effective Dreyfusards (and among the first Protestants) to rally to the cause. To corroborate the French opinions and confirm the objectivity of the enterprise, Mathieu also commissioned handwriting experts from Switzerland, Belgium, England, and the United States. At home and abroad the experts agreed: Dreyfus could not have written the bordereau.

---

[14]Quoted in Maurice Beaumont, *Aux Sources de l'affaire Dreyfus d'après les Archives diplomatiques* (Paris: Productions de Paris, 1959), 150.

Georges Picquart, who had reached the same conclusion, now realized that his comrades had become his enemies. The General Staff, desperate to suppress the secret file and the Esterhazy affair, had engineered his exile. A brief leave in Paris confirmed those suspicions, and after his return to North Africa in April 1897, Picquart added a codicil to his will. "In the event of the death of the undersigned," he wrote, "deliver this envelope to the president of the republic, who alone should have knowledge of it." Summarizing his discovery and pursuit of Esterhazy, Picquart attacked the General Staff for attempting to "smother" the affair and for treating the law with "contempt." He also feared that many of the secret dossier's documents, taken from him by Deputy Chief Gonse, "had been destroyed."[15]

By May and June 1897 rivalries within the General Staff had given way to frontal assaults, with Henry accusing Picquart of deceit and indiscretion. Insubordinate toward one superior, Henry enjoyed the protection of others, above all of Gonse. From his post on the Gulf of Tunis, Picquart protested the content and tone of Henry's "insinuations" and, on his next visit to Paris in June, broke the army's chain of secrecy and confided his discoveries to a civilian friend. In an affair full of watersheds and pivotal moments, Picquart's meeting with the lawyer Louis Leblois marked a major "turning point."[16]

Though sworn to secrecy by his friend, Leblois could not control himself. By July he had reported Picquart's revelations to the sixty-four-year-old vice president of the Senate, Auguste Scheurer-Kestner, one of France's most respected politicians. In 1894 the senator had expressed only a vague sadness that a fellow Alsatian had committed treason. He deplored the bigotry surrounding the case (as a Protestant, he felt Drumont's arrows) but revered the army and accepted its verdict. By 1897, however, Scheurer-Kestner had doubts. They had been fueled by appeals from Lazare, Reinach, and others, and in July they were confirmed by Leblois. The senator announced his intention to mount a campaign for Dreyfus's "rehabilitation" but honored his promise to Leblois that he would neither expose Picquart nor publicly reveal the traitor's name. Through the fall, while he engaged detectives to follow Esterhazy, he presented his doubts about the Dreyfus case to the president of the republic

---

[15]J. Reinach, *Histoire de l'affaire*, 2:701–4.
[16]Douglas Johnson, *France and the Dreyfus Affair* (London: Blandford, 1966), 84.

and minister of war. But Félix Faure "wanted to know nothing and hear nothing," and General Billot promised an investigation he never intended to launch.

By October the General Staff suspected collusion between Scheurer-Kestner and Picquart, and anxieties intensified when the senator informed Billot that he knew the traitor's name. Esterhazy's exposure would shed immediate light on Dreyfus's innocence, and after three years of lies, intrigues, forgeries, and malfeasance, the General Staff wanted nothing less than light. Esterhazy must be informed and protected, and for that job Gonse and Henry pressed into service "their man for all seasons," du Paty de Clam.[17] The evidence points to du Paty as the artisan of an anonymous letter sent to Esterhazy in mid-October 1897. Sprinkled with intentional misspellings and inaccuracies (and probably penned by Henry's wife), it was signed "Your devoted friend, Espérance [Hope]."

[17]The description is Bredin's; see *The Affair,* 189.

ESPÉRANCE

Letter to Esterhazy

October 1897

Your name is going to be the object of a great scandal. The Dreffus family will publicly accuse you of being the author of the document on which the Dreffus trial was based. The family has specimens of your handwriting for a comparative examination. A colonel who was at the ministry last year, a Mr. Picart, delivered the papers to the Dreffus family. This Mr. Picart is now, I believe, in Tonkin.

By publishing your handwriting in the newspapers, the family hopes you will panic and flee to your family in Hungary.

That will indicate that you are the guilty party, and they will profit by demanding a retrial and by proclaiming Dreffus's innocence. . . .

Mr. Picart bought specimens of your handwriting from noncommissioned officers in your regiment in Rouen last year.

Repertoire de l'affaire Dreyfus: Dates et documents, 1894–1898 (Paris: n.p., 1898), 102.

I have all this from a sergeant in your regiment who had been given money for your handwriting. You are now warned about what these scoundrels want to do to destroy you. Now it is up to you to protect your name and your children's honor.

Make haste, for the entire family will do what it can to ruin you.

Your devoted friend,
Espérance

Never show this letter to anyone; it is for you alone, to save you from the great dangers that threaten you.

Clandestine meetings with Esterhazy followed, including one bizarre encounter at Montsouris Park in southern Paris. Aware of the perils involved in contacting the commandant (few fin de siècle spies were shadowed by more detectives), du Paty wore a fake black beard, while Félix Gribelin, the Statistical Section's archivist, donned blue-tinted glasses, and Henry waited in a nearby carriage. The officers in mufti repeated the "Espérance" warnings and pledged to protect Esterhazy, but they insisted that he follow orders and behave. With renewed confidence, the commandant informed Schwartzkoppen of his new protective web and agreed that their dealings should now come to a quiet close. Besides, the attaché was about to depart for a new post in Berlin.

At the same time, journalists and anonymous letter writers showered Scheurer-Kestner with vitriol: "You are an old blackguard, rogue, and traitor, a dirty Prussian like all the rest of your Protestant and Jewish coreligionists." The senator kept repeating his call for Dreyfus's rehabilitation, but, for both enemies and allies, his refusal to name the traitor seemed like a nightmarish tease. And it continued until a stranger to the case appeared in early November. Waiting at an omnibus stop in Paris, a banker named de Castro came across one of the bordereau posters and recognized the handwriting of his most disreputable client, Ferdinand Walsin-Esterhazy. He returned to his office, gathered up a file of the commandant's letters, and contacted Mathieu Dreyfus.

Until that moment, the Dreyfus family had never heard Esterhazy's name or known of what de Castro described as the commandant's "detestable reputation." Hoping to confirm his discovery, Mathieu rushed to Scheurer-Kestner's Paris quarters and announced that Esterhazy was the traitor. With the weight of the promise he had made to Leblois now lifted, the senator responded, "Yes, it's him." On November 15, assisted by Edgar Demange, Mathieu drafted a letter to the minister of war, and the following day the text appeared in *Le Figaro*. At the Quai d'Orsay, the diplomat Maurice Paléologue called the letter "the bursting of a bombshell."[18]

[18]Maurice Paléologue, *Journal de l'affaire Dreyfus, 1894–1899* (Paris: Plon, 1955), 61.

MATHIEU DREYFUS

Letter in Le Figaro

November 16, 1897

The sole basis of the accusation brought against my unfortunate brother in 1894 is an unsigned, undated letter establishing that confidential military documents had been delivered to an agent of a foreign military power.

I have the honor to inform you that the author of that document is Count Walsin-Esterhazy, infantry commandant, placed on nonactive duty since last spring as the result of temporary infirmities.

Commandant Esterhazy's handwriting is identical to that of the document. It will be extremely easy for you to procure a specimen of that officer's handwriting.

Furthermore, I am ready to indicate where you may find letters written by him, letters of indisputable authenticity, which date from a period prior to my brother's arrest.

I have no doubt, Monsieur le Ministre, that, knowing the author of the treason for which my brother has been convicted, you will move quickly to do justice.

Two days earlier Scheurer-Kestner hosted a small luncheon party attended by the lawyer Louis Leblois and a celebrated novelist, Emile Zola. Others had tried to recruit Zola to the Dreyfus campaign, but without success. In 1896 he confessed to Bernard Lazare that he had paid little attention to the Dreyfus case; he had been in Rome at the time of the

Quoted in Mathieu Dreyfus, *L'Affaire telle que je l'ai vécue* (Paris: Grasset, 1978), 200.

captain's arrest, the court-martial seemed pro forma, and he recalled the degradation mainly as a public spectacle that would fit well in a future novel. On the topic of anti-Semitism, however, Zola had not been silent. "For the Jews," published in *Le Figaro* in the spring of 1896, announced the writer's "surprise and growing disgust" with the campaign against Jews in France. He called it "a monstrosity," an "absurd and blind" return to barbarism that defied "all truth and all justice."[19]

But if the essay probed issues common to the Dreyfus case, it made no mention of the prisoner and his plight. Eighteen months passed before Zola, tutored in the details of the affair by Scheurer-Kestner and Leblois, realized that the "gripping" and "horrible" story of Captain Dreyfus was a human drama on "a grand scale," not unlike the series of realist novels, *Les Rougon-Macquart,* that had secured the writer's fame and fortune. The Dreyfus case, dominated from the outset by the popular journalism of anti-Semites and militant nationalists, needed a new interpreter, a powerful advocate of republican justice who could touch the crowd and examine the facts with the precision of a social scientist. Zola entered the Dreyfusard arena with an essay published in *Le Figaro* on November 25, 1897, but he moved, at first, like a locomotive in low gear. Hesitating "to speak of the affair" or to expose its crimes and criminals, he focused instead on "the crystal life" of the heroic Scheurer-Kestner. By the essay's final line, however, a rousing battle cry the Dreyfusard movement would embrace as its slogan, Zola's momentum had gathered, and his challenge had become clear.[20]

[19]Emile Zola, *L'Affaire Dreyfus: La Verité en marche* (Paris: Garnier-Flammarion, 1969), 57–62.

[20]Frederick Brown, *Zola: A Life* (New York: Farrar, Straus, & Giroux, 1995), 726–27.

M. Scheurer-Kestner

November 25, 1897

What a poignant drama, and what superb characters! Life has brought these documents to our attention, and they are of such tragic beauty that, as a novelist, my heart leaps with admiration and excitement. I know of nothing that is of loftier psychological interest.

It is not my intention to talk about the Affair. Although circumstances have enabled me to examine it and reach a firm opinion concerning it, I cannot overlook the fact that an inquiry is under way, that the matter has been brought before the courts and that in all decency we must wait, without adding to the clutter of abominable gossip being used to obscure the Affair, which is so clear and simple in itself.

But already, the characters involved in this Affair belong to me; although I am merely a passer-by, my eyes are open, prepared to look at all that life has to offer. And while the man who was sentenced three years ago and the man who is a defendant today are still sacred to me, as long as the judicial system has not fulfilled its task, the third great character in this drama—the accuser—has nothing to fear from being talked about frankly and honestly.

What follows is what I have seen of M. Scheurer-Kestner, what I believe and what I assert. One day, perhaps, if circumstances allow it, I shall talk about the other two characters in the drama.

A life as clear as crystal, utterly clean and upright; not one blemish, not one flaw. A single and unwavering viewpoint, unwarped by any militant ambition, has led to an elevated political position, due solely to the respect and liking of his peers.

And he is no dreamy-eyed Utopian. He is an industrialist who has spent his life in his laboratory devoting himself to specialized research, in addition to the day-to-day cares of being responsible for a large commercial firm. . . .

There you have it; that is what the man is like. Everyone knows him; no one can contradict me. And yet this is the man within whose breast the most tragic and absorbing of dramas is going to be played out. One day, a doubt enters his mind, for already there is some doubt in the air; already it has disturbed more than one conscience. A court martial has found a captain—

Emile Zola, excerpts from *The Dreyfus Affair: "J'Accuse" and Other Writings,* edited by Alain Pagès, translated by Eleanor Levieux (New Haven: Yale University Press, 1996), 10–14 with cuts. Copyright © 1996 by Eleanor Levieux and Yale University. Reprinted with permission of Yale University Press and CNRS Editions, Paris.

who perhaps is innocent—guilty of treason. The punishment has been appalling.... But great God, what if he were innocent? What a measureless shudder of pity we feel! We break out in a cold sweat at the horrible thought that no amends can possibly make up for the wrong he has suffered....

To cut a long story short, M. Scheurer-Kestner at last feels certain. He knows where the truth lies; he will do what justice requires. This is the excruciating moment.... He fully realized what storms he was going to stir up, but truth and justice are sovereign over all else, for they alone make a nation great. Political interests may blot them out momentarily but any nation that did not base its sole *raison d'être* on truth and justice would today be a nation doomed.

.. ,What was M. Scheurer-Kestner's intention, however? To do his duty and, in so doing, to disappear. He had resolved to tell the government, "Here is the situation. Take the Affair into your hands; if you choose to rectify the error, you will have the merit of being just. All acts of justice lead to triumph." Because of circumstances which I do not wish to go into, his words were not heeded....

How great he was! How wise! He kept silent not only because of the promise he had made but precisely because he was responsible for the truth—the poor, naked, shivering truth that everyone was hissing and booing and seemed to have some interest in strangling to death. His only thought was to shield it from the passion and rage arrayed against it. He had vowed that no one would steal the truth from him and he intended to choose exactly when and how he would make the truth triumph. What could be more natural, more praiseworthy? I know of nothing more sublimely beautiful than M. Scheurer-Kestner's silence these past three weeks while an entire panic-stricken nation has suspected and insulted him. Novelists, there's an exceptional character for you! There's a hero! ...

On the one hand, you have M. Scheurer-Kestner and his crystal-clear life. On the other hand you have the people who are accusing and insulting him. You must judge. You must choose between him and them. Find what motivation he could possibly have, aside from his noble need for truth and justice. Covered with insults, his very soul bruised and rent, feeling his lofty and respected situation totter beneath him, yet prepared to sacrifice everything in order to accomplish his heroic task, he keeps silent. Calmly, he waits. The greatness of this man is exceptional.

I have said already that I do not wish to talk about the Affair itself. And yet, I must repeat, it is as clear and simple as you please once you see it as it really is.

A miscarriage of justice is a deplorable thing but it can always happen. Judges do make mistakes; army officers can make mistakes as well. What would that have to do with the honour of the army? If such a mistake has occurred, the only thing worth doing is to correct it. No wrongdoing has taken place—unless someone persists in refusing to acknowledge, even when confronted with indubitable proof, that a mistake has been made. At bottom, there is no other problem but that. All will be well once the people involved make up their minds to acknowledge that an error may have been made and that afterwards they hesitated because of the embarrassment of admitting it. Those who know will understand what I am talking about.

What about the diplomatic complications that might ensue? All that is merely a smokescreen. No foreign power has had anything to do with the Affair, and this must be stated loud and clear. The only thing we need be concerned with is French public opinion, which is exasperated and over-wrought by the most odious of campaigns. The press is a necessary force; I believe that when all is said and done, it does more good than harm. Nonetheless, certain newspapers are the guilty parties, making some readers panic, terrifying others, feeding on scandals to treble their sales. Idiotic anti-Semitism has fanned this stupidity into flames. On all sides people are being denounced. Even the best and purest individuals no longer dare to do their duty, for fear of getting scorched. . . .

One reason why M. Scheurer-Kestner has maintained a dignified silence before taking action is that he was waiting, I imagine, for each and every person to examine his own conscience. . . .

If, for political considerations, justice were to be delayed, this would constitute an additional wrong that would merely delay the inevitable outcome and make it even more painful.

The truth is on the march, and nothing shall stop it.

5

J'Accuse

Forced by public events to open a formal investigation, the army hoped to dispose of the Esterhazy matter quickly, if possible, and quietly, above all. But while General Staff officers shielded the commandant, they could not make him behave. Indulging his insatiable desire for self-promotion (and letter writing), Esterhazy launched a campaign to save whatever honor his name had left. Beginning in October 1897, he sent a series of appeals to the minister of war and president of the republic. "I have a heritage of glory to defend," he wrote General Billot, and he insisted that his "rare and very open meetings with Schwartzkoppen" were the innocent visits of an old family friend from "the diplomatic world." As for the bordereau, Dreyfus had access to letters sent by Esterhazy to Jewish bankers and army officers; perhaps the captain had forged the commandant's handwriting. To Félix Faure, Esterhazy declared that his family name would not be "dragged through the mud," and when the president did not respond, the officer moved on to threats. Appealing to Faure's high office ("Help me, my prince, to my rescue"), he warned that if the "Pontius Pilates" of the political world ignored him, "my blood will cover their heads."[1]

In late November 1897 the public learned what the inner circles of government and the military already knew: Esterhazy, unbalanced by anger and ambition, lived on the cusp of insanity. The revelation came by way of letters he had sent to his mistress (who was also his cousin and moneylender) thirteen years before. Madame de Boulancy, out for revenge after taking Esterhazy to court for unpaid debts, handed the letters to her lawyer, who in turn showed them to Scheurer-Kestner. Always following the appropriate path, the senator informed the officer

---

[1]See *Repertoire de l'affaire Dreyfus: Dates et documents, 1894–1898* (Paris: n.p., 1898), n.a., 103–17, 125–26.

assigned to investigate Esterhazy, but while General Georges de Pellieux pursued his inquiry, Mathieu Dreyfus and Joseph Reinach obtained copies of the letters and transmitted the most incriminating document, later known as "the Uhlan letter," to *Le Figaro.* It was published three days after Zola's declaration that "truth is on the march."

FERDINAND WALSIN-ESTERHAZY

The Uhlan Letter
November 28, 1897

I am absolutely convinced that these people [the French] are not worth the ammunition it would take to kill them, and all those little cowardly, cloying women to whom men give themselves up confirm my opinion.

For me there is only one human quality, and it is completely lacking in the people of this country. And if tonight someone told me that I would be killed tomorrow as a *captain of the uhlans* [the lance-carrying mounted soldiers of central Europe] *running a sword through the French,* I would certainly be perfectly happy. . . .

You are completely mistaken about my nature and character. Generally speaking, I am certainly worth less than the least of your friends, but I am of a completely different species. That is what people usually misunderstand about me. But right now, inflamed, embittered, furious, in an absolutely atrocious situation, I am capable of great things if the occasion arises, or of crimes if they would revenge me.

I would not hurt a little puppy, but I would kill one hundred thousand Frenchmen with pleasure. All the little gossipy, merrymaking hairdressers throw me into a black rage, and if I could, which is much more difficult than one might imagine, I would be with the Mahdi [in the Sudan] in fifteen days.

Oh! . . . the filthy men who go from one woman to another hawking their malicious gossip, which everyone listens to. What a calamitous show it would be to have Paris taken by storm, and, in the red sun of battle, given over to the pillaging of one hundred thousand drunken soldiers.

Repertoire de l'affaire Dreyfus: Dates et documents, 1894–1898 (Paris: n.p., 1898), 144–45 (emphasis in original).

There is the merrymaking I dream of.
So be it.

The Uhlan letter caused a sensation but made little difference to those who were already converted. Esterhazy's supporters believed his protest that the document was a forgery (or noted its irrelevance to the Dreyfus case), and its mysterious appearance seemed to confirm the presence of a "Jewish Syndicate" (to which Zola responded that the only syndicate at work in the Dreyfus case was open to all and dedicated to truth: "Of that syndicate, ah, yes, I am with it, and I dearly hope that all the courageous people of France will be as well!").[2] Still, Esterhazy's letter, coupled with the campaigns of Scheurer-Kestner and others, raised new doubts among citizens who had either ignored Dreyfus's court-martial or praised its verdict. By late 1897 Georges Clemenceau, who vilified the prisoner three years earlier, had rallied to the cause in the columns of the recently established newspaper *L'Aurore.* "Who is protecting Esterhazy?" he asked on November 29. "Who among our great leaders had contact with this man?"[3]

Hubris had kept Esterhazy and his comrades confident, and a file full of documents had kept them armed. In the closing weeks of 1897, however, they faced a torrent of leaks, a gathering of Dreyfusards (the term had just been coined), and a sense of collective panic. With the press mobilized, the high command had to find a public way out of the Esterhazy affair, and for staff officers practiced in the art of rigging trials, the best escape led through the halls of military justice. They would court-martial Esterhazy, engineer his acquittal, and reaffirm Dreyfus's guilt. At first the commandant resisted the role (though attracted to the spotlight, he was allergic to courtrooms), but he had no choice, and in early December he submitted a "spontaneous" demand to be brought before the court-martial of Paris. The letter had been secretly edited by the same officer, General de Pellieux, to whom it was publicly addressed.

---

[2]Emile Zola, *Le Figaro,* Dec. 1, 1897.
[3]Quoted in *Repertoire de l'affaire,* 147.

FERDINAND WALSIN-ESTERHAZY

Letter to General de Pellieux

December 2, 1897

MY GENERAL: As an innocent man, the torture to which I have been subjected for fifteen days is superhuman.

I believe that you have in your hand all the proof of the infamous plot concocted to destroy me. But that proof must come forward in a judicial debate as extensive as possible. The full light must shine forth.

Neither a suspension of the inquiry nor an order of insufficient cause would now secure the redress that is due me. As an officer publicly accused of high treason, I have the right to a court-martial, the highest form of military justice. Only a decision by that court, an aquittal before the public opinion they dared to address, will discredit the most cowardly slanderers.

From your high sense of justice, I wait to be called before the court-martial of Paris.

Reacting to the Esterhazy appeal, the Chamber of Deputies pressed the government to reassure the army and the nation. In a dramatic parliamentary session on December 4, Prime Minister Jules Méline responded with one of the epoch's more embarrassing and desperate declarations: "I shall say immediately the decisive word in this debate: There is no Dreyfus affair." And General Billot, mounting the rostrum, sent much of the Chamber into "frantic applause" when he declared the case "justly and regularly tried."[4] But if the Dreyfus court-martial stood as a matter legally decided *(une chose jugée)*, the Dreyfus affair was just coming to public life. And the prisoner's defenders were proving Méline wrong in more ways than one.

In mid-December Emile Zola wrote "Letter to the Young," in which he berated those "few French students" who took to the streets inflamed by anti-Semitism and other "stupid political and religious passions." With

---

[4]Maurice Paléologue, *Journal de l'affaire Dreyfus, 1894–1899* (Paris: Plon, 1955), 82–83.

Repertoire de l'affaire Dreyfus: Dates et documents, 1894–1898 (Paris: n.p., 1898), 150.

the rhythmic beat he would soon perfect, Zola opened his final paragraphs with "Young men, young men!" and implored the youth of France to be generous and humane. "We go to combat for humanity," he wrote, and he wanted them to cry out "for justice, and for truth!" On January 6, 1898, four days before Esterhazy's trial, a brochure titled "Letter to France" asked why the people of a great nation had reached "this ferocity of terror, this blackness of intolerance." In the brochure Zola condemned the "filthy press" for spreading lies and dishonoring France, and he raised a timely warning: "Your army, today, is all of you. It is all your children who are ready to defend the territory of France. [But] plumed helmets marching by still make your hearts race. . . . France, if you do not take care, you are moving toward dictatorship." Ending, as usual, on a high pitch of hope, Zola remained confident that France would reawaken "to justice and truth."[5]

On January 10, 1898, however, the France of Zola's dreams slept in, and neither justice nor truth appeared at the Esterhazy trial, held in the same former convent where Dreyfus had been court-martialed. Rejecting the civil suits filed by lawyers for Lucie and Mathieu Dreyfus, the judges ruled that all military witnesses would testify in closed session, so as not to "endanger national defense."[6] Esterhazy, now a Parisian celebrity, drew a large and curious crowd. Mathieu Dreyfus, upon seeing the commandant for the first time, noted "the profile of a great bird of prey," and journalists, for and against the accused, echoed the description; Séverine described Esterhazy's lips moving into "a slight smile."[7] And for good reason: His trial lasted barely two days, and the judges' deliberation took three minutes. Found not guilty by unanimous vote, the commandant left the hall to shouts of "Long live France!" "Long live the Army!" and "Death to the Jews!" On the rue du Cherche-Midi, a crowd of more than one thousand hurled threats at Colonel Picquart, who had been heard in closed session, and at Scheurer-Kestner and Mathieu Dreyfus, whose public testimonies had been interrupted by jeers, hisses, and howls of laughter.

[5]Emile Zola, *L'Affaire Dreyfus: La Verité en marche* (Paris: Garnier-Flammarion, 1969), 91–109.

[6]Quoted in Jean-Denis Bredin, *The Affair: The Case of Alfred Dreyfus,* trans. Jeffrey Mehlman (New York: George Braziller, 1986), 239.

[7]See, for example, Séverine (the pen name of Caroline Rémy), *Vers la lumière: Impressions vécues* (Paris: Stock, 1900), 79. Séverine reported on the trial for the women's newspaper *La Fronde.*

In the forty-eight hours following Esterhazy's acquittal, the Dreyfusard movement struck its nadir and then took its most promising turn. On January 13 the Senate rejected Scheurer-Kestner's bid for reelection as vice president, and Minister of War Billot, citing Picquart's communication of secret materials to his lawyer, ordered the colonel's detention at the Mont Valérien Fortress. On the same morning, however, the Dreyfusard newspaper *L'Aurore* published a special edition of three hundred thousand copies with a bold headline that would soon become the most famous battle-cry of the belle époque.

Emile Zola drafted his letter to the president of the republic over a two-day period, and on the night of the Esterhazy verdict, he read the text aloud to colleagues gathered in the offices of *L'Aurore*. Clemenceau, the paper's codirector, lifted the powerful title, "J'Accuse," from the letter's final paragraphs, and a few hours later a tidal wave of publicity hit the streets. Posters announced the special edition, and hundreds of hawkers cried out its headline. Zola's previous articles had been long on passion but short on names. Now, however, the writer listed the criminals like a taxonomy of poisonous plants. At times he exaggerated, at times he made mistakes; he imbued du Paty with too much power, and Mercier and Gonse with not enough; and he failed to mention the army's most active agent, Commandant Henry. But an open letter to the president of the republic sent by a popular novelist (a French genius for some, an Italian pornographer for others) could not help but push the Dreyfus case into a full-blown political and social affair.

EMILE ZOLA

J'Accuse

January 13, 1898

MONSIEUR LE PRÉSIDENT: Will you allow me, out of my gratitude for the gracious manner in which you once granted me an audience, to express my concern for your well-deserved glory? Will you allow me to tell you that although your star has been in the ascendant hitherto, it is now in danger of being dimmed by the most shameful and indelible of stains?

You have emerged unscathed from libellous slurs, you have won the people's hearts. You are the radiant centre of our apotheosis, for the Russian alliance has been indeed, for France, a patriotic celebration. And now you are about to preside over our World Fair. What a solemn triumph it will be, the crowning touch on our grand century of diligent labour, truth and liberty. But what a blot on your name (I was about to say, on your reign) this abominable Dreyfus Affair is! A court martial, acting on orders, has just dared to acquit such a man as Esterhazy. Truth itself and justice itself have been slapped in the face. And now it is too late, France's cheek has been sullied by that supreme insult, and History will record that it was during your Presidency that such a crime against society was committed.

They have dared to do this. Very well, then, I shall dare too. I shall tell the truth, for I pledged that I would tell it, if our judicial system, once the matter was brought before it through the normal channels, did not tell the truth, the whole truth. It is my duty to speak up; I will not be an accessory to the fact. If I were, my nights would be haunted by the spectre of that innocent man so far away, suffering the worst kind of torture as he pays for a crime he did not commit.

And it is to you, M. le Président, that I will shout out the truth with all the revulsion of a decent man. To your credit, I am convinced that you are unaware of the truth. And to whom should I denounce the evil machinations of those who are truly guilty if not to you, the First Magistrate in the land?

First of all, the truth about the trial and the verdict against Dreyfus.

One wicked man has led it all, done it all: Lt-Col du Paty de Clam. At the time he was only a Major. He *is* the entire Dreyfus Affair. Not until a fair inquiry has clearly established his actions and his responsibilities will

Emile Zola, excerpts from *The Dreyfus Affair, "J'Accuse" and Other Writings,* edited by Alain Pagès, translated by Eleanor Levieux (New Haven: Yale University Press, 1996) 43–53, with cuts. Copyright © 1996 by Eleanor Levieux and Yale University. Reprinted with the permission of Yale University Press and CNRS Editions, Paris.

we understand the Dreyfus Affair. He appears to have an unbelievably fuzzy and complicated mind, haunted by implausible plots and indulging in the methods that litter cheap novels — stolen papers, anonymous letters, rendez-vous in deserted places, mysterious women who flit about at night to peddle damaging proof. It was his idea to dictate the bordereau to Dreyfus; it was his idea to examine it in a room entirely lined with mirrors; it was du Paty de Clam, Major Forzinetti tells us, who went out with a dark lantern intending to slip into the cell where the accused man was sleeping and flash the light on his face all of a sudden so that he would be taken by surprise and blurt out a confession. And there is more to reveal, but it is not up to me to reveal it all; let them look, let them find what there is to be found. I shall simply say that Major du Paty de Clam, in charge of investigating the Dreyfus Affair, in his capacity as a criminal police officer, bears the greatest burden of guilt — in terms of chronological order and rank — in the appalling miscarriage of justice that has been committed.

For some time already, the bordereau had been in the possession of Colonel Sandherr, head of the Intelligence Bureau, who has since died of total paralysis. There were "leaks," papers disappeared, just as papers continue to disappear today; and efforts were being made to find out who had written the bordereau when a conviction slowly grew up that that person could only be an officer from the General Staff, and an artillery officer at that. This was a glaring double error, which shows how superficially the bordereau had been examined, since a close and rational scrutiny of it proves that it could only have been written by an infantry officer.

Accordingly, they searched throughout the premises; they examined handwriting samples as if it were a family matter; a traitor was to be caught by surprise in the offices themselves and expelled from them. Now, the story is partly familiar to us and I do not wish to repeat it all over again; but this is where Major du Paty de Clam comes into it, as soon as the first suspicion falls on Dreyfus. From that moment on, it was du Paty de Clam who invented Dreyfus. The Affair became *his* affair. He was sure that he could confound the traitor and wring a complete confession from him. Of course, there is the War Minister, General Mercier, whose intelligence seems to be on a mediocre level; and of course there is the Chief of the General Staff, General de Boisdeffre, who appears to have been swayed by his intense clericalism, and there is the Deputy Chief, General Gonse, whose conscience managed to make room for a good many things. But to begin with, there was really only Major du Paty de Clam. He led those men by the nose. He hypnotized them. Yes indeed, he also dabbles in spiritism and occultism; he converses with spirits. The experiments to which he subjected the unfortunate Dreyfus and the whole demented system of torture — the traps he attempted to make him fall into, the foolish investigations, the monstrous fabrications — are beyond belief.

Ah, for anyone who knows the true details of the first affair, what a nightmare it is! Major du Paty de Clam arrests Dreyfus and has him placed in solitary confinement. He rushes to the home of Madame Dreyfus and terrifies her, saying that if she speaks up, her husband is lost. Meanwhile the unfortunate man is tearing out his hair, clamouring his innocence. And that is how the investigation proceeded, as in some fifteenth-century chronicle, shrouded in mystery and a wealth of the wildest expedients, and all on the basis of a single, childish accusation, that idiotic bordereau, which was not only a very ordinary kind of treason but also the most impudent kind of swindle, since almost all of the so-called secrets that had supposedly been turned over to the enemy were of no value. I dwell on this point because this is the egg from which the real crime—the dreadful denial of justice which has laid France low—was later to hatch. I would like to make it perfectly clear how the miscarriage of justice came about, how it is the product of Major du Paty de Clam's machinations, how General Mercier and Generals de Boisdeffre and Gonse came to be taken in by it and gradually became responsible for this error and how it is that later they felt they had a duty to impose it as the sacred truth, a truth that will not admit of even the slightest discussion. At the beginning, all they contributed was negligence and lack of intelligence. The worst we can say is that they gave in to the religious passions of the circles they move in and the prejudices wrought by esprit de corps. They let stupidity have its way.

But now, here is Dreyfus summoned before the court martial. The most utter secrecy is demanded. They could not have imposed stricter silence and been more rigorous and mysterious if a traitor had actually opened our borders to the enemy and led the German Emperor straight to Notre Dame. The entire nation is flabbergasted. Terrible deeds are whispered about, monstrous betrayals that scandalize History itself, and of course the nation bows to these rumours. No punishment can be too severe; the nation will applaud the traitor's public humiliation; the nation is adamant: the guilty man shall remain on the remote rock where infamy has placed him and he shall be devoured by remorse. But then, those unspeakable accusations, those dangerous accusations that might inflame all of Europe and had to be so carefully concealed behind the closed doors of a secret session—are they true? No, they are not! There is nothing behind all that but the extravagant, demented flights of fancy of Major du Paty de Clam. It's all a smokescreen with just one purpose: to conceal a cheap novel of the most outlandish sort. And to be convinced of this, one need only examine the formal indictment that was read before the court martial.

How hollow that indictment is! Is it possible a man has been found guilty on the strength of it? Such iniquity is staggering. I challenge decent people to read it: their hearts will leap with indignation and rebellion when they think of the disproportionate price Dreyfus is paying so far away on Devil's Island. So Dreyfus speaks several languages, does he? This is a crime. Not one compromising paper was found in his home? A crime. He occasionally pays a visit to the region he hails from? A crime. He is a hard-working man, eager to know everything? A crime. He does not get flustered? A crime. He does get flustered? A crime. And how naively it is worded! How baseless its claims are! They told us he was indicted on fourteen different counts but in the end there is actually only one: that famous bordereau; and we even find out that the experts did not all agree, that one of them, M. Gobert, was subjected to some military pressure because he dared to come to a different conclusion from the one they wanted him to reach. We were also told that twenty-three officers had come and testified against Dreyfus. We still do not know how they were questioned, but what is certain is that not all of their testimony was negative. Besides, all of them, you will notice, came from the offices of the War Department. This trial is a family conclave; they all *belong*. We must not forget that. It is the General Staff who wanted this trial; it is they who judged Dreyfus; and they have just judged him for the second time.

So all that was left was the bordereau, on which the experts had not agreed. They say that in the council chambers, the judges were naturally leaning towards acquittal. And if that is the case then you can understand why, on the General Staff, they are so desperately insistent today on proclaiming, in order to justify the judgement, that there was a damning but secret document; they cannot reveal it but it makes everything legitimate and we must bow before it, as before an invisible and unknowable God! I deny the existence of any such document, I deny it with all my strength! Some ridiculous piece of paper, possibly; perhaps the one that talks about easy women and mentions a man named D . . . who is becoming too demanding; no doubt some husband or other who feels they're not paying him enough for the use of his wife. But a document that concerns the national defence, a document that would cause war to be declared immediately if ever it was produced? No! No! It's a lie! And what makes the whole business all the more odious and cynical is that they are lying with impunity and there is no way to convict them. They turn France inside out, they shelter behind the legitimate uproar they have caused, they seal mouths by making hearts quake and perverting minds. I know of no greater crime against society.

These, M. le Président, are the facts that explain how a miscarriage of justice has come to be committed. And the evidence as to Dreyfus's character, his financial situation, his lack of motives, the fact that he has never ceased to clamour his innocence — all these demonstrate that he has been a victim of Major du Paty de Clam's overheated imagination, and of the clericalism that prevails in the military circles in which he moves, and of the hysterical hunt for "dirty Jews" that disgraces our times.

Now we come to the Esterhazy affair. Three years have passed. Many people's consciences are still profoundly uneasy; worried, they look further, and ultimately they become convinced that Dreyfus is innocent.

I will not retrace the story of M. Scheurer-Kestner's doubts and then of the certainty he came to feel. But while he was conducting his investigation, very serious events were taking place within the General Staff itself.

Colonel Sandherr had died and Lt-Col Picquart had succeeded him at the head of the Intelligence Bureau. And it is in that capacity and in the exercise of his functions that Picquart one day held in his hands a special delivery letter addressed to Major Esterhazy by an agent of a foreign power. It was Picquart's strictest duty to launch an investigation. It is clear that he never acted otherwise than with the consent of his superior officers. So he outlined his suspicions to his hierarchical superiors—General Gonse, then General de Boisdeffre, then General Billot, who had succeeded General Mercier as Minister of War. The famous Picquart file that has been talked about so much was never anything more nor less than the Billot file, by which I mean the file that a subaltern prepared for his Minister, the file that they must still have in the War Ministry. The inquiry lasted from May to September 1896, and two things must be stated in no uncertain terms: General Gonse was convinced that Esterhazy was guilty, and neither General de Boisdeffre nor General Billot questioned the fact that the bordereau was in Esterhazy's handwriting. Lt-Col Picquart's investigation had led to that indubitable conclusion. But feeling ran very high, for if Esterhazy was found guilty, then inevitably the Dreyfus verdict would have to be revised, and that was what the General Staff was determined to avoid at all costs.

At that point there must have been an instant of the most intense psychological anguish. Note that General Billot was not compromised in any way; he had just come on stage; it was within his power to reveal the truth. But he dared not do it—terrified of public opinion, no doubt, and certainly afraid as well of handing over the entire General Staff, including General de Boisdeffre and General Gonse, not to mention the subalterns. Then there was but one minute of struggle between his conscience and what he thought was in the best interests of the army. Once that minute was over, it was already too late. He had made his choice; he was compromised. And ever since then his share of responsibility has grown and grown; he has taken the others' crime upon himself; he is as guilty as the others; he is guiltier than the others, for he had the power to see that justice was done and he did nothing. Understand that if you can! For a year now, General Billot, General de Boisdeffre and General Gonse have known that Dreyfus is innocent, and they have kept this appalling knowledge to themselves! And people like that sleep soundly! And they have wives and children, and love them dearly!

Lt-Col Picquart had done his duty as a decent man. In the name of justice, he insisted to his superior officers. He even begged them; he told them how impolitic their dithering was, what a terrible storm was building up, how it was going to burst once the truth became known. Later on, M. Scheurer-Kestner used the same words to General Billot; out of patriotism, he implored him to get a grip on the Affair instead of letting it go from bad to worse until it became a public disaster. But no, the crime had been committed and the General Staff could no longer confess to it. And

Lt-Col Picquart was sent away on mission; they sent him farther and farther away, all the way to Tunisia where one day they even tried to do his bravery the honour of assigning him to a mission that would assuredly have got him slaughtered, in the same region where the Marquis de Morès had been killed. Mind you, Picquart was not in disgrace; General Gonse had a friendly exchange of letters with him. Only, there are some secrets it is not wise to have discovered.

In Paris, the all-conquering truth was on the march, and we know how the predictable storm eventually burst. M. Mathieu Dreyfus denounced Major Esterhazy as the real author of the bordereau just as M. Scheurer-Kestner was about to place in the hands of the Minister of Justice a request for a revision of the Dreyfus trial. And this is where Major Esterhazy appears. Witnesses state that at first he panicked; he was on the verge of suicide or about to flee. Then suddenly he became boldness itself and grew so violent that all Paris was astonished. The reason is that help had suddenly materialized in the form of an anonymous letter warning him of his enemies' doings; a mysterious lady had even gone to the trouble one night of bringing him a document that had been stolen from the General Staff and was supposed to save him. And I cannot help suspecting Lt-Col du Paty de Clam, for I recognize the type of expedients in which his fertile imagination delights. His achievement—the decision that Dreyfus was guilty—was in danger, and no doubt he wished to defend his achievement. A revision of the verdict? Why, that would put an end to the far-fetched, tragic work of cheap fiction whose abominable last chapter is being written on Devil's Island! He could not allow that to happen. Henceforth, a duel was bound to take place between Lt-Col Picquart and Lt-Col du Paty de Clam. The one shows his face for all to see; the other is masked. Soon we will see them both in the civil courts. Behind it all is the General Staff, still defending itself, refusing to admit to its crime, which becomes more of an abomination with every passing hour.

In a daze, people wondered who Major Esterhazy's protectors could be. Behind the scenes there was Lt-Col du Paty de Clam, first of all; he cobbled it all together, led the whole thing. The means used were so preposterous that they give him away. Then, there are General de Boisdeffre and General Gonse and General Billot himself, who are obliged to get Esterhazy acquitted since they dare not let Dreyfus's innocence be acknowledged lest the War Office collapse as the public heaps scorn on it. It's a prodigious situation and the impressive result is that Lt-Col Picquart, the one decent man involved, the only one who has done his duty, is going to be the victim, the person they will ride rough-shod over and punish. Ah justice! what dreadful despair grips my heart! They are even claiming that Picquart is the forger, that he forged the letter-telegram purposely to cause Esterhazy's downfall. But in heaven's name, why? To what end? State one motive. Is he too paid by the Jews? The funniest thing about the whole story is that in fact he was anti-Semitic. Yes, we are witnessing an infamous sight: men heavily in debt and guilty of evil deeds but whose innocence is being proclaimed while the very honour of a man whose record is spotless is being dragged in the mud! When a society comes to that, it begins to rot away.

This, M. le Président, is the Esterhazy affair: a guilty man who had to be proved innocent. For almost two months now, we have been following every single episode of this pitiful business. I am simplifying, for by and large this is only a summary of the story, but one day every one of its turbulent pages will be written in full. So it is that we saw General de Pellieux, first of all, then Major Ravary, conduct a villainous investigation from which the scoundrels emerged transfigured while decent people were besmirched. Then, the court martial was convened.

Did anyone really hope that one court martial would undo what another court martial had done in the first place?

I am not even talking about the judges, who could have been chosen differently. Since these soldiers have a lofty idea of discipline in their blood, isn't that enough to disqualify them from arriving at an equitable judgement? Discipline means obedience. Once the Minister of War, the supreme commander, has publicly established the authority of the original verdict, and has done so to the acclamations of the nation's representatives, how can you expect a court martial to override his judgement officially? In hierarchical terms, that is impossible. General Billot, in his statement, planted certain ideas in the judges' minds, and they proceeded to judge the case in the same way as they would proceed to go into battle, that is, without stopping to think. The preconceived idea that they brought with them to the judges' bench was of course as follows: "Dreyfus was sentenced for treason by a court martial, therefore he is guilty; and we, as a court martial, cannot find him innocent. Now, we know that if we recognize Esterhazy's guilt we will be proclaiming Dreyfus's innocence." And nothing could make them budge from that line.

They reached an iniquitous verdict which will forever weigh heavy on all our future courts martial and forever make their future decisions suspect. There may be room for doubt as to whether the first court martial was intelligent but there is no doubt that the second has been criminal. Its excuse, I repeat, is that the commander in chief had spoken and declared the previous verdict unattackable, holy and superior to mere mortals—and how could his subordinates dare to contradict him? They talk to us about the honour of the army; they want us to love the army, respect the army. Oh yes, indeed, if you mean an army that would rise up at the very first hint of danger, that would defend French soil; that army is the French people themselves, and we have nothing but affection and respect for it. But the army that is involved here is not the dignified army that our need for justice calls out for. What we are faced with here is the sabre, the master that may be imposed on us tomorrow. Should we kiss the hilt of that sabre, that god, with pious devotion? No, we should not!

As I have already shown, the Dreyfus Affair was the affair of the War Office: an officer from the General Staff denounced by his fellow officers on the General Staff, sentenced under pressure from the Chiefs of the General Staff. And I repeat, he cannot emerge from his trial innocent without all of the General Staff being guilty. Which is why the War Office employed every means imaginable—campaigns in the press, statements and innuendoes, every type of influence—to cover Esterhazy, in order to convict Dreyfus a second time. The republican government should take a broom to that nest of Jesuits (General Billot calls them that himself) and make a clean sweep! Where, oh where is a strong and wisely patriotic ministry that will be bold enough to overhaul the whole system and make a fresh start? I know many people who tremble with alarm at the thought of a possible war, knowing what hands our national defence is in! and what a den of sneaking intrigue, rumour-mongering and back-biting that sacred chapel has become—yet that is where the fate of our country is decided! People take fright at the appalling light that has just been shed on it all by the Dreyfus Affair, that tale of human sacrifice! Yes, an unfortunate, a "dirty Jew" has been sacrificed. Yes, what an accumulation of madness, stupidity, unbridled imagination, low police tactics, inquisitorial and tyrannical methods this handful of officers have got away with! They have crushed the nation under their boots, stuffing its calls for truth and justice down its throat on the fallacious and sacrilegious pretext that they are acting for the good of the country!

And they have committed other crimes. They have based their action on the foul press and let themselves be defended by all the rogues in Paris—and now the rogues are triumphant and insolent while law and integrity go down in defeat. It is a crime to have accused individuals of rending France apart when all those individuals ask for is a generous nation at the head of the procession of free, just nations—and all the while the people who committed that crime were hatching an insolent plot to make the entire world swallow a fabrication. It is a crime to lead public opinion astray, to manipulate it for a death-dealing purpose and pervert it to the point of delirium. It is a crime to poison the minds of the humble, ordinary people, to whip reactionary and intolerant passions into a frenzy while sheltering behind the odious bastion of anti-Semitism. France, the great and liberal cradle of the rights of man, will die of anti-Semitism if it is not cured of it. It is a crime to play on patriotism to further the aims of hatred. And it is a crime to worship the sabre as a modern god when all of human science is labouring to hasten the triumph of truth and justice.

Truth and justice—how ardently we have striven for them! And how distressing it is to see them slapped in the face, overlooked, forced to retreat! I can easily imagine the harrowing dismay that must be filling M. Scheurer-Kestner's soul, and one day, no doubt, he will wish that when he was questioned before the Senate he had taken the revolutionary step of revealing everything he knew, ripping away all pretence. He was your true good man, a man who could look back on an honest life. He assumed that truth alone would be enough—could not help but be enough, since it was plain as day to him. What was the point of upsetting everything, since the sun would soon be shining? He was serene and confident, and how cruelly he is being punished for that now! The same is true of Lt-Col Picquart: out of a lofty sense of dignity, he refrained from publishing General Gonse's letters. His scruples do him honour, particularly since while he was being respectful of discipline, his superior officers were busy slinging mud at him, conducting the investigation prior to his trial themselves, in the most outrageous and unbelievable way. There are two victims, two decent, stout-hearted men, who stood back to let God have His way—and all the while the devil was doing his work. And where Lt-Col Picquart is concerned, we have even seen this ignoble thing: a French court first allowed the rapporteur to bring charges against a witness publicly, accuse him publicly of every wrong in the book, and then, when that witness was called to give an account of himself and speak in his own defence, that same court held its session behind closed doors. I say that that is still another crime, and I say that it will arouse the conscience of all mankind. Our military tribunals certainly do have a peculiar idea of justice.

That, M. le Président, is the plain truth. It is appalling. It will remain an indelible blot on your term as President. Oh, I know that you are powerless to deal with it, that you are the prisoner of the Constitution and of the people nearest to you. But as a man, your duty is clear, and you will not overlook it, and you will do your duty. Not for one minute do I despair that truth will triumph. I am confident and I repeat, more vehemently even than before, the truth is on the march and nothing shall stop it. The Affair is only just beginning, because only now have the positions become crystal clear: on the one hand, the guilty parties, who do not want the truth to be revealed; on the other, the defenders of justice, who will give their lives to see that justice is done. I have said it elsewhere and I repeat it here: if the truth is buried underground, it swells and grows and becomes so explosive that the day it bursts, it blows everything wide open along with it. Time will tell; we shall see whether we have not prepared, for some later date, the most resounding disaster.

But this letter has been a long one, M. le Président, and it is time to bring it to a close.

I accuse Lt-Col du Paty de Clam of having been the diabolical agent of a miscarriage of justice (though unwittingly, I am willing to believe) and then of having defended his evil deed for the past three years through the most preposterous and most blameworthy machinations.

I accuse General Mercier of having been an accomplice, at least by weak-mindedness, to one of the most iniquitous acts of this century.

I accuse General Billot of having had in his hands undeniable proof that Dreyfus was innocent and of having suppressed it, of having committed this crime against justice and against humanity for political purposes, so that the General Staff, which had been compromised, would not lose face.

I accuse Generals de Boisdeffre and Gonse of having been accomplices to this same crime, one out of intense clerical conviction, no doubt, and the other perhaps because of the esprit de corps which makes the War Office the Holy of Holies and hence unattackable.

I accuse General de Pellieux and Major Ravary of having led a villainous inquiry, by which I mean a most monstrously one-sided inquiry, the report on which, by Ravary, constitutes an imperishable monument of naive audacity.

I accuse the three handwriting experts, Messrs Belhomme, Varinard and Couard, of having submitted fraudulent and deceitful reports—unless a medical examination concludes that their eyesight and their judgement were impaired.

I accuse the War Office of having conducted an abominable campaign in the press (especially in *L'Eclair* and *L'Echo de Paris*) in order to cover up its misdeeds and lead public opinion astray.

Finally, I accuse the first court martial of having violated the law by sentencing a defendant on the basis of a document which remained secret, and I accuse the second court martial of having covered up that illegal action, on orders, by having, in its own turn, committed the judicial crime of knowingly acquitting a guilty man.

In making these accusations, I am fully aware that my action comes under Articles 30 and 31 of the law of 29 July 1881 on the press, which makes libel a punishable offence. I deliberately expose myself to that law.

As for the persons I have accused, I do not know them; I have never seen them; I feel no rancour or hatred towards them. To me, they are mere entities, mere embodiments of social malfeasance. And the action I am taking here is merely a revolutionary means to hasten the revelation of truth and justice.

I have but one goal: that light be shed, in the name of mankind which has suffered so much and has the right to happiness. My ardent protest is merely a cry from my very soul. Let them dare to summon me before a court of law! Let the inquiry be held in broad daylight!

I am waiting.

M. le Président, I beg you to accept the assurance of my most profound respect.

Zola knew he would not wait long. He had paved the legal path to his arrest for defamation when he stated that the second court-martial had

Figure 8. One of the most famous headlines in the history of journalism. Published on January 13, 1898, Emile Zola's "J'Accuse . . . ! Letter to the President of the Republic" turned the judicial case into an international affair.

"knowingly" acquitted a guilty man. Based on that passage alone, Minister of War Billot submitted a formal complaint to the minister of justice, and Zola's trial was set for February 7. Held at the Palais de Justice on Paris's Ile de la Cité, the ten-day process drew the entire cast of characters from the General Staff, the high offices of government, and the Dreyfusard ranks. Outside the courtroom a grotesque atmosphere conjured up the spectacle of a public hanging. At the close of each day's session, gangs mobilized by Jules Guérin (Drumont's associate and leader of the Antisemitic League of France) applauded generals, cried out "Death to the Jews!" and threatened to throw Dreyfusards into the Seine. On the trial's second day, police pushed back more than five hundred demonstrators, many of whom wielded leaded canes. On later days the mix of curious onlookers and activist thugs reached six thousand.

Shouts resounded through the palace as well, where the court ordered that no mention be made of the Dreyfus case. The traitor had been convicted, and res judicata would be respected. With every attempt by Zola's lawyer, Fernand Labori, to attack the absurdity of such a rule, the judges called out, "The question will not be raised!" Military witnesses, on the other hand, testified with little interruption and constantly alluded to evidence proving Dreyfus's guilt—and, by extension, Zola's defamation. When interrogated by the defense, however, du Paty, Henry, and others refused to answer questions of substance, and Esterhazy turned his back. By the end of the trial's first week, the farce was clear to all but the most myopic anti-Dreyfusards, and when Picquart completed his testimony, with its account of the Esterhazy inquiry, much of the audience rose to applaud. Newspaper reports described the colonel's performance and the clear theatricality of the entire process, but the journalists were not alone. Marcel Proust, a Dreyfus supporter who would later thread the affair through the plot of his masterpiece *Remembrance of Things Past,* took copious notes and included descriptions of Picquart, General Boisdeffre, and other witnesses in *Jean Santeuil,* a forgettable novel about a memorable moment.

More than three years earlier, when the Dreyfus court-martial had drawn to a close, the General Staff had sent du Paty to the judges armed with the secret dossier. Now, in the late stages of the Zola trial, General de Pellieux aimed for his own coup de grâce. In public he would counter Picquart's testimony with hard evidence of Dreyfus's treachery. The "pact of silence" had been broken by witnesses who had mentioned the

1894 trial, and Pellieux felt free to quote from memory the file's most devastating document—the letter from the Italian attaché in which the traitor's name had been spelled out in full. But while Pellieux's revelation captivated judges and spectators, it sent chills through the inner circle of the General Staff. Unaware of the document's origins and acting on his own, Pellieux had quoted the forgery inserted by Henry into the Dreyfus dossier two years after the captain's court-martial.

When Zola's lawyer demanded that the incriminating letter be placed in evidence, the army quickly leaned on the crutch of national security and rolled out "the old warhorse" (Proust's description), Chief of Staff Boisdeffre. At that point the general, like Pellieux, may have been unaware that the letter was a forgery. He knew, however, that the exposure of state secrets might spark an international crisis. Much like Henry at Dreyfus's court-martial, though with more elegance and influence, Boisdeffre called for faith in the word of the high command.

Neither Zola's prepared text ("by my forty years of work I swear that Dreyfus is innocent") nor his lawyer's "herculean" closing argument could slow the momentum established by Boisdeffre. Only the slightest peripheral vision was needed to see the relevance of the Dreyfus affair to the Zola case, but this was a tribunal with blinkers firmly fixed, and the prosecution had little trouble convincing the court that "J'Accuse" had been defamatory. After thirty-five minutes of deliberation, the judges convicted Zola and his codefendant, Perrenx, the managing director of *L'Aurore,* by a majority vote. Sentenced to the maximum penalty of one year in prison and a fine of three thousand francs, Zola left the courtroom to a chorus of jeers. Watching military officers in joyous celebration and hearing gangs shout, "Drown the kikes! Long live the army!" Zola, whose novels had portrayed mob hysteria in graphic detail, described the crowd as "cannibals."[8]

Seven months passed between the publication of "J'Accuse" and its author's flight to London following his retrial (on a technicality) and reconviction in mid-July. During that period Prime Minister Jules Méline repeated his litany of denial. "There is no longer a Zola case," he announced in February, "nor an Esterhazy case, nor a Dreyfus case. There is no case at all."[9] But the proclamation was both useless and wrong. The

[8] Quoted in Bredin, *The Affair,* 270.
[9] Quoted in *L'Affaire Dreyfus de A à Z,* ed. Michel Drouin (Paris: Flammarion, 1994), 75.

Dreyfus battle was joined in countless arenas, including, in March, the riding arena of the Ecole Militaire, where Picquart wounded Henry in a duel of swords. A few days earlier, on February 26, Clemenceau and Drumont had exchanged six pistol shots without drawing blood. And during the same period Picquart, in the sharpest gesture of disdain an officer could inflict, refused Esterhazy's challenge to a duel. As a point of honor, he would not meet on equal terms a man he knew to be a traitor.

Beyond the circle of veterans, however, the affair now exploded on the streets of Paris and provincial cities. It reached into the halls of academe, aristocratic salons, and the marketplaces of Algeria, where Jews had been under attack since the young republic had granted them citizenship in 1871. Grafting colonial hatreds to the metropole's widely publicized affair, Max Régis, director of the newspaper *L'Antijuif,* incited pogroms in Algiers starting in late January, and in May helped secure the election of his mentor and friend Edouard Drumont as the Algiers deputy. "We will water our liberty tree," Régis proclaimed, "with Jewish blood."[10]

Within France the Dreyfus affair had little direct impact on election campaigns in the spring of 1898, although the extent to which it provided a subplot, which it surely did, defies measurement. But the affair's politics thrived on many sites, and during the months prior to the legislative contests, the combined impact of the Esterhazy and Zola trials triggered a wave of riots. Most prevalent in eastern France, with its significant Jewish population and deep habits of anti-Semitism, riots also erupted in Lyons, Marseilles, Toulouse, Rouen, and more than a dozen other cities and towns. Priests, teachers, and politicians helped link the affair to local issues, but the Zola trial sparked the greatest number of "patriotic" demonstrations. Although gangs of youths, students, and "self-styled students" dominated the crowds shouting "Death to Zola! Long live the army!" industrial workers, artisans, shopkeepers, and professionals joined in as well.[11] In towns with Jewish residents, mobs pillaged stores, desecrated synagogues, and attacked rabbis. Evidence of murder came from Algiers, and serious injuries were reported in many parts of France.

---

[10]Quoted in Pierre Birnbaum, *L'Affaire Dreyfus: La République en péril* (Paris: Gallimard, 1994), 64.

[11]Stephen Wilson, *Ideology and Experience: Antisemitism in France at the Time of the Dreyfus Affair* (Rutherford, N.J.: Fairleigh Dickinson University Press, 1982), 106–24.

Reading about the provincial assaults and witnessing the riots in Paris, the writer and Zionist Max Nordau imagined the possibility of "a general slaughter of Jews throughout the country."[12]

But France was not Russia (or Algeria), at least not yet, and the republic's government, however tolerant of abuses within its military, would not support pogroms or permit social disorder. By the late spring of 1898 the gendarmes had done their job, and although organized anti-Semites regrouped, the young hooligans who had turned on Jews as a winter pastime found other outlets for their anger or boredom. With few exceptions, the conflicts of the affair—after their short, violent run down streets and back alleys—were again confined to newspaper columns, caricatures, café and salon conversations, and debates within the halls and cloakrooms of the Chamber of Deputies. One of the affair's most celebrated images, Caran d'Ache's "A Family Dinner," which appeared in *Le Figaro,* captured the power of the debate in a private setting. A peaceful dinner party fills the cartoon's first frame, and the caption reads, "Absolutely no talk of the Affair." The second frame, titled "They talked about it," shows throats throttled, fingers pointed, and chairs overturned. Only the dog seems to bark for order.[13]

The sticks and stones diminished, but the words and pictures aimed to hurt. Emile Zola, like Joseph Reinach in the political realm, had long been the object of vicious portraits in prose and caricature. Scatalogical images had depicted the author of *Les Rougon-Macquart* as a pig wallowing in the filth of his vulgar work. Following "J'Accuse" the nationalist press reminded readers of the recent novel, *La Débacle,* in which Zola was critical of the General Staff during the 1870 war. One print showed the writer stuffed into a garbage bin marked with the novel's title and carried by comrades portrayed as German officers and hook-nosed members of the "Jewish Syndicate." Another caricature, displayed on a cardboard pull toy and titled "The Foundation of the Dreyfus Affair," had Zola baring his buttocks with the inscription "My Heart Belongs to Dreyfus." Newspaper reports were no less crude. Drumont pounded the xenophobic drum in diatribes against Zola's Italian heritage, and the

---

[12]Quoted in Michael R. Marrus, *The Politics of Assimilation: The French Jewish Community at the Time of the Dreyfus Affair* (Oxford: Oxford University Press, 1980), 266.

[13]On Caran d'Ache's cartoon drawing and more, see Michael R. Marrus, " 'En Famille': The Dreyfus Affair and Its Myths," *French Politics and Society* 12 (1994): 77–90.

— Surtout ! ne parlons pas de l'affaire Dreyfus !

... Ils en ont parlé...

Figure 9. Caran d'Ache's "A Family Dinner" appeared in *Le Figaro* on February 13, 1898. Not all French households were divided by the affair, but for those citizens engaged in the case the early months of 1898 were the most violent. Riots erupted in Paris and provincial cities, and in the French colony of Algeria.

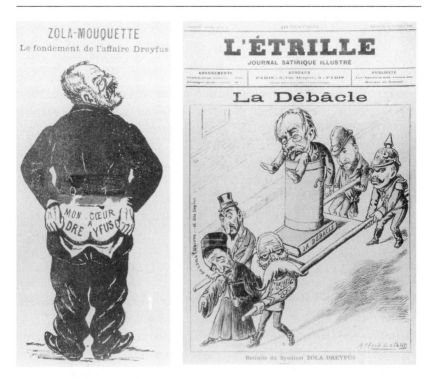

Left: **Figure 10.**   With the strategically placed inscription "My heart belongs to Dreyfus," this paper novelty from 1898 mocks Emile Zola, the captain's most notorious defender. Critics often used scatalogical images to attack the "pornographic" novelist.

Right: **Figure 11.**   Critical of the French high command in his novel *The Debacle,* Emile Zola was excoriated as part of a German-Jewish "Syndicate" in *L'Etrille* and other anti-Dreyfusard publications. This image appeared on February 27, 1898.

editor in chief of the mass-circulation *Le Petit Journal* used information supplied by Henry to slander the memory of Zola's father; he also called the novelist "a fool, a peacock, a vice monger, a smut fancier."[14]

At the same time, literati, artists, scientists, and academicians mounted loftier, but no less divisive, campaigns. The day after "J'Accuse"

---

[14]Ernest Judet of *Le Petit Journal* is quoted in Frederick Brown, *Zola: A Life* (New York: Farrar, Straus, & Giroux, 1995), 746–77.

was published, Zola, joined by Emile Duclaux, director of the Pasteur Institute, drew up one of the first public petitions demanding the revision, or judicial review, of the Dreyfus case, and over the weeks that followed, *L'Aurore* published the names of nearly fifteen hundred supporters. Georges Clemenceau, in one of the affair's most celebrated proclamations, used the front page of *L'Aurore* to praise the courage of those Dreyfusard "intellectuals," a word he underscored. "They have come from all corners of the horizon," he wrote. "They have rallied around an idea," and through their "peaceful revolt," they formed "the origins of a movement of opinion that rises above all diverse interests."[15]

Hardly new, the word *intellectual* had been in vogue for more than two decades (it appeared in the novels of Barbey d'Aurevilly and Guy de Maupassant), and more than a century had passed since a celebrated writer (Voltaire) had rallied to the defense of an innocent man (Calas) and sparked a notorious "affair." Later, Victor Hugo, playwright and poet, attacked the politics of Napoleon III and ended up in exile. But Voltaire, Hugo, the novelist George Sand, and other engaged intellectuals had worked alone or in a loose confederation of friends, while the petitioners for Dreyfus proclaimed themselves part of a collective, a modern movement of the high-minded assembled to fight an injustice. This was new, and it was considered outrageous by other writers, artists, scientists, and teachers who believed in Dreyfus's guilt or in res judicata and who accused the new "intellectuals" of portraying themselves as magisterial oaks in a forest full of trash trees. As one literary critic and historian put it, they aimed to elevate themselves "to the rank of supermen." Maurice Barrès, a novelist deeply involved in politics, launched the most vigorous attack against the Dreyfusard "demi-intellectuals," members of what Barrès dismissed as "the phone book of the elite."[16]

In February 1898 the expanding group of Dreyfusard intellectuals formed the League of the Rights of Man, with its first general assembly held in June. Pledged to protect all those whose liberty was endangered and whose rights were violated, the league was progressive but far from radical. Its president, the former minister of justice Ludovic Trarieux, had no time for socialists, anarchists, or trade unionists. Later, anti-

---

[15] *L'Aurore,* Jan. 23, 1898.
[16] Maurice Barrès, *Scènes et doctrines du nationalisme* (Paris: Félix Juven, 1902), 45–47.

Dreyfusards, more resistant to group enterprises, established the League of the French Fatherland, with the poet François Coppée as its first president and an inaugural charter signed by academicians, members of the French Institute, and eminent doctors, lawyers, journalists, and artists. Both leagues espoused causes that reached far beyond the Dreyfus case. In fact, it was by now almost universally acknowledged that the prisoner on Devil's Island served best, in the journalist Séverine's words, as a "pretext for the grand combat of ideas." Even the affair, as Zola noted, sometimes became "very trifling."[17]

While the League of the Rights of Man placed the separation of church and state high on its agenda, the League of the French Fatherland, in an effort to draw moderates as well as reactionaries, championed a vague crusade for moral order and defense of the military and state policy *(raison d'état)*. They left the street work to other groups with more muscular members, including Paul Déroulède's League of Patriots and Guérin's Antisemitic League. And yet another nationalist organization born of the Dreyfus affair spilled both ink and blood over the evil trinity of Jews, Protestants, and Freemasons that threatened the fiber of Catholic France. The neo-royalist Action Française attracted gifted writers and cane-wielding toughs *(Camelots du roi)* who would play principal roles in the affair's twentieth-century incarnations.

French women, as absent from the leagues as they were from parliament, found other arenas in which to engage the fight for or against Dreyfus. The aristocratic and bourgeois salons depicted in Proust's fiction had their equivalents—and, at times, their models—in the gatherings hosted by Dreyfusard women such as the marquise Arconati-Visconti and Madame Strauss, and by their anti-Dreyfusard rivals, including the Comtesse de Loynes, who not only entertained nationalists but subsidized their newspapers. Less privileged women used the press to comment on the affair and, in many cases, to assert the citizenship still denied them.[18] The newspaper *La Fronde,* founded by Marguerite Durand in December 1897, with the veteran journalist Séverine

---

[17]*La Fronde,* Jan. 15, 1898. Zola is quoted in Douglas Johnson, *France and the Dreyfus Affair* (London: Blandford, 1966), 125.

[18]Maíre Cross, Colette Cosnier, and other scholars examined this issue at a 1994 conference in Tours, France. See Eric Cahm, "Les Représentations de l'affaire Dreyfus dans la presse en France et à l'étranger," *Société Internationale d'histoire de l'Affaire Dreyfus* 2 (Autumn 1996): 28–30.

on its staff, ran the entire text of "J'Accuse" on the day following its appearance in *L'Aurore*. Simultaneously with *Le Siècle* (another Dreyfusard paper), *La Fronde* also launched petitions under the title *"Appel aux Femmes"* (Call to Women). Along with names came comments on the tragedy of Lucie Dreyfus and support for her desire to join her husband in exile (common for the wives of deportees, but denied to her). Full of "tears" for the prisoner and his family, letters to the editor also confirmed the diversity of Dreyfusard "feminism" and put the lie to Séverine's comment that the petitioners were "simply obeying the impulse of their heart . . . the feelings of pity and sympathy" for a suffering "compatriot." Tears, many women made it clear, "were not enough."[19]

[19]*La Fronde,* Mar. 26, 1898. See also Cahm, "Les Représentations," 29; and Helen Rodney, "Séverine," in *L'Affaire Dreyfus de A à Z,* ed. Drouin 282–87.

LE SIÈCLE

Call to Women
March 25–27, 1898

May our voices be heard, may they awaken benumbed consciences and make the ill-fated man's jailers realize the horror of the *needless* torture they inflict upon him.

MME. DE TAVERNIER

Before the cowardice and infamy of certain men, women are weighed down by silence, and so I am persuaded that letters will come from everywhere.

This is a faint token of respect and pity toward Madame Dreyfus and the poor martyr on Devil's Island, but however faint it may be, I am happy to give it.

BLANCHE LEMOINE

There is no honest woman who would not instantly put herself in the place of her husband, who would not feel his pain and despair! For her [Lucie Dreyfus] . . . her husband is a martyr whom she follows, through her thoughts, along the path of suffering!

Le Siècle, Mar. 25–27, 1898 (emphasis in original).

And so! we, the women of France, ask Dreyfus's judges to allow the poor martyr to join her husband on his rock of exile.

When a man is taken to the scaffold, is he not given a priest? It is his consolation. I cannot believe that in France, with our great love of humanity, we do not understand the feelings of that sad victim, Madame Dreyfus!

JEANNE THIRIAT

Compassion, courage, vigor, all the lofty actions of the human spirit seem forever lost in the outburst of evil, unjust, and criminal passions that the sad spectacle of this unfortunate Dreyfus affair has brought about.

As you have so rightly said, it is in the hearts of French women that one must seek and find those feelings of goodness.

Women and mothers, we protest in the name of humanity and justice. Outraged, we demand from the minister of colonies a little compassion for that unfortunate man and his admirable wife . . . whose sufferings exceed all one can imagine. We ask that she be able to rejoin her husband . . . and we send her our admiration for her courage and our ardent sympathy.

REINE LEHMAN
LUCIE BERNARD
MARGUERITE LEHMAN
MARIA DERUPPE
V. MAYER
HENRIETTE D. NADILLE
SARA FRAENNEL
A. VAN LEE
V. SCHWOB
ANNA LEFÈVRE
Y. PAULINE GEORGES

For a few years now, French novels have been based almost exclusively on that feeling of compassion we portray as a design for living. Compassion for worthy and unworthy sufferings; . . . compassion for the guilty; compassion for the innocent; human compassion! . . . But how unfortunate that that eloquence does not give way to action, that it remains like an embalmed corpse buried in books!

Remember that in early Christian times the greatest criminals found inviolable sanctuary in churches, at the foot of altars.

Let us remain Christian, and may all condemned men, without exception, find sacred refuge in women.

ISABELLE DE PONTOIS

Daughter, sister, and widow of republicans of long standing, who fought their entire lives for the good cause, I believe it is my duty to join your appeal in favor of the unfortunate Madame Dreyfus.

This is neither a political nor a religious question; it is a question of the heart, to which no one should remain unfeeling.

VEUVE CHARLES GUICHARD

Convinced of the illegality of Captain Dreyfus's conviction, revolted by the bias of the judges in the Esterhazy and Zola affairs, shocked by the unjust and barbaric behavior of the government toward Madame Dreyfus, I ask that my name be added to the list of French women who have responded to the appeal published by *Le Siècle.*

MME. PIERRE BONNIER

Even though your appeal is addressed to French women, allow me, a foreigner who has made France her second homeland, to join . . . the wishes warmly expressed by so many noble French women for the triumph of truth, justice, and humanity.

May the men who govern the affairs of this beautiful country of France be touched by the heart-rending distress of that innocent victim of so many inexplicable mysteries! . . .

This wish comes spontaneously from the anguished hearts, not only of French women but of all women. . . . It is shared, I know, by every one of my compatriots; . . . by American, English, Russian women, and, I have no doubt, by those women of all nations who have not been able to read about the cruel rejection of Madame Dreyfus's request without painful astonishment and a profound sense of grief.

MARY CHALMER

I am Jewish, and as a Jew my name on your appeal to the women of France does not carry great weight, for I am too involved in this stirring question.

But in the name of ALL Israelites whose hearts beat in unison with the noble and courageous Madame Dreyfus, and whose modesty keeps them from sending in their names, I express thanks to all the Christian women who have not forgotten that their religion is about love and charity, and to those freethinking women who believe that the feminine heart should express tender compassion toward all suffering.

L. LÉVY

Although Séverine had few rivals among women journalists in the Dreyfusard camp, she had keen competition across the literary barricades. Sibylle-Gabrielle Marie-Antoinette de Riqueti de Mirabeau, Comtesse de Martel de Janville, had a short nom de plume (Gyp) and an impressive résumé as novelist, reporter, and salon hostess. The "feminine center of nationalism" numbered Barrès and Déroulède among her guests. One biographer calls Gyp a notorious and talented enfant terrible of the affair, and her mocking articles, with their unbridled anti-Semitism, prove the point.[20] Covering the Zola trial for *La Libre Parole,* she coined the term Izolâtres to describe the novelist's allies, all of whom, no matter what their religion, were "Jews."

[20]See Willa Z. Silverman, *The Notorious Life of Gyp: Right-Wing Anarchist in Fin-de-Siècle France* (New York: Oxford University Press, 1995).

GYP

Les Izolâtres
March 3, 1898

They are ugly! and whatever they do, the primitive stigmata persist, despite their easy life, mixed marriages, and tidiness. The Jewish women (authentic Jews, of course) who filled the court benches for fifteen days were, in general, chubby, even obese, and of an oily fat. . . .

Their slender waists, bosoms, and bouncing hips give to their short little bodies—topped by enormous heads—the look of a pillow knotted in the middle. The strong perfume they seem to suck up like a sponge cannot overpower the particular smell that Schopenhauer calls the *foetor judaicus* [the Jewish stink].

The men are even uglier, but the type is more varied. There are as many thin Jewish men as there are fat ones. . . .

Next to the witnesses' entrance, against the courtroom wall, behind the journalists' bench, a skewerful of Jewish lawyers. Not one Christian! And, without prejudice, they are truly appalling to see! . . . During the fifteen sessions that bench of Jewish lawyers, even as they replaced themselves, remained just as hideous. Oh no! certainly! those men are not and can never be French, no matter what is done. They come, in this case, to prove once again that they are the born and sworn enemies of our race, that they want to lessen and defile in order to raise themselves up and seek revenge. . . .

The Frenchman certainly has more character than the Jew, however baptized he may be.

A Jew, from his office, bank, or by telegram or telephone, may affect a large number of Christians. Face-to-face or elbow-to-elbow, a Christian is easily worth three Jews. . . . Therefore, during the court session the French, though of an inferior number, often carried the day. . . .

Colonel Picquart is the pretty Jew, or rather the pretty Jewish blond. About his religion I have no hint, though I'd wager Protestant. He sways back and forth at the witness rail, moving his hips, which he shows off a bit too much, and tips his head toward his right shoulder as he speaks, a very graceful and catlike posture.

He expresses himself stylishly, with a blank, arid voice. He has the wheedling look of a snake charmer, who will become the soul of the Izolâtre society and who will certainly be . . . the most intelligent and agreeable recruit. . . .

No one—in my corner at least—questions the disinterestedness of M. Zola. But one reckons that by becoming, unconsciously or not, the man of the Syndicate; by tearing to pieces, in concert with a handful of Jews, the country of adoption that had applauded his great talent, he has committed a vile and wicked act. Behind him, one smells the Jews. . . .

If M. Zola went down to the lion's den, he would be hooted, [and if] M. Joseph Reinach was imprudent enough to venture there as well, he would spend, I believe, a nasty quarter of an hour.

It is certain that abroad Herr Zola, Herr Reinach, and the Izolâtres are considered to be, for the moment, the elite among Frenchmen. . . . But it is no mistake that in France the Izolâtres are not worth two cents.

Beyond Gyp, who was hard to miss, anti-Dreyfusard women rarely expressed their sentiments in public. A few Catholic organizations mobilized letter-writing campaigns, and a small group of "patriotic feminists" contributed cash and commentaries to a nationalist fund drive late in 1898. But no widely publicized petitions were launched on the scale of *La Fronde, Le Siècle,* and *L'Aurore.*[21]

Meanwhile, in the well-documented male domain of organized politics, the third year of the Dreyfus case—the first of the affair—marked a pivotal moment in the history of French socialism. At least five socialist parties made up the French left in the 1890s, and since emerging from the long repression that had followed the Commune (the "coma" imposed upon them, as one historian described it[22]), socialists had entered the Chamber of Deputies in increasing numbers. The elections of 1893 had raised the tally to forty. Authoritarian theorists argued with

---

[21]Although Stephen Wilson mentions the "patriotic feminists" among anti-Dreyfusards, a full history has yet to be written. See Wilson, *Ideology and Experience,* 142.

[22]D. W. Brogan, *The Development of Modern France, 1870–1939* (Gloucester, Mass.: Peter Smith, 1970), 1:288.

reform-minded socialists over the revolution's timing and tactics (though not over its inevitability), with the strongest voice coming from Jules Guesde's *Parti ouvrier,* France's first modern socialist party and the largest of the fin de siècle left. Adhering to the strict Marxist rule of nonparticipation in bourgeois governments, the Guesdists, along with many unaligned socialists, insisted that revolutionary change could never emerge from a capitalist cabinet. At the same time, most of the left still believed that "huckstering" Jewish financiers blocked the revolution by keeping the bourgeois system afloat.

At the outset, and not surprisingly, the majority of socialists, including those who condemned anti-Semitism, showed little or no interest in the case of an army officer from a family of affluent industrialists. They shared that view with anarchists, without sharing the nihilism and fanaticism that aimed toward destruction alone. During the three years following Dreyfus's court-martial and deportation, socialists of every stripe either abstained from the debate or condemned it as a distraction from the class struggle. Only in the winter of 1897–98, when the evidence of criminal actions on the part of the General Staff mounted, did a few socialists awaken to the combat that pitted individual rights against an authoritarian high command. The most influential of those early advocates emerged from the library of the Ecole Normale Supérieure, one of France's most prestigious institutions of higher learning.

Mentor to a small army of ardent young socialists, Lucien Herr, the Ecole Normale's librarian, held informal tutorials on the affair's revolutionary dimensions. An Alsatian by birth and a socialist for nearly a decade, Herr joined the Dreyfusard movement later than some but earlier than most. By the final weeks of 1897 he had "no doubt about Dreyfus's innocence" and looked forward to overcoming "the desperate resistance of military men who see themselves ruined and dishonored." Elevating "the duty to question" over "the duty to obey," the librarian drew to the affair an impressive coterie of students, graduates, and visitors, including the twenty-five-year-old poet Charles Péguy, who would gather proselytes in his turn; the literary critic, Léon Blum, the same age as Péguy and later to become France's first socialist prime minister; and, at nearly forty years old, Jean Jaurès, the most powerful independent socialist in the Chamber of Deputies.[23]

Herr's "greatest convert," Jaurès took a long time to convince. He had

---

[23]Daniel Lindenberg, "Lucien Herr," in Drouin, *L'Affaire Dreyfus,* 212–16.

greeted Dreyfus's 1894 conviction with an angry comment about treasonous officers being exiled while simple soldiers were shot for minor crimes, and even after Scheurer-Kestner's campaigns, the socialist continued to define the case as a bourgeois struggle. By early 1898, however, Herr's influence and Zola's public attack on the high command had convinced Jaurès that revolutions come in many forms and that the anti-Dreyfusard crusade signaled a danger "not only for the bourgeois republic but the social republic."[24] When he lost his parliamentary seat in the May 1898 elections (for reasons that had more to do with the economy of his region of southwestern France than with the Dreyfus affair in Paris), Jaurès battled his way back through the newspaper *La Petite République*. And when he did—when he rallied to the republic in peril by rallying to Dreyfus—he helped lead French socialism toward more direct involvement in the established order. His goals, like his rhetoric, remained revolutionary, but unlike many of his comrades, he finally saw in the plight of Dreyfus the plight of the oppressed writ large. And no less important, he came to care about the man on Devil's Island, the prisoner whose need for practical politics was paramount.

[24]Quoted in Bredin, *The Affair*, 295.

JEAN JAURÈS

The Socialist Concern

1898

On that day [when the crimes of General Mercier and the court-martial judges are exposed], we will have the right, we socialists, to rise up against all the leaders who wage war against us in the name of the principles of the French Revolution.

"What have you done," we will shout to them, "to the declaration of the rights of Man and individual liberty? You have treated them with contempt. You have turned all that over to the insolence of military power. You are the turncoats of the bourgeois Revolution." . . .

There are two parts to capitalist and bourgeois legality. There is an en-

Jean Jaurès, *Les Preuves: l'affaire Dreyfus* (Paris: La Petite République, 1898), 11–13.

tire set of laws destined to protect the fundamental inequity of our society, laws that consecrate the privilege of capitalist property, the exploitation of the wage earner by the owner. We want to break those laws, through revolution if necessary, and . . . give rise to a new order. But next to those laws of privilege and plunder, made by one class for itself, there are others that sum up . . . the modest safeguards that, little by little, humanity has gained through the long effort of the centuries and the long series of revolutions.

Now among those laws, the one that prohibits the conviction of a man, no matter who he may be, without debate is perhaps the most essential of all. Contrary to the nationalists, who want to maintain . . . everything that protects Capital and turn over to the generals everything that protects man, we revolutionary socialists want to abolish the capitalist portion and save the humane portion of today's legality. . . .

If Dreyfus has been convicted illegally, and if, in fact, as I will soon demonstrate, he is innocent, he is no longer an officer or a bourgeois. He is stripped, by the very violence of misfortune, of every quality of class. He is no longer anything but humanity itself, at the highest point of misery and despair one can imagine.

If they have convicted him contrary to every law, if they have wrongly condemned him, what a mockery it is to count him still among the privileged! No, he is no longer part of that army that degraded him through criminal error. He is no longer part of those ruling classes who, because of cowardly ambition, hesitate to reestablish for him lawfulness and truth. He is only a model of human suffering at its most poignant. He is the living witness of the military lie, of political cowardice, of the crimes of authority.

Certainly, without contradicting our principles and without putting aside class conflict, we can listen to the cry of our compassion. In our revolutionary combat, we can preserve our humane heart. In order to remain socialists, we are not obliged to run away from humanity. . . .

Who, then, is today most threatened by the despotism of the generals, by the violence, always glorified, of military repression? Who? The proletariat. It is therefore a concern of the first order to hasten the moral disrepute and fall of that high reactionary army which is ready to strike tomorrow.

Since the highest branches of the army have, this time, inflicted their arbitrary and deceitful scheme on a son of the bourgeoisie, middle-class society is profoundly shaken and roused. We should profit from that shock by lessening the moral force and aggressive power of that retrograde General Staff, which is a direct threat to the proletariat.

Launched in mid-August 1898 and soon to reach a circulation of 100,000, Jaurès's *La Petite République* series had been prompted by the actions of a new minister of war. Unlike his precedessors, Godefroy Cavaignac did not try to suppress the affair. He reveled in it. Convinced that Dreyfus and Esterhazy were accomplices in treason, he announced that he would open the file, spread the news, and bring the affair to its final close. And he would do this, he said with some sincerity, not only for the prisoner's enemies but for his defenders as well, many of whom were good patriots who had been led astray. Although more than three hundred documents now filled the dossier, the most incriminating letter remained the Henry forgery, which Cavaignac, like General de Pellieux at Zola's trial, took to be authentic. On July 7 he read the document aloud in the Chamber of Deputies, and by an overwhelming vote (and with "a delirious standing ovation"), the assembly ordered that the speech and the incriminating letter be posted in every one of France's thirty-six thousand town halls. For all but a few socialists in the Chamber (and the moderate Jules Méline, who still wanted the affair to go away), Cavaignac had triumphed. "They did not know," Jaurès said of the majority, "because they did not dare to know."[25]

Georges Picquart, who had been dismissed from the army in late February, lost no time. He informed the minister of war that the document naming Dreyfus "had every appearance of being a forgery." Cavaignac acted no less quickly. On July 13 he had Picquart arrested for the communication of secret papers, the same charge for which the colonel had been detained following Zola's trial. Now, however, the arrest held, and the imprisonment would last eleven months. The minister also moved against Esterhazy, who defended himself by pointing his bejeweled fingers first at the Jews and then, as desperation took hold, at du Paty and others on the General Staff. Although Cavaignac noted those troubling revelations, he was not about to play the fool. Brought before a court of inquiry, Esterhazy avoided the charge of treason (the evidence remained too elusive, the witnesses too unwilling) but was cashiered from the army, to no one's surprise, for habitual misconduct.

Also in August one man with a magnifying glass made a discovery that would soon cut through the confusion of recent events and return the affair to the path of revision. Captain Louis Cuignet had been ordered by Cavaignac to examine the Dreyfus documents. The order should have come before the speech to parliament, but the minister was

[25]Joseph Reinach, *Histoire de l'affaire Dreyfus* (Paris: Fasquelle, 1929), 4:25.

often more keen than careful. The Italian attaché's now notorious note, Cuignet learned, had been cobbled together from two letters, and the paper of its middle section, where Dreyfus's name appeared, was of a slightly different color. The "absolute proof" of the traitor's guilt, uncovered by Henry in 1896, was a forgery. Cuignet repeated the examination for Cavaignac, who then called Henry in for questioning on August 30. Confronted with the letter, the colonel first swore that he had fabricated nothing, and then, pressured by the minister of war for nearly an hour, he confessed. Expressing shock at Henry's deception, Boisdeffre submitted his resignation, as did General de Pellieux, who was right to call himself the "dupe of dishonorable men."[26]

Imprisoned at the Mont-Valérien Fortress, Henry spent the next day writing to his wife ("I see that except for you everyone is going to abandon me") and to General Gonse ("I absolutely must speak to you"). One cryptic comment from Henry to his wife—"You know in whose interest I acted"—has never been explained. Perhaps he referred to Esterhazy, the beneficiary of his paperwork; or to Sandherr, the dead chief he revered; or to the glory of France and its military. Only Henry had the answer, and Henry did not live to tell. Continuing his letters while downing a half-bottle of rum, he stopped in the midst of another note to his wife ("I am like a madman"), picked up a shaving razor, and slit his throat. Rumors of murder soon spread. The colonel had been searched on the day of his arrest, the reports went, and no razor had been found. But the most straightforward explanation remains the most plausible. As one historian has remarked, Henry's suicide "fits in with what one knows of his character, his devotion and loyalty, his submission, even a certain ponderousness."[27]

If, upon reading the Havas news release of Henry's death, Dreyfusards believed that victory drew near, their opponents fought on. At first Drumont, Rochefort, and other nationalists condemned the "hapless" Henry for having aided the enemy with his "odious" and "imbecilic" act.[28] But two articles in the royalist newspaper *La Gazette de France* prompted them to join a chorus of praise for the hero who had sacrificed his life for the fatherland. Young Charles Maurras's apologia

---

[26]Quoted in Brogan, *Development of Modern France,* 1:338.
[27]Johnson, *France and the Dreyfus Affair,* 145.
[28]See Drouin, *L'Affaire Dreyfus,* 81, note 114.

for Colonel Henry—that gallant soldier whose "patriotic forgery" ranked among his "finest feats of war"—would become the foundation text for the new Action Française. Maurras and his followers, like the Dreyfusard intellectuals they abhorred, defined the affair—and carried it into the twentieth century—as a struggle for the soul and future of France.

CHARLES MAURRAS

First Blood

September 6–7, 1898

Colonel, your blood, which streamed to the middle of the cell from the cot where you lay, has been, according to the newspapers, carefully sponged clean by order of the Mont Valérien commandant. But that is a great fallacy. Know that along with your precious blood, the first French blood shed by the Dreyfus affair, there is not a single drop that does not still steam wherever the heart of the nation beats. That blood . . . will cry out until its shedding is expiated not by you, who has given way to a noble despair, not even by the offensive ministerial coterie of Cavaignac, but, rightly, by your chief executioners, and I name them, by members of the syndicate of treason.

Given the current state of disorder among nationalist parties, we have not been able to arrange the grand funeral your martyrdom deserves. . . . It will be our shame not to have tried, but even though the national sentiment is dispersed and divided against itself, and still incapable of action, it is nonetheless coming to life again. Wait, colonel, for it to awaken and reform. Give it some credit. It will vanquish all, and you will be avenged. Before long, in Paris, in your village, monuments to expiate our cowardice will rise from the soil of the fatherland. There one will call witness to what a truly humane person you have been among us.

Strength, determination, finesse, you lacked nothing except a little good fortune on your last day. That failure born of chance will not make us forget your intelligence, your character, your daring spirit of enterprise, that slightly cunning subtlety of mind that called you to the service you discharged. In the most difficult moments, you acted with consistency and independence, with a feeling of responsibility that has become so rare among us that one associates it with the Anglo-Saxons. You are portrayed by others as a brute with a bayonet, a simple slave to commands and a sense of duty you misunderstood. [But] you have shown in every circumstance, in your office and in the courtroom, where everyone admired the good nature and power of your presence, the superior gifts of initiation and resolve. You have called on them with a frantic determination, going so far as to mislead your superiors, your friends, your colleagues, your compatriots for the welfare and honor of all. Your motto "Onward!" which became a proverb, now takes on a mysterious and profound significance. It remains a soldier's motto and becomes, moreover, the motto of the moralist and statesman. We will make it immortal, and it will contain, like a tomb, your memory. . . .

The public spirit freed from anarchist servitude delivers Dreyfus to prison, and it will dedicate statues to you. Your ill-starred "forgery" will be counted among your best feats of war, and that which is most lamentable, its failure, has been paid and overpaid by your blood. . . .

In your memory, my colonel, count on the French to redeem that excess of noble blood.

6

High Courts

Esterhazy took no time to pack. News of Henry's suicide had just broken when the former officer boarded a train bound for Maubeuge, near the Belgian frontier. After shaving the huge handlebar mustache made famous by Parisian caricaturists, he crossed the border on foot, found his way to Brussels, and a few days later sailed to England. Now two of the affair's most renowned players waited out events in London (though Esterhazy enjoyed few of Zola's comforts). With no money and poor English, Schwartzkoppen's old agent turned from the commerce of secrets to the commerce of notoriety: He sold interviews on sensational topics leavened by occasional grains of truth.

A few months earlier, at a dinner party in Paris, Esterhazy had met a British writer just out of jail. Oscar Wilde, whose case rivaled the Dreyfus affair as the most publicized scandal of the fin de siècle, considered Esterhazy eminently "more interesting" than the prisoner on Devil's Island. "It's always a mistake to be innocent," he reportedly said. "To be a criminal takes imagination and courage." During one of their evenings together, Wilde displayed another example of his callous wit when, with a laugh, he told Esterhazy, "The innocent always suffer, it is their métier. . . . The interesting thing surely is to be guilty and wear as a halo the seduction of sin."[1] On that topic the commandant needed no lessons from Wilde, and their brief encounters would be nothing more than perverse footnotes to the affair were it not for the contacts Esterhazy made through Wilde, and were it not for Wilde's role in ruining the plans of an important, if little-known, English Dreyfusard named Carlos Blacker.

An intimate friend of the Italian attaché Alessandro Panizzardi, Blacker had learned of Dreyfus's innocence and Esterhazy's treason. The attaché had given Blacker copies of key documents, and as he

[1]Quoted in Richard Ellman, *Oscar Wilde* (New York: Alfred A. Knopf, 1988), 563–64.

worked in secret to prepare his revelation, he shared the news with another intimate friend, Wilde, who then, unbeknownst to Blacker, mentioned it to Rowland Strong, the Paris correspondent of the *New York Times* and *London Observer*. Strong, a supporter of Esterhazy's, exposed Blacker's secrets in the spring of 1898 and suggested that his documents were forgeries. When the news reached Paris, the anti-Dreyfusard press smeared Blacker as a foreign ally of the "Jewish Syndicate." With the element of surprise lost and his credibility attacked, the Englishman aborted his campaign.[2]

Strong reappeared a few months later, when Esterhazy, in flight and out of cash, peddled to the journalist his most explosive interview. After years of intrigue and months of public denial, he admitted to having written the bordereau, but on the order, he insisted, of intelligence chief Sandherr and as part of a counterespionage ploy to uncover Dreyfus's work for the German high command. First appearing in September 1898 and repeated over the months that followed, the story changed with its teller's moods and needs. At times Esterhazy denied the confession; at other times he embellished it for a price. With Sandherr and Henry dead and Schwartzkoppen silent in Berlin, the risks were small and the rewards substantial. As time passed, however, the wolf cried too often, and his interviews went cheap.[3]

In France newspapers advocating revision of the Dreyfus case rose from 2 percent to 40 percent within hours after Henry's suicide. Increasing numbers of moderates joined the ranks of radicals and socialists, and so did a few powerful voices on the right, including the Bonapartist Paul de Cassagnac. "Revision is the sole and unavoidable solution," he announced. "Without revision, there is no way out of the affair."[4] Nationalists like Cassagnac cared less about the legal details of the case than about the toll it was taking on France, and at home and abroad the nation was not doing well.

By the midsummer of 1898, after a two-year trek from the western

[2]J. Robert Maguire, "Carlos Blacker," in *L'Affaire Dreyfus de A à Z,* ed. Michel Drouin (Paris: Flammarion, 1994), 136–42. See also J. Robert Maguire and France Reinach Beck, "Un document inédit de l'affaire Dreyfus: les confidences de Carlos Blacker à Salomon Reinach," *Les Cahiers naturalistes* 67 (1993): 326–34.

[3]On the Sept. 25, 1898, *London Observer* article, see Patrice Boussel, *L'Affaire Dreyfus et la presse* (Paris: Armand Colin, 1960), 191.

[4]Quoted in Eric Cahm, *L'Affaire Dreyfus: Histoire, politique et société* (Paris: Le Livre de Poche, 1994), 154.

coast of Africa, a French expeditionary force had reached the Egyptian Sudan, where the British, professed masters of the territory, aimed to turn their imperial rivals back. In September, while French troops occupied the fort at Fashoda on the Nile, the two powers stood at the brink of war. Foreign Minister Théophile Delcassé wanted a peaceful resolution (he had always ranked Germany above England as France's greatest threat), but the "paroxysms" of the Dreyfus affair, anti-British chauvinism, and strikes by workers preparing for the 1900 World's Fair in Paris — strikes that mobilized sixty thousand troops — frustrated his diplomatic efforts. Needing a united nation, or at least the appearance of one, the minister called for an end to the politics of the affair. Diplomat Maurice Paléologue recorded the perils and consequences of September 1898.

MAURICE PALÉOLOGUE

My Secret Diary of the Dreyfus Case

September 26, 1898

In the Fashoda affair the French public, alarmed as it is by the threatening attitude adopted by Britain, does not realise the poverty, the hopeless inadequacy, of our naval resources. There is not a single point along our coast . . . which is capable of resisting an attack by the British Fleet; and at Guadeloupe, Dakar, Jibouti, Diégo Suarez and Tonking matters are still worse. . . .

The terrible way in which France is rent by the Dreyfus crisis, which for some weeks has reached a state of paroxysm, greatly aggravates the difficulties, not to say the dangers, of the external situation.

Delcassé has therefore been vigorously applying himself to removing the Dreyfus case from the political field in order to confine it to the judicial field; he hopes that the sheer slowness, methodicalness, complication, and unintelligibility of legal procedure will end by blunting the sharp edge of the irritant provided by the hateful case.

Maurice Paléologue, "Monday, September 26th, 1898" (excerpt) from *My Secret Diary of the Dreyfus Case,* translated by Eric Mosbacher (London: Secker and Warburg, 1957), 124–125. Reprinted with the permission of Librarie Plon and Random House UK, Ltd.

Thus, at the Cabinet meeting which was held this morning . . . on the question of reopening the case, the Foreign Minister fought with all his strength the opposition of the majority of his colleagues to a reconsideration of the 1894 verdict. He gained his point by six votes to four. The Cour de Cassation [France's highest court] will be seized of the matter tomorrow. It is expected that hearings will begin in the Criminal Chamber of the Cour de Cassation in a month.

Taking the first step in that new judicial process, Lucie Dreyfus had formally requested an appeal of her husband's case on September 3. Over the next two months, Prime Minister Henri Brisson, a recent convert to revision, tried to find a like-minded minister of war. Since the birth of the Third Republic, cabinet members had been revolving like the front doors of Paris's grand department stores, and they continued to turn in the fall of 1898. First, Godefroy Cavaignac, still convinced of Dreyfus's guilt, rejected his government's stand and resigned. (Having shined "light" on the affair, writes one historian, Cavaignac then "refused to see it."[5]) The next minister lasted barely ten days, and his successor fell with the entire Brisson government in late October.

Through it all, however, the Criminal Chamber of the Cour de Cassation went about its work. Acting on Lucie Dreyfus's petition, on the cabinet's vote of late September, and on Esterhazy's long-distance confessions, the court voted on October 29 to open an inquiry into the Dreyfus case. For the first time, the matter would be reviewed by a civilian tribunal.

But if the judicial process moved forward, it traveled, as Foreign Minister Delcassé had predicted it would, at a snail's pace through a maze of legal complications. Further delays came when antirevisionists accused the president of the criminal court, Justice Loew, of conspiring with his Alsatian Jewish comrades to set Dreyfus free. To undercut Loew's influence, the opponents of revision in parliament—led by Charles Dupuy, the new prime minister, for whom courage was not "a primary virtue"[6]— enacted a law stating that all Criminal Chamber inquiries must be judged by all three chambers of the Cour de Cassation. Gambling that the majority of judges would kneel before the altar of res judicata, the

[5]Drouin, *L'Affaire Dreyfus,* 80.
[6]Maurice Paléologue, *Journal de l'affaire Dreyfus, 1894–1899* (Paris: Plon, 1955), 172.

antirevisionists, after a series of defeats, entered the new year with reason for hope.

Georges Picquart entered it still behind bars. Held since the summer of 1898 on the old charge of communicating secret documents, he had also been accused of forging the *petit bleu* in order to frame Esterhazy. Transferred from the civilian Santé Prison to Cherche-Midi, that clearinghouse of the affair, he faced a new round of military justice in September, and he knew the dangers involved. On the eve of his transfer, during a court session that would lead to postponement of his case and nine more months in prison, Picquart confronted the witnesses called against him, and as he addressed the president of the court, he stared down Henry's partner, Deputy Chief of Staff Gonse.

GEORGES PICQUART

I Have Had My Say

September 21, 1898

Tonight I will probably go to the Cherche-Midi Prison. This is probably the last time, in front of this secret investigation, that I can say a word in public. I want it known that if the noose of Lemercier-Picard [a freelance forger believed to have been in the pay of the Statistical Section and found hanged] or the razor of Henry is discovered in my cell, it will be murder, because a man like me could never for an instant think of committing suicide. I will face this prosecution with my head held high and with the same serenity that I have brought before my accusers. There you are; I have had my say.

The Dreyfusard camp now had a shining hero for public consumption. The prisoner on Devil's Island, distant in geography and personality, never fit the role, and Zola, Lazare, Jaurès, and other allies, however courageous, never cut the figure. Picquart, though, had a flair for theater and the look of a dandy, which led allies to call him cultivated and ene-

---

Francis de Pressensé, *Un Héros: Le lieutenant-colonel Picquart* (Paris: Stock, 1898), 377.

mies, like the journalist Gyp, to hint at homosexuality. A decorated veteran whose anti-Semitism kept all but the most ferocious anti-Dreyfusards from placing him among the "Jewish Syndicate," he emerged in the closing months of 1898 as another martyr of the affair. Petitions condemning his imprisonment drew thousands of signatures (*L'Aurore* alone secured ten thousand names); a book of nearly four hundred pages carried the title *Un Héros;* an English author dedicated a volume on the Dreyfus case to Picquart, "the true, the dutiful and the brave"; and an English tobacco company ran advertisements with his picture over the slogan "For a Good Man." In Paris public rallies in support of Picquart, organized by the League of the Rights of Man and the Masonic Grand Orient, filled conference halls, and in literary journals and newspaper columns, the intelligentsia of revision published manifestos of praise and commitment. "For Dreyfus we were only a handful," wrote novelist and playwright Octave Mirabeau. "For Picquart we will be an entire army, even more united, even more fervent." Mirabeau was right, if only for a moment. Moderates, socialists, and anarchists stood shoulder to shoulder in protest against "all military tyranny," as Joseph Reinach announced, "against all social injustice."[7]

Henry's suicide had evaporated most of the anti-Dreyfusard center and hardened all of the right. In the face of overwhelming evidence that miscarriages of justice had occurred in the Dreyfus case, only the most resolute advocates of *raison d'état* or racism could carry on the fight, in good conscience or bad. And while Picquart became a Dreyfusard hero, Colonel Henry's widow became, for militant nationalists, the symbol of a suffering France.

When Joseph Reinach announced in *Le Siècle* that Henry had been Esterhazy's accomplice in treason (a claim based on strong rumors but no hard evidence), *La Libre Parole* advertised a national fund drive for the legal defense of Henry's widow. Contributions poured in (more than 130,000 francs from 25,000 subscriptions by January 1899), and along with the cash came occasional diatribes. Most signatories refrained from comment, and not all contributors were motivated by anti-Semitism, but the fact that Joseph Reinach, the target of bigotry for

---

[7]Reinach is quoted in Cahm, *L'Affaire Dreyfus,* 166. Mirabeau's article appeared in *L'Aurore,* Nov. 24, 1898. See also Francis de Pressensé, *Un Héros: Le lieutenant-colonel Picquart* (Paris: Stock, 1898). For examples of Picquart's popularity in England, see Douglas Johnson, *France and the Dreyfus Affair* (London: Blandford, 1966), 210.

over a decade, expressed shock at the statements attests to their extreme violence. Published in book form in 1899, the lists of the "Henry Monument" filled more than seven hundred pages.

The Henry Monument
December 1898–January 1899

A lieutenant of the colonial infantry. For the shame of the Jews and the triumph of honest men. 3 francs.

L.M., ex–second lieutenant of the 159th infantry. Long live France! Down with the kikes and freemasons who insult the army! 5 fr.

Koechlin (Marcel), veteran officer of the 1st Regiment of the [French] foreign legion and of the 90th artillery regiment. In memory of his commanders, comrades, and men who died for the fatherland. 1,000 fr.

An administrative officer, in retirement. For the expulsion of the Yids. 5 fr.

A superior officer who would be delighted to see France in the hands of the French. 5 fr.

A section of officers from a frontier fortress who await with impatience the order to try new cannons and new explosives on the one hundred thousand Jews who poison the country. 25 fr.

A veteran of 1870, who considers the Jews the ten plagues of Egypt reunited. 2 fr.

Galey (Abbot), for the defense of the eternal law against Puritan quackery and Judeo-Huguenot swindling. 5 fr.

A rural priest, who offers up the most ardent prayers for the extermination of the two enemies of France: the Jew and the Freemason. 5 fr.

A missionary from Tonkin, who would like to see all the millions of the syndicate of treason used for the construction of a railroad from Hanoi. . . .

A teacher, sworn enemy of stateless people. 1.50 fr.

A teacher from the Jura, who does not fail to tell his students that Jews and their friends are the vampires of France. 1 fr.

A future medical student, already sharpening his scalpels to dissect the Maccabee Dreyfus, bored through by the dozen bullets of a firing squad. 0.25 fr.

Pierre Quillard, *Le Monument Henry: Listes des souscripteurs classées méthodiquement et selon l'ordre alphabétique* (Paris: Stock, 1899), 37–38, 43, 50, 58–59, 80, 95, 100–102, 149, 186, 215, 226, 410–11, 427, 440–41, 494–95 (emphasis in original).

Three students from the Bordeaux Faculty of Medicine, shouting "Long live the Army" and spitting their contempt in the face of the turncoat Jaurès . . . and the stinking gorilla Reinach. 3 fr.

A group of policemen, respectful of discipline, not wanting to say what they think of Dreyfus, but heartily supporting the subscription opened in favor of the wronged widow of Colonel Henry and the poor orphan. 15 fr.

A group of policemen, who would be very happy to thump hard and fast on Dreyfusards and filthy Yids, while, *by command and under pain of dismissal,* they are compelled to protect those rogues. 12.50 fr.

A royalist widow who misses the old bygone days when Jews were kept in their place. 2 fr.

A widow, who raises her son for God and France and in hatred of Freemasons and Jews. 0.15 fr.

A woman with great admiration for Drumont, who would like to see him govern France with the power of a king or emperor. 0.15 fr.

Fashoda-Dreyfus. Shame and treason! 5 fr.

Mother of a family who wants to mark the difference between her sex and the divorcées of *La Fronde*. 2.50 fr.

Sabatier (Madame Achille). Saint Joan of Arc, patron of our sweet France, deliver us from the Jews! 20 fr.

H.L., brother of an infantry lieutenant, for Félix Faure when he kills as many kikes as rabbits. 0.50 fr.

XXXX. Finding not enough Jews to massacre, I propose cutting them in two, in order to get twice as many. 0.50 fr.

Down with the sheeny *La Fronde!* Long live the women of the household! 1 fr.

A Protestant woman vigorously protesting the accusation that her coreligionists are all Dreyfusards. 5 fr.

When will the alarm bell sound to rid France of the evil Yids? 1 fr.

On February 16, 1899, death removed yet another barrier from the revisionist path. President Félix Faure had just passed the halfway mark of his term when he died in office, or, more precisely, in a bedroom annex to his office, where an afternoon rendezvous had ended with the chief of state suffering an apoplectic fit in the arms of his mistress. Among Dreyfusards the president's exit raised more hopes than eyebrows, especially for Mathieu Dreyfus, who had long believed that the Elysée Palace, with its "vain" and "hostile" tenant, stood as "the strongest center of resistance" to the revisionist campaign. To a certain extent, Mathieu's anger clouded his assessment. Widespread "indifference" did not greet the president's demise (his talents in the realm of international relations would be missed), but antirevisionists had clearly lost in Faure a "devoted servant."[8]

If the Third Republic was ever in serious danger during the affair, which is easier to imagine than prove, the six months following Faure's death marked the period of greatest peril. Though elected by a comfortable margin in the National Assembly, Faure's successor, the prudent and capable Emile Loubet, had formidable enemies on the right. As prime minister at the beginning of the decade, he had been accused of suppressing the Panama scandal and, by some critics, of profiting from it; and the charges, though unfounded and unjust, had stuck like tar on the back of a village outcast.

On the day of Loubet's election, when he went to the Elysée to pay his respects at Faure's coffin, nationalists followed his entourage, shouting "Panama!" and calling the new president "the elect of the synagogue." One week later, on the day of Faure's funeral, Paul Déroulède, with banknotes, gold, and manifestos on his person and a vague promise of support from General de Pellieux on his mind, gathered his patriots at the Place de Bastille, the first stop on the way to a coup d'état, or so the plan had it. Déroulède's legions numbered barely two hundred (he had hoped for five thousand), but they came to sweep France clean of Loubet, the Dreyfus affair, the constitution, and every other barrier standing between the nation and the glory that only Déroulède and his comrades could define. The attempt was serious (Maurice Barrès, anything but frivolous, joined in); the outcome was not.

Pellieux recognized the folly and withdrew support, and another officer, General Roget, leading troops back from Père Lachaise Cemetery, refused Déroulède's appeal "to have pity on the fatherland, to save France and the Republic, to move on to the Elysée!" Arrested and tried for provocation and "seditious cries," Déroulède proudly announced his "guilt" of wanting to overthrow the corrupt republic. After he declared, "Citizens . . . if you want me to begin again, acquit me!" the jury did just that.[9]

Déroulède's judicial "triumph" of late May had come in a Palais de Justice courtroom only yards from the hall in which the united chambers

[8]Mathieu Dreyfus, *L'Affaire telle que je l'ai vécue* (Paris: Grasset, 1978), 181–82, 206.
[9]Bertrand Joly, "La Ligue des patriotes et l'affaire Dreyfus," in *L'Affaire Dreyfus,* 421–22.

of the Cour de Cassation neared the end of their inquiry into the Dreyfus case. On May 29, to a packed audience, presiding justice Ballot-Beaupré presented his official opinion on the bordereau, "the principal basis of the accusation and conviction. . . . Is it or is it not written in Dreyfus's hand?" the justice asked, and as the hall fell silent, he answered, "After an in-depth examination, I have, for my part, reached the conclusion that the bordereau was written not by Dreyfus but by Esterhazy."[10]

The obvious had become official. Drawing the same conclusion, the attorney general of the Cour de Cassation asked the court to annul the verdict of 1894 and to send Captain Dreyfus before a new court-martial. This is what the prisoner had always wanted: to be judged by his peers, but in the light of day. As the session drew to a close, Lucie Dreyfus's lawyer, Henri Mornard, described the new trial that awaited Dreyfus and, with the flourish of a smart lawyer, praised the army: "It is with joy in their hearts that the military judges, proclaiming an error committed in all sincerity and loyalty, will declare that their unfortunate brother-in-arms . . . has never fallen afoul of the law of honor. . . . I await your decision as though it were the blessed dawn of the day that will allow the great light of concord and truth to shine over the nation."[11] With antirevisionist judges fighting in retreat, the final deliberations took more than two days, but on June 3, 1899, the chief justice, who carried on his shoulders more than the weight of his scarlet and ermine robe, read the decision aloud. Rescinding and annulling the 1894 verdict, the judgment called for the accused to be brought before a new court-martial, far from Paris, in the Breton city of Rennes.

The greatest Dreyfusard victory to date sparked another round of nationalist violence. In *L'Intransigeant* Henri Rochefort had dreamed of "lining up" the high court justices and having "a torturer cut off their eyelids" so that "poisonous spiders could gnaw away at their pupils. . . . Then the hideous blind men would be brought to a pillory with signs reading 'This is how France punishes traitors who try to sell her to the enemy.' "[12] After the June decision, other journalists described the judges as "old monkeys" in the pay of the "Jewish Syndicate." And on Sunday, June 4, at the steeplechase races at Auteuil in the Bois de

---

[10]Quoted in Jean-Denis Bredin, *The Affair: The Case of Alfred Dreyfus*, trans. Jeffrey Mehlman (New York: George Braziller, 1986), 381–82.

[11]Ibid., 382.

[12]*L'Intransigeant*, Oct. 18, 1898. See also Bredin, *The Affair*, 361.

Boulogne, nationalists stepped up their attacks on President Loubet. Surrounded by hundreds of demonstrators—"society people and stable boys," in Joseph Reinach's description[13]—Loubet heard the epithets that did not surprise him. But he also saw a cane come crashing toward his head. Baron Fernand Cevreau de Christiani had emerged from a crowd of young men wearing the floral badges of their allegiance—the white carnations of royalists, the bluets of anti-Semites. Meticulous in dress but careless in aim, Christiani only creased the president's top hat, and after a thirty-minute confrontation, police made fifty arrests. The baron had acted on a bet, but his cane thrust was the punctuation mark of a deeper crisis. "This," Loubet said to Prime Minister Dupuy, by his side, "is a lesson."[14]

It was also the beginning of Dupuy's end, for the disorder did not stop at Auteuil. One week later nearly one hundred thousand defenders of the republic and its president marched to Longchamp, where thoroughbreds ran on the flat rather than over fences, and where the grandstand, at least, had always attracted citizens of more modest means than the tribune at nearby Auteuil. Paris workers, singing "La Marseillaise" and armed with clubs in anticipation of a nationalist ambush, acted as Loubet's bodyguards, and thousands of police and soldiers stood by (a force equal to Bonaparte's army in Egypt, according to Reinach). Skirmishes gave way to more arrests, and within forty-eight hours those deputies who still cared about the Third Republic voted Dupuy's government out. "The defense of the institutions of the Republic," writes Jean-Denis Bredin, "was henceforth at the center of the debate between the partisans and enemies of Dreyfus."[15]

The crisis continued through June, as generals and colonels hinted at mutiny, and as Loubet searched for a new prime minister. The call went out to René Waldeck-Rousseau, senator from the Loire and the lawyer who had recommended Edgar Demange to the Dreyfus family five years earlier. A supporter of revision and a confirmed anticlerical, Waldeck-Rousseau was dour in appearance (he had "the cold eye of a jellied fish," remarked one observer), but bold in action. His government proved the point. He chose the first socialist cabinet member in the history of the Third Republic (Alexandre Millerand, in the supremely ironic post of

---

[13]Joseph Reinach, *Histoire de l'affaire Dreyfus* (Paris: La Revue Blanche, 1901–11), 5:156.

[14]Ibid., 5:117.

[15]Bredin, *The Affair,* 387.

minister of commerce) and then turned right for a minister of war. His appointment of General Gaston de Galliffet, reviled by the left as the "butcher" who had led troops against the Paris Commune thirty years before, triggered a parliamentary uprising. But Waldeck-Rousseau knew that his old friend Galliffet would keep the army in check and that his presence in the government, though angering socialists, would soothe conservatives.

The gamble almost failed. On June 26 deputies on the margins of the right and left responded to "the cabinet of republican unity" with jeers and hisses (prompting Clemenceau to note that Waldeck-Rousseau needed "men and not wild beasts" as his adversaries).[16] As yet another crisis gained force, it fell to a former prime minister to save the government. Henri Brisson, not old but ill, mounted the tribune with difficulty, called on the Chamber to defend the republic, and then raised his arms in the gesture that many deputies recognized (and the far right reviled) as the Masonic sign of distress. The government won its vote of confidence, owing the victory not only to Brisson but also to Jaurès, who had convinced socialists still reeling from the Galliffet appointment—and still clinging to the dogma of nonparticipation in bourgeois governments—that the republic mattered to the working classes and that the republic was in danger.

The court decisions of June 1899 opened the way for homecomings. Emile Zola returned to France from England, and Georges Picquart walked out of prison (and into a banquet organized by the League of the Rights of Man) after eleven months in the cells of Santé, and Cherche-Midi. By late June Alfred Dreyfus, whose status had changed from convict to prisoner awaiting justice, was en route from South America to Rennes, confident that his rehabilitation drew near.

He knew virtually nothing about his own affair. On Devil's Island guards whispered occasional rumors, but most of them followed the order of silence. Dreyfus's correspondence, when not arbitrarily interrupted, was always reviewed, frequently censored, and sometimes discarded by the odd sadistic functionary. Family letters contained expressions of love and encouragement but never touched on the politics of the affair and rarely on the judicial case. Nor did government officials ever respond to the prisoner's letters of appeal. Living with the memories and

---

[16] *L'Aurore,* June 27, 1899.

nightmares of the winter of 1894–95, Dreyfus held to the belief that a few officers had made a tragic mistake and to the hope that once the real traitor was uncovered, men of honor like General Boisdeffre would right the wrong and call the captain home.

Family letters could only hint that the end was near. "Our hopes are stronger than ever," Mathieu Dreyfus had written in 1898, and in the fall of that year, Lucie had spoken of the "final phase of the case. . . . My hand trembles I am so happy." But when nothing concrete followed, Dreyfus's rising expectations crashed into the deepest depression he had known in exile. Battling malarial fever and dysentery, he fought off the seduction of suicide with weapons of faith—faith in the God he worshiped but never defined; faith in the family whose honor would be ruined by his death in exile; faith in the French fatherland, whose justice, he still believed, stood "above all human passion, above all human error. . . . It will be my supreme judge."

Finally, in the closing weeks of 1898, a letter from Lucie, followed by a telegram from colonial officials, announced that the high court had moved to review the case. In December Dreyfus read the attorney general's summary of events and learned the bare outlines of Esterhazy's treachery (the "miserable wretch" now had a name) and Henry's forgery and suicide.[17] Always thinking it would be "a matter of weeks" before his return, Dreyfus waited through yet another long season of silence, and then, anticipating the court's decision, he sent Lucie his last letter from Devil's Island. Written three days before the official call for a new military trial, the letter alludes to the question of whether the case would be sent before a second court-martial *(avec renvoi)* or be decided by the civilian high court itself *(sans renvoi)*.

[17]On Dreyfus in exile, see Michael Burns, *Dreyfus: A Family Affair, 1789–1945* (New York: HarperCollins, 1991), 195–217 and passim.

ALFRED DREYFUS

Letter to Lucie Dreyfus

June 1, 1899

My Dear Lucie, A few lines of talk with you, during these days when, more than ever, if it is possible, my thoughts and heart are with you, with everyone. . . .

Whether the court of appeal hands down a decision *avec renvoi* or *sans renvoi* is of little importance to us. My confidence in the justice of my country is the same, be it the justice of the high court or the court-martial.

And so I write with the deepest emotion, thinking not only of the indescribable happiness of holding you in my arms again, of holding our dear children, . . . of coming at last to the end of these horrible tortures, . . . but also with all the joy that fills the heart of a Frenchman and soldier, because the denouement of this frightening judicial error, and its reparation, will resound to the honor of this noble country of France, as it will resound to the honor of our beloved army.

I stop here, my pen unable to convey such sublime emotions, and I hope that I arrive back in our precious country simultaneously with these few lines.

Shortly after noon on June 5, 1899, the chief guard of Devil's Island entered Dreyfus's prison hut and handed him a document.

Alfred Dreyfus, *Souvenirs et correspondance* (Paris: Grasset, 1936), 189–90.

Announcement of the Second Court-Martial
June 5, 1899

The Court rescinds and annuls the judgment rendered on 22 December 1894 against Alfred Dreyfus by the First Court-Martial of the military government of Paris and sends the accused before the Court-Martial of Rennes, etc.

It is agreed that the present decision will be printed and transcribed on the margin of the annulled verdict in the record books of the First Court-Martial. . . ; in virtue of this decision, Captain Dreyfus ceases to be submitted to the regime of deportation. He becomes a simple suspect, is restored to his rank, and may recover his uniform.

Arrange for the order of release by the prison administration, and withdraw the military guards from Devil's Island. At the same time, place the prisoner in charge of the troop commandant and replace the guards with a brigade of gendarmes. . . .

The cruiser *Sfax* departs today from Fort-de-France [Martinique] with the order to take the prisoner from Devil's Island and return him to France.

Dreyfus sent a final telegram to his wife: "My heart and soul with you, children, everyone. Departing Friday. Await with immense joy the moment of supreme happiness of holding you in my arms. Thousand kisses." The warship *Sfax,* its prisoner on board, lifted anchor on June 9 and arrived three weeks later off the southern coast of Brittany. At night and under heavy rain, a lifeboat brought Dreyfus ashore, where gendarmes, ordered to remain silent, took him by carriage to a special train bound for the outskirts of Rennes. At dawn another carriage rushed through empty streets to a military prison close by the school (lycée) that would be used for the court-martial proceedings. Emaciated, exhausted, and injured when transferred in stormy weather from the *Sfax,* Dreyfus was confused by the "mysterious goings and comings" that marked his arrival. As an officer whose conviction had been annulled by France's highest court, he had expected a dignified welcome at least, followed by a moment of celebration with family and friends. He found instead gendarmes "with anxious faces."[18]

[18]Alfred Dreyfus, *Cinq années de ma vie* (Paris: La Découverte, 1994), 212.

Alfred Dreyfus, *Cinq années de ma vie* (Paris: La Découverte, 1994), 207.

Those mixed emotions of joy and trepidation intensified as he prepared to meet Lucie for the first time in more than four years. Though only thirty-nine years old, his thin hair had gone almost completely white; sudden flushes of malarial fever turned his skin from chalk to crimson; malnutrition had rotted his teeth; and he could speak only in a hoarse whisper, as the years of silence and sickness had damaged his larynx and vocal chords. But he could still call on the "stoicism" his wife had always admired. Later that night Lucie described in a letter to her husband the hour they had passed together under the watch of a prison guard.

LUCIE DREYFUS

Letter to Alfred Dreyfus

July 1, 1899

MY VERY DEAR ALFRED, For four years I have been fighting, praying, and ardently hoping to see this blessed day finally arrive. I prepared myself for the emotion; I wanted to be strong, to have no weakness. But we both needed to make a superhuman effort . . . in order to endure that great test with courage.

How the hour passed quickly! It seemed like a dream, a beautiful dream, full of affection and worthy suffering.

I wanted to tell you a thousand things, to talk about our children, our family, all those we love together, but I feared that I would hurt you by raising those tender subjects. My poor friend, you who have not spoken in nearly five years, you who have suffered every martyrdom, you are still gallant and courageous. You are worthy of all the praise and many testimonies I am receiving for you from France and the entire world. They confirm, you will see, how much you are honored and loved.

Finally, a few more weeks and we will have happiness. These will be days of work for you. You will have much to do to acquaint yourself with all that has happened, to learn to know the characters of the men who have taken part in this terrible drama. Some are base and vile and deserve only pity; others are superior souls, of a purity, eminence, and devotion that makes us forget much that is evil.

Alfred Dreyfus, *Souvenirs et correspondance* (Paris: Grasset, 1936), 192–93.

With that letter Dreyfus learned that his military case had become a national and international affair. His first meetings with Mathieu, Edgar Demange, and his new co-counsel, Fernand Labori, also served as tutorials on the events that had transpired since his deportation. He read the transcript of Zola's trial, the inquiry of the united chambers of the Cour de Cassation, and the eloquent final report of Lucie's lawyer, Henri Mornard. And he learned the lineup of Dreyfusards and anti-Dreyfusards. Shocked by the betrayal of General Boisdeffre, he was, at the same time, full of gratitude for "the courage of all those people, great or humble, who had valiantly joined the struggle for the triumph of truth and justice."[19] Scores of letters arrived from allies he had yet to meet. Reinach, Scheurer-Kestner, the novelist Anatole France, and others praised his courage and patriotism, and Emile Zola sensed what the captain longed to hear. It is "the honor of the army that you will save," Zola wrote on July 6, "this army that you have loved so much. . . . It is we who are its true defenders."[20]

Military officials and brigades of journalists made last-minute preparations for the trial, scheduled to begin on August 7. Reacting to rumors of assassination plots against Dreyfus (if acquitted, "it will be the duty of every patriot to kill him," announced one nationalist newspaper), authorities assigned nearly two hundred mounted police to a restricted zone between the prison and the Rennes lycée. Concerned that the captain's skeletal frame would shock observers, they ordered a padded uniform for his courtroom appearance. Meanwhile, more than three hundred journalists descended on Rennes from "all parts of the world," as the *New York Sun* announced.

The Dreyfus affair, already central to the history of modern France, had become a major event in the history of modern journalism, and timing played a role in its enormous popularity. With the Spanish-American War just over and the Boer War in southern Africa and the Boxer Rebellion in China not yet headline news, Dreyfus's second court-martial provided rich material at the right moment for a roving army of foreign correspondents. Britain and the United States dominated the pool; Japan and Turkey sent reporters; and one Austrian newspaper paid $20,000 for

---

[19]Ibid., 215.
[20]Zola's letter and others appear in Alfred Dreyfus, *Souvenirs et correspondance* (Paris: Grasset, 1936), 237–38 and passim.

the "urgent" rates charged by telegraph companies. The city's chamber of commerce provided a "vast editorial room," with telephones, telegraph equipment, and 150 tables; and on the first day of the court-martial, more than 650,000 words would go out over six telegraph lines.[21]

While photographers captured scenes of the formal process and informal recesses, a new band of reporters, armed with motion picture cameras, met with less luck. Barely a half-decade old, the technology of documentary filmmaking could record only shadowy images of Dreyfus and his seven judges, and of the prisoner's wife walking with Edgar Demange. At the same moment, however, in his Paris studio, Georges Méliès, who had just completed a dramatization of the Spanish-American War, produced *L'Affaire Dreyfus,* the longest and most "realistic" motion picture of its epoch. Its eleven reels ran nearly fifteen minutes, and its actors resembled the familiar players of the affair. Méliès, a committed Dreyfusard, kept the heroes and villains in sharp focus and presented Lucie Dreyfus and the journalist Séverine as the affair's two heroines. Within a few days the Pathé brothers, confirming that the competitive business of motion pictures had begun, filmed their own six-part "docudrama" of the captain's case.[22]

Along with journalists and filmmakers, the mass migration to Rennes included leaders and followers of the affair's two camps. Like belligerents contesting a city under siege, they settled into separate enclaves. Dreyfusards made the Hotel de France and the Auberge des Trois Marches in the nearby countryside their "veritable general headquarters," and local members of the League of the Rights of Man, led by Victor Basch, professor at the University of Rennes, supplemented their ranks. Anti-Dreyfusards, joined by homegrown nationalists and anti-Semites, gathered around a house rented by former minister of war General Mercier. For city residents indifferent to the trial, the onslaught of outsiders (dubbed "Parisians" regardless of origin) proved irritating but profitable. Among shopkeepers sympathetic to the captain's cause, the foreign coins in circulation became known as "dreyfusards."[23]

---

[21]See the report by the *New York Sun* in Louis L. Snyder, *The Dreyfus Case: A Documentary History* (New Brunswick, N.J.: Rutgers University Press, 1973), 329–34.

[22]Stephen Bottomore, "Dreyfus and Documentary," *Sight and Sound* 53, no. 4 (1984): 290–93. See also Shlomo Sand, "Dreyfus, Made in Hollywood," *L'Histoire,* January 1994, 120–123.

[23]See Johnson, *France and the Dreyfus Affair,* 164.

To veterans of the affair, the retrial at Rennes was just that, a return to the testimonies and documents deposed, assembled, and forged over a span of nearly five years. A parade of familiar witnesses appeared during the twenty-nine sessions that lasted four weeks, and French trial procedure allowed them to intervene almost at will. They raised objections, made speeches, and introduced hearsay evidence. In the dead of summer, in a somber provincial town, the endless hours of old news—of staff officers repeating the events of late 1894, of police agents respreading the rumors of Dreyfus's gambling and womanizing, of Alphonse Bertillion rehashing his graphological fantasies—sent many observers into slumber or off on stolen holidays in the Breton countryside. The most sensational event occurred outside the courtroom, when an unknown assailant shot Dreyfus's co-counsel in the back and escaped into the hinterlands. Fernand Labori recovered quickly and returned to work, hailed as a man of steel by his admirers, reviled as a man of intrigue by anti-Dreyfusards who accused him of stage-managing the event to turn the tide of a doomed case.

Inside the courtroom a surprise witness for the prosecution, Eugene Lazare de Cernuszki, an Austrian and former officer, caused a brief flutter of interest when he claimed to have seen proof of Dreyfus's guilt. (Friends in the diplomatic circles of Vienna, he testified, held a list of German spies in France, with Dreyfus's name on top.) But Cernuszki was soon exposed as "a scoundrel and false witness."[24] As for the affair's legitimate witnesses, the most crucial quartet never appeared: Esterhazy dared not leave London, du Paty was ill, and Sandherr and Henry were dead, though the presence of Henry's widow ensured that he was not forgotten.

Journalists and other commentators made "theater" the metaphor of preference. Dreyfus's seven judges sat on the proscenium stage of the lycée's great hall under a white plaster crucifix (not the only reminder of the first court-martial) and in front of an audience that on some days approached one thousand. News reports described spectators coming to the trial "as if to the theatre," Maurice Paléologue called each recess an entr'acte, and Joseph Reinach defined Rennes as the last act "in the fever of the battle, and then the curtain will fall, the lights will dim, and the ac-

[24]Reinach, *Histoire de l'affaire,* 5:492.

Figure 12.   "The most famous man in the world," back from Devil's Island, appears before judges, witnesses, and journalists at the Rennes retrial in the summer of 1899. Dreyfus (fourth from the right), flanked by his defense lawyers, Edgar Demange and Fernand Labori, faces his judges.

tors will give up their costumes and become themselves again, the good, the mediocre and the others."[25] The most anticipated moment, Dreyfus's first appearance, was portrayed in scores of articles as the grand entrance of a tragic hero (or villain) onto the stage of world opinion. During the past few years, hundreds of thousands of caricatures, paintings, lithographs, and song-sheet illustrations had made Dreyfus the most familiar public figure in France since the two Napoleons. For the first time he faced an open, public trial, and for the first time journalists laid eyes on "the most famous man in the world."

[25]Ibid., 143.

G. W. STEEVENS

The Tragedy of Dreyfus

August 7, 1899

The Trial was to begin at half-past six. . . . A line of mounted gendarmes, pushing the crowd out of the neighbouring streets, proclaimed that they were taking Dreyfus across the road from the military prison to the High School, in whose lecture-hall he was to be arraigned.

A moment later the line opened, and the crowd of journalists, waving their passes, pushed through. They jammed in at a narrow door, up stone steps, through another doorway, round a corner, inside a cordon of infantry, and they were in the court. It was a lofty, oblong, buff-plastered hall. . . . With large windows on each side—square in the lower tier, circular in the upper—it was almost as light as the day outside; round the cornice were emblazoned the names of Chateaubriand, Lamennais, Renan, and the intellectuals of Brittany. At the top was a stage, its front filled with a long table, behind this seven crimson-covered seats for the judges. A white Christ on a black cross, hanging on the back wall above the President's chair proclaimed the place a Court of Justice. On the right, as you faced the stage, were a small raised table and seats for the counsel of the accused; on the left a similar erection for the prosecuting Commissary of the Government and his assistants. Down each side of the body of the hall was a strip of extemporized match-board bench and desk for the Press. In the broader centre were seats for the witnesses, then, behind a bar, for the favoured public. Behind all this ran another bar lined by a guard of the 41st Infantry. Behind their homely peasant faces and between their fixed bayonets peered the general public, five deep, in the shallowest of strips at the very back of the hall.

The Press stampeded and trampled over the match-board, and in the fulness of time sorted itself into its appointed places. The general public shifted and scrunched behind the barrier. The centre of the hall began to fill up with witnesses, with officers of infantry in red pantaloons and gunners in black. Behind the daïs appeared a sprinkling of selected spectators. Then, on the waxing bustle of the hall, came in men in black gowns with little white-edged tippets and white bands, with queer high black caps like birettas. Now we should see. And next moment—it was already past seven—there was a hoarse cry from behind—present arms!—rattle— and there filed in the seven officers in whose hands rests the conscience of France. The President—a small but soldierly man in eyeglasses, with

---

G. W. Steevens, *The Tragedy of Dreyfus* (New York: Harper and Bros., 1899), 41–43.

black hair and a small face, a huge white moustache and imperial—saluted and sat down. Bring in the accused.

Instantly the black, rippling hall is still as marble, silent as the grave. A sergeant usher went to a door—the tramp of his feet was almost startling—on the right hand of the top of the hall. It opened and two officers stepped out. One of them was the greatest villain or the greatest victim in France—and for the moment men wondered which was he. It seemed almost improper that the most famous man in the world was walking in just as you or I might.

Then all saw him, and the whole hall broke into a gasp. There came in a little old man—an old, old man of thirty-nine. A middle-statured, thickset old man in the black uniform of the artillery; over the red collar his hair was gone white as silver, and on the temples and at the back of the crown he was bald. As he turned to face the judges there was a glimpse of a face both burned and pale—a rather broad, large-featured face with a thrusting jaw and chin. It was not Jewish in expression until you saw it in profile. The eyes under the glasses were set a trifle close together, and not wholly sympathetic either; you might guess him hard, stubborn, cunning. But this is only guessing: what we did see in the face was suffering and effort—a misery hardly to be borne, and a tense, agonized striving to bear and to hide it. Here is a man, you would say, who has endured things unendurable, and just lives through—maybe to endure more.

He walked up two steps to his seat with a gait full of resolve yet heavy, constrained, mechanical—such a gait as an Egyptian mummy might walk with if it came to life in its swathing grave-clothes. He saluted the President with a white-gloved hand, took off his *képi,* sat down. An officer of gendarmes followed and sat down behind him. The recorder, rising from beside the prosecuting officer, read out the general order constituting the court; then . . . the President, in a small voice, put a question to the prisoner. Another sudden stillness; then came the voice of Dreyfus. No one heard what he said—thin, sapless, split, it was such as might rustle from the lips of a corpse.

If few journalists, French and foreign, excelled at objectivity, nearly every account, hostile and sympathetic, stressed Dreyfus's rigid presence and "automatic step." *L'Aurore* called him a hero with the bearing of "an impeccable functionary." Writing for *La Fronde,* Séverine found him "precise, poised, self-controlled," and with "a spirit of incredible strength and a disdain for posturing." For Maurice Barrès, who was not without sympathy or insight, the prisoner was a "poor little man . . . a ball of living flesh" who comes "rolling from South America [from Devil's Island] into the midst of our battle" and is "fought over by the players of two teams."

But Barrès also showed his colors; not all the "perfumes of Arabia or waters of the Jordan," he wrote, "could conceal the stench of treason."[26]

Above all, allies, enemies, and unaligned observers wanted the gavel brought down firmly and finally on the affair, and they wanted Dreyfus to demonstrate his innocence or guilt with some grand gesture. But he could not please the crowd, nor would he, even if he had the strength, for unlike the majority of men and women who surrounded him, he had come to Rennes for a trial and not for a tragedy. "What was needed was an actor," Joseph Reinach thought, and Dreyfus "was a soldier." His voice rose above a faint monotone only on a few occasions, and it rose to a shout only once. On August 12, when Mercier declared from the witness stand, "if the slightest doubt had crossed my mind, I would be the first to say to . . . Captain Dreyfus, 'I erred in good faith,'" the prisoner lunged forward and cried out "That is what you should do!" And when Mercier tried to continue, Dreyfus shot back, "It is your duty!"[27]

Dreyfusards applauded the outburst, as did spectators who were relieved that the prisoner had come to life. But the effort could not be sustained, and the advantage shifted back to the former minister of war. More than any other participant, Mercier dominated the court-martial. He interjected comments, cross-examined witnesses, and reminded the judges by his presence alone — in full uniform and medals — that he was their superior and that Rennes marked a choice between the accused and the military leaders of France. The general still treated the documents of the case as evidence of Dreyfus's guilt, and he added innuendo. In court and via the anti-Dreyfusard press, he intimated that the bordereau had been traced from an original document that had made its way to the German kaiser and that Wilhelm II had annotated its margins. It could never be exposed, the minister added, for an international crisis, if not war, would ensue. Mercier's authority remained great, much of his audience remained gullible, and the absurd legend of the "annotated memorandum" took a long time to die.

On the counterattack, the Dreyfusard press portrayed Mercier as a threadbare remnant of France's reactionary past, a bitter and deluded officer with "the face," as *L'Aurore* put it, "of a lying and evil old woman."[28] In court the most notable witness in Dreyfus's defense, for-

---

[26]Maurice Barrès, *Scènes et doctrines du nationalisme* (Paris: Félix Juven, 1902), 137ff.

[27]Reinach, *Histoire de l'affaire,* 5:295; and Theodore Reinach, *Histoire sommaire de l'affaire Dreyfus* (Paris: Ligue des droits de l'homme, 1924), 177.

[28]*L'Aurore,* Aug. 8, 1899.

mer president Casimir-Périer, challenged Mercier. The affair and its documents had never endangered France's relations with Germany, he testified. There had never been a "historic night" shortly after Dreyfus's conviction when, as Mercier had insisted, "we were two steps away from war."[29] The fiery Fernand Labori wanted to press even harder, to humiliate the general and condemn the high command for five years of felonies.

Labori's tirades, brilliant and unbridled, worried those Dreyfusards who believed in reason over rancor and who preferred the more respectful Demange. Even Bernard Lazare, an anarchist ready to condemn the military, criticized Labori's methods as counterproductive and perilous. Clemenceau and Picquart, however, championed their friend's pugnacity. In early September, with the final arguments approaching, Mathieu Dreyfus, anxious for the alliance he had helped forge, tried to mediate. But Labori had no taste for compromise. Disgusted with the caution of the Dreyfus family and their inner circle—with what he defined as their obsequious respect for established authority—he stepped aside for Demange.

Closing arguments stretched across three sessions. The military prosecutor read a prepared text drafted (unbeknowst to the audience) by a nationalist lawyer and close friend of Mercier's. It reminded the judges that they were under no obligation to explain their decision; they should simply "declare what they believe in their hearts. . . . France anxiously awaits your verdict." Demange's summation took five hours and, in tone and content, infuriated Labori. Emphasizing the doubt surrounding Dreyfus's guilt rather than the certainty of the army's crimes, Demange told the court, "I have confidence in you because you are soldiers." The presiding judge, Colonel Albert Jouaust, then acknowledged the prisoner's rank for the first time. "Captain Dreyfus," he asked, "have you anything to add in your defense?" The audience could barely hear the reply of the man, who, according to Maurice Paléologue, looked "like a corpse" and "muttered some indistinct words." Reaffirming his innocence and quest to save his family's name, Dreyfus felt assured, at last, that justice would be done.[30]

One reporter, who had arrived in Rennes "neither for nor against Dreyfus," kept a diary of the court-martial. Convinced of the prisoner's

---

[29]Quoted in Bredin, *The Affair,* 409.
[30]Paléologue, *Journal de l'affaire,* 263. See also, Bredin, *The Affair,* 427.

innocence after the "unforgettable trial," he described the final hours and the judges' verdict.

JEAN-BERNARD

Impressions of a Spectator

September 9, 1899

We have arrived at the last stage of this sad calvary. The opening of the [final] session has been delayed one hour, and precautions have increased. At the entrance, the guard is quadrupled; not only is your name taken, and the name of your newspaper, but two police agents frisk your clothes; even opera glasses are prohibited. . . . All women are formally barred from the hall; the order is absolute. . . . Several women who made it into the public gallery were ushered out. Only six female journalists, with official passes, have been able to take their customary places. Gendarmes surround the area, and in the courtyard artillerymen are at the ready. . . .

Colonel Jouaust opens the session; he is more pale than usual. . . . The judges slowly take their places, and Demange continues his summation, examining the bordereau, proving not only that others could have written it but that Dreyfus could not have written it, nor could he have furnished the documents it lists. Today the judges listen with restless attention. . . . Lieutenant Colonel Brongniart takes notes incessantly, with the same nervousness as yesterday, and the argumentation unfolds, without high-flown phrases, without grand gestures. One sees that Demange wants to speak in an unpretentious way, so that he is understood by these simple souls. . . .

The court retires, and during those moments, which seem to us like long, sleepless nights, they deliberate.

In a corner of the large courtyard, leaning against the pillars, we close our eyes, also collecting our thoughts, and we deliberate in our turn.

In our hearts and minds we sum up the long debates, we weigh everything that could possibly be brought against that victim. . . .

Face-to-face with our conscience, face-to-face with the readers who examine our thoughts, before that God who endures as one of the faiths of our maturity, Dreyfus is innocent!

But now the judges return.

With an emotion that grips us all, we listen to the verdict:

Jean-Bernard, *Le Procès de Rennes: Impressions d'un spectateur* (Paris: Alphonse Lemerre, 1900), 391–95.

By a vote of five to two, Dreyfus is found guilty.
But he is granted extenuating circumstances and sentenced to ten years' imprisonment!

Prepared for an uprising, military officials got a wake. Only a few whispers and sobs were heard within the hall, and even Dreyfus's enemies, who would shout their victory from the pages of the next day's papers, "seemed struck dumb." Demange collapsed in tears, and Labori brought the news to the prisoner. In accordance with military law, Dreyfus had not been present for the public proclamation of his verdict. "Take care of my wife and children," he asked the lawyer, and then, just as he had done in the winter of 1894, he stood at attention, flanked by guards, to hear the judgment read.[31]

Absurd but legal, the decision to convict with "extenuating circumstances" had emerged from last-minute negotiations within the deliberation room. The judges had voted in ascending order of rank, and after the five junior officers ("imbued with the quasi-unanimous opinion of the army") moved to convict,[32] Commandant de Bréon, a devout Catholic who had prayed for guidance in the church next to the Rennes lycée, voted to acquit, as did the presiding judge, Colonel Jouaust, an anticlerical who shared de Bréon's courage, if not his faith. At that point at least one of the junior officers, "mortified" by the break with his superiors, asked that the vote be taken again. But military regulations would not allow it. Scrambling for a compromise, the judges agreed on "extenuating circumstances" and a reduced sentence. They emerged from the deliberation room looking "horribly pale."[33]

"When the report of the Rennes process is published *in extenso*," Emile Zola wrote in *L'Aurore*, "there will exist no more detestable monument to human infamy. . . . The ignorance, folly, madness, cruelty, deceit, and crime" that ran throughout the court-martial will lead "tomorrow's generations to tremble with shame." Maurice Barrès saw it differently: "Let us no longer remember the traitor, except to love those who punished him. . . . We acknowledge with immense hopefulness the victory of Rennes."[34]

[31]Jean-Denis Bredin, *L'Affaire* (Paris: Juillard, 1983), 394.
[32]Michel de Lombarès, *L'Affaire Dreyfus* (Paris: Lavauzelle, 1985), 156–57.
[33]Paléologue, *Journal de l'affaire*, 264.
[34]Emile Zola, *L'Affaire Dreyfus: La Verité en marche* (Paris: Garnier-Flammarion, 1969), 161. Barrès is quoted in Bredin, *The Affair*, 428.

7

The World's Affair

Emile Zola and Maurice Barrès, in their postmortems of Rennes, looked beyond the nation to world opinion. And they were not alone. For Dreyfusards the verdict dishonored France and shamed its army in the eyes of the world. For anti-Dreyfusards it marked a victory over "foreigners both inside and outside of France" who, in the words of Barrès, "wanted to 'put one over on us.' "[1] Reacting to the attacks on France and French justice that began in earnest with the Esterhazy trial and peeked with Rennes, Drumont, Rochefort, Maurras, and their followers accused foreigners of mounting slanderous campaigns through an international press controlled by Jews. Those accusations—fueled by a combination of xenophobia, paranoia, and the economics of selling newspapers—were neither new nor confined to journalists. For over a year French ambassadors and attachés had been submitting reports on the growing wave of anti-French sentiment across Europe and America. They described newspaper hawkers in Holland selling translations of "J'Accuse" and shouting, "The Dreyfus affair, the greatest scandal of the century!" They portrayed the "entire" press of New York attacking France "with extreme violence and conspicuous bad faith." And more often than not, French commentators abroad, like anti-Dreyfusards at home, traced the assaults to a single source. Vast Jewish funds lay behind the campaign for Dreyfus, went the rumor from the French embassy in London. The Austrian press was "almost entirely in the hands of the Jews," reported another agent. And in Germany the French ambassador pointed to the "semites" who shaped opinions of the affair.[2]

---

[1]Maurice Barrès, *Scènes et doctrines du nationalisme* (Paris: Félix Juven, 1902), 211. See also Jean-Denis Bredin, *The Affair: The Case of Alfred Dreyfus,* trans. Jeffrey Mehlman (New York: George Braziller, 1986), 428.

[2]For these and other foreign reactions, see Archives Nationales, BB/19 96 and 106, Feb.–May, 1898. Parts of this chapter are drawn from Michael Burns, "The Policy of Par-

Substituting bigotry for analysis, those commentators struck one true note: The majority of Dreyfusards resided abroad. Indifference also greeted the affair in foreign lands, as it did in many parts of France, and anti-Dreyfusard sentiments could be found among some Catholics in the United States (who vilified Zola's "pornography") and among some Québecois (who believed what they read in bellicose newspapers such as *L'Action nationale*). But foreign opinions, when expressed, were overwhelmingly pro-Dreyfus and ecumenical. Jews, though clearly interested in the fate of their coreligionist and his affair, neither engineered nor dominated the protests. Even France's closest international partner, czarist Russia, had significant numbers of "educated" subjects, as one report put it, who were "incensed" by their ally's handling of the affair—and that from an empire awash in anti-Semitism. The Italian poet Gabriele D'Annunzio detested Jews but could not deny the evidence. "There is no doubt about it," he told a French diplomat. "This time Judas is innocent!" Foreign clubs, organizations, and ad hoc groups rallied to the Dreyfusard side—from the Swedish Association of the Blind and the Dreyfus Agitation Committees of America, to the sixty-five Englishmen and five Germans who reacted to the Rennes verdict with a telegram to the French president ("You are, sir, the leader of a filthy people"). Mark Twain skewered France with his rapier wit, and the American philosopher William James, "deeply saddened by the behavior of the French," gave thanks that he, at least, "lived in a Republic."[3]

One of the most detailed critiques of the affair by a foreign commentator—and one that reached the world's most powerful sovereign—came from Britain's lord chief justice. Sent to Rennes to observe the court-martial, he prepared a paper for Queen Victoria, who would later call the verdict "a defiance of good sense." The chief justice underplayed the role of anti-Semitism, expressed impatience with socialist Dreyfusards, and chastised the foreign press for its sweeping indictment of the French nation. But he was clear on the prisoner's

---

doning: Dreyfus and the World's Fair in 1900," in *L'Affaire Dreyfus et l'opinion publique en France et à l'étranger,* ed. Michel Denis et al. (Rennes: Presses universitaires de Rennes, 1995), 27–37.

[3]William James is quoted in David Levering Lewis, *Prisoners of Honor: The Dreyfus Affair* (New York: William Morrow, 1973), 299. On D'Annunzio, see Maurice Paléologue, *My Secret Diary of the Dreyfus Case, 1894–1899,* trans. Eric Mosbacher (London: Secker and Warburg, 1957), 105.

innocence and the affair's global dimensions, and insightful on the topic of grand judicial cases in the modern age of the telephone and telegraph.

LORD RUSSELL OF KILLOWEN

Report to Queen Victoria
September 16, 1899

I have followed the Dreyfus case from its earliest to its latest stage with close interest; and, while I have come to the clear conclusion that the case against Dreyfus was supported by no solid evidence, I at the same time think that a harsh judgment has been pronounced by the foreign Press generally, and notably by that of Great Britain, not only upon some of the persons concerned, but even upon the French nation as a whole.

To begin with, it is necessary to bear in mind the almost sacred character with which the imagination of the French people has invested their army. Nor is this without some natural explanation. Looking to the numerous divisions of political parties, even amongst those who advocate constitutional government in some form or another, and remembering besides the large and increasing number of socialists (to say nothing of the anarchistic element), it is hardly wonderful that large masses of the people have come to doubt the stability of its government and to regard the army as the sole ark of safety in France. When, therefore, the original Conseil de Guerre [court-martial] pronounced against Dreyfus, it was quite natural that the people of France should believe in its judgment. . . .

Later, when facts began to leak out which made thoughtful people doubt the justice of the condemnation, it was unfortunate for Dreyfus that amongst the most prominent advocates for revision were to be found (1) foreign journals [newspapers], and in France (2) among the class of men like Clemenceau and . . . Jaurès. . . .

These men were only too glad, while advocating the rehabilitation of Dreyfus, to make his cause the opportunity for an attack upon the army as an institution. I do not mean to say that there were not others in France who advocated revision who were free from these imputations.

As to foreign journals, France has not yet realised the fact that every great drama, whether in the Courts of Justice or elsewhere, is now played

R. Barry O'Brien, *The Life of Lord Russell of Killowen* (London: Smith, Elder and Co., 1901).

before the whole world as an audience, and is therefore subject to the criticism of the whole world. France has not realised that the telegraph and the telephone have almost brought the ends of the earth together, and that it is quite impossible to treat, as a purely domestic concern, any question which, like this one, appears to touch the very foundations of justice. In all circumstances it not only distrusts the motive of foreign advice or interference, but repudiates and grievously resents it.

In fact, France does not regard any of the great communities of the world, except Russia and perhaps the United States of America, as friendly to her. The result has been that the adverse comments in the German and in the British Press, so far from helping the cause of Dreyfus, have been appealed to and paraded by those who profess to believe in his guilt, as if they afforded corroborative evidence of his guilt. . . .

What has especially troubled the French people is that these attacks have not been confined to those immediately concerned as judges or as military officers in the Dreyfus case, but have been extended to the French nation as a whole, and against that nation has been levelled the charge of a general decadence of moral tone and sense. Indeed, the latest form that these comments have taken is an attack upon the [Catholic] religion of the mass of the people of France, which is also the religion of a not unimportant section of her Majesty's subjects at home and in her empire abroad. . . .

It is quite true, unhappily, that so-called religious papers, like *La Croix,* have written abominably against Dreyfus, just as avowedly non-religious papers have done; but I do not think there is any ground for the suggestion that the prejudice against Dreyfus was at all considerably accentuated by the fact of his being a Jew. That the Jews are unpopular in France is undoubted; but it is equally true that they are unpopular in Germany and in Russia, and indeed in most countries where they reside, but assuredly not only on religious, but on racial and social grounds. . . .

As to Dreyfus himself, I was disappointed [at Rennes]. I was full of pity for him, and entered the Court with every desire to be impressed by him; but I was not. He does *not* impress one favorably. He is mean-looking, with a hard, unsympathetic face; and, so far as expression goes, I must reluctantly admit that there was no openness, frankness or nobility in his expression. He did, I think, display a great deal of dignity in the passionless immobility with which he, almost throughout the entire proceedings, listened to the injurious and, as I believe, often lying statements launched against him. . . .

The explanation of the erroneous judgment, as I conceive it to be, at which [the judges] arrived I take to be this: they were unversed in the law, unused to legal proceedings, with no experience or aptitude to enable them to weigh the probative effect of testimony; they were steeped in prejudice and concerned for what they regarded as the honour of the army; and thus, impressed or overawed by the heads of their profession, they gave undue weight to the flimsy rags of evidence which alone were presented against the accused man. . . .

I am glad to learn, upon what I believe is good authority, that, with a view to a general appeasement, the Government do contemplate granting at an early date a free pardon to Dreyfus. . . . Although a pardon is no reparation to an innocent man, it will at least restore him to his family, and will give him the time and the leisure to work out, even to the satisfaction of his countrymen, still largely hostile to him, his complete vindication.

It seems to me that good may come for the world in general out of the sufferings of this man.

In the first place, it will render impossible the continuance of courts-martial, at least without more complete legal safeguards and control than now exist. . . .

In the next place, I think it will bring home to the Powers of the world the impossibility of continuing to use the services of their military attachés at foreign courts for the purposes of espionage. It seems intolerable that an officer in a noble service would be called upon to perform duties which in any degree call upon him to play the part of espion [spy]. . . .

A final word. France is undoubtedly just now passing through the throes of a crisis. I think that, in the end, truth and a sense of justice will completely reassert themselves. They are beginning to do so. It is not to be forgotten that the rehabilitation of Dreyfus (almost complete in the eyes of the onlooking world) has been brought about mainly by the efforts of Frenchmen . . . and, with all his grossness and exaggeration, the name of Zola ought not to be omitted.

It must be remembered also that recent proceedings cast no slur on the administration of justice in the civil Courts of the land; for surely it might have been predicted with certainty, that, if the revision trial had taken place before the Cour de Cassation (which is the highest court in the land), Dreyfus would now be a free man.

If overly optimistic about the end of espionage in diplomatic circles, the chief justice had it right about the move to pardon Dreyfus. Within hours of the Rennes verdict, Minister of War Galliffet broached the idea to President Loubet, citing Dreyfus's health (physicians declared that he would not survive another prison term) and the "higher political interest" of healing the nation's wounds.[4] On September 11 Joseph Reinach publicly proposed the pardon in *Le Siècle,* and Prime Minister Waldeck-Rousseau, though skeptical at first, quickly agreed. Loubet, however,

---

[4]Galliffet quoted in W. Harding, *Dreyfus: The Prisoner of Devil's Island* (New York: Associated, 1899), 365–66.

worried about the army. A legally established court-martial had reconvicted Dreyfus, and an immediate pardon would surely be viewed as a re-
buke of military justice. It could infect rather than heal.

At the same time, during the week following the verdict, the Dreyfusard alliance, never tightly knit, unraveled. One camp, led by Reinach
and Bernard Lazare, argued that a presidential pardon would save the
prisoner and, if proclaimed quickly, send a signal of his innocence from
France's highest authority. But Jean Jaurès hesitated, and Georges
Clemenceau, speaking for Picquart and others, argued that a pardon im-
plied guilt, which meant defeat, and besides, the great ideological battles
of the affair mattered more than the man whose name it carried.

Mathieu Dreyfus, after failing to mediate the clash between Labori
and Demange, tried to referee yet another Dreyfusard conflict. Day and
night in Paris, he implored his comrades to act in concert. His own stand
was clear: "A pardon is essential, a pardon without delay, or my brother
will die."[5] But Mathieu insisted on a unanimous vote from the allies who
had become his friends. Finally, Jaurès agreed with his socialist partner,
Minister of Commerce Alexandre Millerand, and supported the pardon.
Clemenceau remained defiant (he had earned the nickname "Tiger")
and conceded only when the votes went against him and the decision became an affair of the heart. "If I were the brother," he admitted to Mathieu, "I would accept the pardon."[6]

Reinach kept an extraordinary journal of those busy days and intense
negotiations. Written in the heat of the moment *(à chaud),* with haphazard punctuation and in a style that approached stream of conscious-
ness, it summarized the meetings with Waldeck-Rousseau and
Millerand; it excoriated Clemenceau for caring more about the "daily
bread" of his journalism than about the prisoner waiting in Rennes; and
above all, on the eve of the Universal Exposition to be held in Paris in
1900, it stressed the need to preserve "the honor of France before the
world."

---

[5] For Mathieu Dreyfus's comments, see the account by Joseph Reinach in Pierre Vidal-
Naquet, *Les Juifs, la mémoire et le présent* (Paris: La Découverte, 1991), 2:137–58.
[6] Mathieu Dreyfus, *L'Affaire telle que je l'ai vécue* (Paris: Grasset, 1978), 242.

JOSEPH REINACH

The Pardon

September 10–13, 1899

SUNDAY, SEPTEMBER 10

In the night from Saturday to Sunday, the idea of a pardon for Dreyfus enters my mind, becoming an obsession. I see there two great advantages. The one, human: to cut short, to put an end to the unjust tortures inflicted on that ill-fated man, to return him to his wife and children, to allow him to die, if he is going to die, as some have announced, in peace, and to save the Republic the shame of his death in its prisons. The other, a general political advantage, still more decisive: The entire world is going to rise up with a shout of horror against the Rennes verdict—and not only against the five judges, against the deceitful generals, against the forgers, against the band of nationalists, but against France itself. Either we resign ourselves to this dishonor, becoming complicitous in the crime of Rennes, or we set France apart from it. How? . . .

A Pardon is the only way, but on the formal and necessary condition that it be immediate. A pardon tomorrow separates France from the five judges of Rennes before the world. A pardon in a month is nothing more than an act of pity. Tomorrow it is the resounding disavowal of the verdict, the proclamation of Dreyfus's innocence by the Republic's government itself. And on the initiative . . . of the minister of war, because he alone can countersign the pardon decree; and it will surely not be an ordinary thing to have the chief of the army tear to pieces the military judgment before its ink is dry. . . . All that can still be saved of France's honor will be saved. The pardon only annuls the verdict itself . . . ; but Dreyfus, free, pardoned . . . will pursue his final and official rehabilitation. And if he dies before then, we will pursue it: The pardon prevents nothing. . . .

MONDAY, SEPTEMBER 11

. . . In front of the Foreigner, before the world, we must break with the judges at Rennes. Waldeck is very impressed by the argument: France must be extricated, rescued. The entire world press covers France with insults and sarcasm. Everywhere, there are cries of anger and horror. Yesterday, during demonstrations in twenty large cities, shouts were heard: "Down with Mercier! Long live Dreyfus!" and also "Down with France!" The French consulates at Budapest, at Antwerp, in America had to be protected. . . .

Pierre Vidal-Naquet, *Les Juifs, la mémoire et le present* (Paris: La Découverte, 1991), 2:137–58.

Millerand, minister of commerce, hits upon this point: "And the Exposition [the World's Fair of 1900]? Is the Exposition not in danger? Is there not a veritable foreign plot in the works to stay away from the Exposition, to put Paris, to put France, in quarantine?"

The point is unexpected; the point is very true. . . .

Clemenceau has given in; he promises his cooperation. . . . "Of course," says Jaurès, "Captain Dreyfus and Mathieu will continue to fight along with us." "Yes," says Mathieu, who can no longer contain his joy. . . . "And I ask you to draft my brother's declaration, confirming that when he leaves prison, he will pursue the struggle to the end, to revision." Jaurès and I draft it. Mathieu takes a copy. . . . The declaration will be published by the Havas Press Agency on the very day of the pardon, one hour after Mathieu will have left [Rennes] with his brother. . . .

Clemenceau, suspicious, intervenes: "And in a word, Millerand, are you certain the pardon will be granted tomorrow?"

Millerand turns to Mathieu: "I give you my word of honor that if [it] is not granted tomorrow, as promised, I will submit my resignation."

Mathieu left at ten o'clock for Rennes.

TUESDAY, SEPTEMBER 12

This pardon [agreed upon in principle by a unanimous cabinet vote the previous evening], three days after the infamous verdict, this response of the republic—bold, noble, immediate—to the immense indignation of the civilized world, was too beautiful.

Picquart is right, as he told me a short time ago: "One must never have faith in the success of something 'beautifully' conceived." I tell him: "For the past two years, we have definitely been living in a world that is too heroic, too Wagnerian, outside ordinary humanity. We have lost the idea of what that is. We insist on believing that we are capable of everything. We must give up that illusion."

What was accomplished last night has been undone this morning by the president of the Republic in the cabinet council.

. . . Loubet . . . believes there are drawbacks to granting the pardon without delay; it would irritate the army, . . . it would be advisable to put it off until next week.

Waldeck-Rousseau observes that an immediate pardon is a response, a signal to the world that France separates itself from the five judges at Rennes. The more the measure is delayed, the more its high meaning is lost.

Heated debate. [Foreign Minister] Delcassé supports Loubet, who asks if it is simply a game of signatures.

Then Millerand recalls the word of honor he gave to Mathieu. . . . If the pardon is not immediately decided, he will resign.

Waldeck responds that he will submit his resignation as well. It is a crisis. . . .

Loubet, like Félix Faure, begins to tremble in fear of the gutter press.

The movement of condemnation and of hatred against France reaches frightening proportions throughout the world. And Loubet's horizon still reaches no farther than [his hometown of] Montélimar. This postponement . . . is loathsome for Dreyfus and criminal for France. . . .

WEDNESDAY, SEPTEMBER 13
Mathieu . . . saw his brother yesterday morning [in Rennes]. For the first time they were alone. The captain has decided to withdraw his appeal [which he must do to receive a pardon] only if our opinion is unanimous. "In your place," went Clemenceau's last word to Mathieu, "I would do what you are doing.". . .

Mathieu speaks to his brother about the future battles for his complete and official rehabilitation. The captain will take on the most active role himself: He will speak out; he will write.

He receives hundreds of letters and telegrams from the entire world. He senses that he has become a symbol.

If the republic lets this man die in its prisons, it is a new and indelible disgrace.

Support for the pardon extends and intensifies in newspapers everywhere. What a pity not to realize the role of poetry in politics!

Reinach's text ends in medias res, with the pardon proposed but unsigned. By the fifth day after the Rennes verdict, Dreyfus had withdrawn his appeal, and most of his supporters had acquiesced with regret. Like Clemenceau, they were long on courage but short on sympathy for the survivor of Devil's Island. "We were prepared to die for Dreyfus," said Charles Péguy, "but Dreyfus was not."[7] The prisoner had completed a process that Péguy had seen coming. From the mystical plane of high idealism, the affair had fallen to the hard ground of politics and self-interest, though not all his former allies would agree. For Jaurès and other socialists with whom Péguy would eventually break, the affair, despite the pardon, had been a grand struggle triumphantly waged.

Still, in September 1899 Loubet continued to take the army's pulse. During that crucial period, the foreign demonstrations alluded to by Reinach intensified, and external pressures reinforced the Dreyfusards' internal campaign. Through the second week of September, in Rome, Milan, Brussels, London, New York, and other cities and towns, crowds

---

[7]Quoted in Douglas Johnson, *France and the Dreyfus Affair* (London: Blandford, 1966), 179, note 14.

shouted slogans and carried placards praising Dreyfus and vilifying the French army. Protesters in Chicago burned the tricolor flag, and a demonstration in London's Hyde Park drew a crowd of more than thirty thousand. President Loubet, whose entire political life had been accompanied by angry shouts, was not likely to be moved by similar diatribes in foreign tongues. But protesters also wielded the stick of international commerce, and when they threatened to refuse participation in the World's Fair of 1900, Loubet, who had helped launch the idea nearly eight years earlier, took notice. And so did French politicians and businessmen, for whom the Dreyfus affair was old news and the World's Fair a major investment.

In fact, the Exposition and the Dreyfus case had intersected long before. In 1898 reports described foreign manufacturers and suppliers contemplating a *"boycottage,"* a word that entered the French lexicon during the affair's last phase.[8] One German newspaper, as if to wave a red flag at the Gallic bull, advised its readers to "abstain from visiting the great French Exposition . . . because they will not be safe in a country where all rights are violated, where only the antisemitic and chauvinist population makes the law [and] threatens to throw into the Seine anyone who does not share their passions." By the summer of 1899, the Protestant bishop of Calcutta was advising British authorities in India to boycott the Exposition, "since France had ceased to be a member of civilized nations."[9]

Previous world's fairs in Paris had served as "recovery rites" after national traumas. The 1878 Exposition had followed a parliamentary upheaval that had nearly toppled the Third Republic, and the 1889 World's Fair, a record setter in every way, had come on the heels of the Boulanger crisis. But in 1900 the international community linked the questions of commerce and human rights for the first time. Although sovereign states never reached the point of calling for an official boycott (indeed, many governments rejected the idea), thousands of private citizens and scores of organizations, from San Francisco to Berlin, forged the connection between Dreyfus's civil liberties and the economics of

---

[8]Richard Mandell, *Paris 1900: The Great World's Fair* (Toronto: University of Toronto Press, 1967), 89 and passim; and Mandell, "The Affair and the Fair: Some Observations on the Closing Stages of the Dreyfus Case," *Journal of Modern History* 37 (1967): 253–65.

[9]Archives Nationales, BB/19 103, French consul general, Hamburg, Mar. 10, 1898; and Mandell, "The Affair and the Fair," 258.

the World's Fair. On that score, their campaigns were more typical of the century to come than of the century just past.[10]

Emile Zola referred to the World's Fair and the reputation of France in an article published at the height of the foreign protests and in the midst of the debate over the presidential pardon. "The Fifth Act," like "J'Accuse" before it, confirmed Zola's keen sense of timing.

[10]For more on this, see Burns, "Policy of Pardoning," 34–36. For political philosopher Hannah Arendt, "the wrong done to a single Jewish officer in France was able to draw from the rest of the world a more vehment and united reaction than all the persecutions of German Jews a generation later" (*The Origins of Totalitarianism* [New York: Harvest, 1973], 91).

EMILE ZOLA

The Fifth Act

September 12, 1899

I am terrified. What I feel is no longer anger, no longer indignation and the craving to avenge it, no longer the need to denounce a crime and demand its punishment, in the name of truth and justice. I am terrified, filled with the sacred awe of a man who witnesses the supernatural: rivers flowing backwards toward their sources and the earth toppling over under the sun. I cry out with consternation, for our noble and generous France has fallen to the bottom of the abyss.

We had assumed that the trial in Rennes was the fifth act of the dreadful tragedy in which we have been ensnared for nearly two years. All of the dangerous obstacles had been overcome, it seemed: we believed we were moving towards a conclusion of concord and pacification. . . . But no, we were mistaken! A new obstacle has arisen, the most unexpected and dreadful of them all, making the drama more sombre still, prolonging it, dragging it out toward some unforeseeable end. Our minds shudder and reel at the prospect.

Beyond a doubt, the trial in Rennes was only the fourth act. But great

Emile Zola, excerpts from *The Dreyfus Affair: "J'Accuse" and Other Writings,* ed. Alain Pagès, trans. Eleanor Levieux (New Haven: Yale University Press, 1996), 136–43, with cuts. Copyright © 1996 by Eleanor Levieux and Yale University. Reprinted with the permission of Yale University Press and CNRS Editions, Paris. See also Emile Zola, *L'Affaire Dreyfus: La Verité en marche* (Paris: Garnier-Flammarion, 1969), 162ff.

God in Heaven, what will the fifth act be like? What new pain and suffering will it be composed of? Into what supreme expiation will it plunge this nation? One thing is certain: an innocent man cannot be convicted twice without the sun turning dark and the peoples of the world rising up. . . .

When the complete and detailed minutes of the trial in Rennes are published, they will constitute the most loathsome monument imaginable to human infamy. It outdoes everything. Never will History have seen a more villainous document. Such blatant ignorance, stupidity, madness, cruelty and lies—in a word, crime—are displayed in it that the generations to come will shudder with shame. . . . That is why I am terrified: because any nation that is capable of holding such a trial, such a consultation on its moral and intellectual condition, in front of the civilized world, must be going through a horrendous crisis. Is that nation's death imminent? We are drowning in poisonous mud—will we ever find a fountain of goodness, purity and justice that can wash us clean? . . .

And there we are, in this fine situation, for all Europe and all the world to see. The entire world is convinced that Dreyfus is innocent. . . . We have lost our moral battle of Sedan, and this is a hundred times more disastrous than the other Sedan [where Prussia defeated France in 1870], which involved only bloodshed. . . .

The worst part is that we have a rendez-vous with glory. France has decided to celebrate its century of diligent labour, science and struggles for freedom, truth and justice. Never has there been a century of more admirable effort, as future generations shall realize. And France has invited the nations of the world to come and glorify France's victory. . . . And what will they find? An innocent man convicted twice, truth slapped in the face, justice slain. We have become the object of contempt and they will come to snigger at us, and they will guzzle our wines and kiss our servant girls, as if they were slumming in some low dive. Can we really be on the verge of such a thing? Are we going to let our World [sic] Fair become an evil den where the whole world will scornfully condescend to have a good time? No! We must perform the fifth act of our monstrous tragedy now, without delay, no matter how painful the penance we have to do. We must regain our honour so that we can welcome the peoples of the earth to a healed and regenerated France.

I am haunted by that fifth act; I keep coming back to it, trying to picture it. Has no one noticed that this Dreyfus Affair, this gigantic drama that has aroused the universe, seems to have been staged by some sublime playwright, determined to make it an incomparable masterpiece? . . . The genius behind this living drama is fate. . . . Surely it wants this masterpiece to be complete; surely it is preparing some superhuman fifth act which will recreate a glorious France, leading the procession of nations. . . .

Before the Assize Court of the Seine [in 1898], I swore that Dreyfus was innocent. I swear it before the entire world and now the entire world joins me, as in a chorus. I repeat: the truth is on the march, and nothing shall stop it. At Rennes, it has just taken a giant step. I have but one fear now: that the truth will arrive in a thunderbolt hurled by the avenging Nemesis and will shatter our country, unless we ourselves hasten to let the truth shine forth, like a sunburst over France.

For years Zola had been hurling his own thunderbolts, and in the crowded pantheon of France's secular gods, he had no rival as the nation's modern Nemesis, the voice of indignation at the crimes of human presumption. His "Fifth Act" kept up that assault, but it also touched on themes—the global reputation of France and the nation's regeneration—that transcended domestic divisions and struck a timely chord. His article came at a moment when the vast majority of the French population, including many of those who would never acknowledge Dreyfus's innocence, agreed that the honor of France in the eyes of the world mattered more than a protracted struggle over the case of one man. Furthermore, with Dreyfus pardoned and about to return home, and with Picquart out of jail and feted by Parisian notables, the battle for justice had lost its urgency. And finally, though states might not suffer exhaustion, people do, and though the affair's grand conflicts—between individual rights and *raison d'état,* between civilian government and military authority, between church and state—would not go away, nearly all French citizens wished by the fall of 1899 that Alfred Dreyfus would.

And so he did, with a promise to return. On the day the presidential pardon took effect, Dreyfus issued a public proclamation that Jaurès and Reinach had helped draft.

ALFRED DREYFUS

Declaration of Innocence

September 19, 1899

The government of the Republic restores my liberty. It is nothing for me without honor. From today on I will continue to pursue the reparation of the hideous judicial error of which I am still the victim. I want all of France to know, by a final judgment, that I am innocent. My heart will be at rest only when there is no longer a single Frenchman who imputes to me a crime that another has committed.

Dreyfus and the few allies who remained by his side were about to confront the most formidable enemies of all: short memories and the deep desire to forget. Two days after the pardon, General Galliffet issued his own proclamation, and although it was aimed at the army, French citizens were ready to march to its request.

Quoted in Mathieu Dreyfus, *L'Affaire telle que je l'ai vécue* (Paris: Grasset, 1978), 242, note 1.

MINISTER OF WAR GASTON DE GALLIFFET

Proclamation to the Army

September 21, 1899

The incident is closed! The military judges, with the respect of all, pronounced the verdict in complete independence. With absolutely no mental reservation, we bow before their decision. We will also bow before the act that a feeling of profound pity has dictated to the president of the republic. There can no longer be a question of reprisals, whatever they may be. Therefore, I repeat, the incident is closed.

I ask you and, if it becomes necessary, I would order you to forget the past in order to think only of the future. With all my comrades, I shout with all my heart, "Long live the Army!" which belongs to no party, but only to France.

Quoted in Jean-Denis Bredin, *L'Affaire* (Paris: Juillard, 1983), 399–400.

8

Encores and Legacies

The "World's Fair truce," as contemporaries called the cease-fire of the Dreyfus case, lasted through the summer and fall of 1900, and then, as if exercising an option on tranquillity, the National Assembly voted an amnesty bill covering every individual, crime, and misdemeanor connected with the affair over its six-year history. By letting the Rennes verdict stand, the government waved a carrot at both sides: Although the "traitor's" enemies could revel in the reconviction, Dreyfus could still appeal to the Cour de Cassation, but only if he uncovered a "new element" in the case. Infuriated by the legislation, Zola penned his second open letter to a president of the republic. "Today, in the place of justice," he wrote Loubet, "comes this villainous and outrageous amnesty . . . [that] not only wounds the nation's conscience, it corrupts the nation's morals."[1] Alfred Dreyfus, writing from his sister's home in southern France, where he had gone to recuperate after Rennes, attacked the bill while still in committee. "[It] extinguishes prosecutions," he told the chairman, "from which I had hoped revelations, perhaps confessions, would result. . . . It benefits only scoundrels who . . . knowingly had an innocent man condemned through lies, perjury, and forgery; and who cast me into the abyss." Picquart argued that the bill "would grant me an amnesty for an offense which I did not commit."[2] And even Esterhazy, still in England, opposed the legislation as a crime against his cash flow; along with peddling interviews, he had been blackmailing his former protectors.

But a few veterans of the affair could not stop the push for peace, and the amnesty bill became law on December 27, 1900. Neither the century

---

[1]Emile Zola, *L'Affaire Dreyfus: La Verité en marche* (Paris: Garnier-Flammarion, 1969), 197–210.

[2]Dreyfus and Picquart quoted in Louis L. Snyder, *The Dreyfus Case: A Documentary History* (New Brunswick, N.J.: Rutgers University Press, 1973), 366–68.

nor the judicial case closed with the "sunburst" of enlightenment that Zola had hoped would fall on the affair's "Fifth Act." Still, Dreyfusards fought on. With the publication of three major books in the first year of the new century, they moved from the amnesty battle to the war against amnesia. *La Verité en marche* (Truth on the March) presented Zola's articles and open letters on the affair; the first volume of Joseph Reinach's *Histoire de l'affaire Dreyfus* offered a dramatic overview of the arrest, conviction, and degradation; and Dreyfus's memoir, *Cinq années de ma vie* (Five Years of My Life), with its detailed account of Devil's Island, enjoyed immediate success in France and abroad.

From the southern town of Carpentras, Alfred and Lucie Dreyfus had moved with their children to a small villa overlooking Lake Geneva in Switzerland. Between bouts of malarial fever and the exhaustion that came with incessant nightmares, Dreyfus studied the documents of his case and traveled to Paris to work with Demange and Mornard. He took the reins of his own affair, while Mathieu Dreyfus, having returned to the textile business in Mulhouse, acted as consultant from afar. The core of Dreyfusard allies continued to search for the "new element" needed for a second revision, but by 1903 death had diminished their highest ranks. Auguste Scheurer-Kestner had died of natural causes on the day of Dreyfus's pardon in 1899, and on the morning of September 29, 1902, Emile Zola was found in the bedroom of his Paris apartment, asphyxiated by the fumes of a defective fireplace. Rumors of murder, inevitable and rampant, were never proven.

On the eve of Zola's funeral, the anti-Dreyfusard press returned to its old ways, slandering the memory of the "dung-drenched" novelist and threatening violence if Alfred Dreyfus joined the cortege. To pay homage to his most renowned defender while avoiding turmoil, Dreyfus slipped into the Montmartre cemetery flanked by Mathieu, Jaurès, Lazare, and other colleagues acting as human shields. More than twenty thousand mourners heard two hundred protesters shouting "Zola to Charenton!" (a Paris prison and insane asylum), while beside the grave the novelist Anatole France honored his fellow Dreyfusard.[3]

---

[3] On the protests and other events surrounding Zola's funeral, see Archives de la Préfecture de Police, Paris, B/A 1309, reports and newspaper clippings, Oct. 6, 1902; and Michael Burns, *Dreyfus: A Family Affair, 1789–1945* (New York: HarperCollins, 1991), 299–301.

Figure 13. Alfred Dreyfus, right, and his "admirable brother" Mathieu, the principal organizer of the Dreyfusard campaign. This photograph was taken after the presidential pardon, while Alfred recuperated at his sister's home in southern France.

ANATOLE FRANCE

Eulogy for Emile Zola

October 5, 1902

Rendering to Emile Zola, in the name of his friends, the honors due him, I will hold back my grief and theirs. It is not through mourning and lamentation that we best celebrate those who leave behind a noble memory; it is through manly praise and the honest description of their work and life. . . .

Is it possible for me, as I recall the struggle waged by Zola for justice and truth, to remain silent about those men intent on ruining an innocent man, those men who, feeling they would be doomed if he was saved, crushed him with the brazen desperation of fear? How do I put them out of sight, when it is my place to show you Zola, weak and unarmed, rising up against them? How can I silence their lies? That would be to silence his integrity. Can I silence the outrages and slander with which they pursued him? That would be to silence his reward and honor. Can I silence their shame? That would be to silence his glory. No! I will speak out!

With the calm and stability that the spectacle of death bestows, I will recall the dark days when selfishness and fear were seated in the councils of government. The injustice started to come to light, but, feeling that it was supported and defended by such powerful public and secret forces, the strongest hesitated. Those whose duty it was to speak out remained silent. The best among them, who did not fear for themselves, were afraid to engage their parties in such terrible dangers. Led astray by monstrous lies, inflamed by hateful oratory, the mass of people, believing they had been betrayed, became enraged. . . .

The darkness deepened. A sinister silence reigned. Then Zola wrote the president of the Republic that measured and powerful letter denouncing the forgery and breach of duty.

With what fury he was attacked by the criminals, their mercenary defenders, their unwitting accomplices, all the united parties of reaction, the deluded mob—you know and you have seen innocent souls, with pious simplicity, join that cortege of barking dogs on the make. You have heard the shrieks of rage and murderous shouts that pursued Zola into the Palais de Justice, during that long trial judged in willful ignorance . . . on the basis of forged evidence, amidst the rattle of swords.

I see here some of those who stood by his side, who shared his peril: Let them say if more insults had ever been hurled at a righteous man. Let them also say with what steadfastness he endured it all. Let them say if his hearty goodness, his manly compassion, his anguish flagged one single time, and if his loyalty ever wavered. . . .

Everything was saved. Zola not only revealed a judicial error, he denounced the conspiracy of all the forces of violence and oppression united to kill social justice, the republican idea, and free thought in France. His courageous words awakened France. The consequences of his action are incalculable.

They unfold today with powerful force and majesty; they reach beyond measure; they have inspired a movement of social equity that will not stop. From his action emerges a new order of things founded on a finer sense of justice and on a more profound understanding of the rights of one and all. . . .

There is only one country in the world in which these noble things could be accomplished. How admirable is the genius of our fatherland! How glorious this soul of France, which, in past centuries, taught Europe and the world the rule of law. France is the country of splendid reason and benevolent thought, the land of just magistrates and humane philosophers, the country of Turgot, Montesquieu, Voltaire, and Malesherbes. Zola, for not having lost faith in the justice of France, deserves well of his country.

Let us not pity him for having suffered and endured. Let us envy him. Atop the most prodigious mound of outrages that folly, ignorance, and wickedness have ever heaped up, his glory reaches an inaccessible height.

Let us envy him: He has honored his fatherland with an immense body of work and a noble act. Let us envy him: His destiny and his heart endowed him with the greatest fate of all; he was a moment in the conscience of humanity.

One year later Bernard Lazare died of cancer at the age of thirty-eight. Less celebrated than Zola and always less fortunate (he died in poverty), he was never less committed to justice. And he stood out, said Charles Péguy, as the affair's one secular "saint" and as Israel's modern "prophet." Misunderstood, rarely appreciated, and soon forgotten, he was, in Péguy's apologia, the premier hero of a movement tarnished by ambition, politics, and self-interest.

CHARLES PÉGUY

Reflections on Bernard Lazare

1910

The prophet, in that great crisis of Israel and the world, was Bernard-Lazare. Let us salute here one of the greatest names of modern times . . . one of the greatest among the prophets of Israel. . . .

Vast numbers of imbeciles . . . still believe that Bernard-Lazare was . . . a young writer come to Paris, like so many others, to make his way, to make his fortune in the world of letters . . . a young Jew from Nîmes or Montpellier. I would not be surprised, I am even certain, that the young Bernard-Lazare believed it himself. The prophet is the first not to know himself. . . . And during the affair, I would not be surprised that the Dreyfus high command, the Dreyfus entourage, the Dreyfus family, and Dreyfus himself always considered Bernard-Lazare a paid agent, a sort of legal consultant . . . a salaried maker of memoirs, a publicist, a hired pamphleteer. . . .

I will draw a portrait of Bernard-Lazare. He had, undeniably, the qualities of a saint, of holiness. And . . . I am not speaking in metaphors. He had a sweetness, a goodness, a mystical tenderness, an evenness of temperament, an experience of bitterness and ingratitude, a perfect ability to deal with bitterness and ingratitude, a sort of kindness that one does not show off. . . . He lived and died for [the Jews] as a martyr. He was a prophet. It was therefore fitting that he was prematurely entombed in silence and oblivion. . . .

He was dead before he died. . . . It is quite remarkable that the only newspaper that ever treated our friend with dignity . . . while undoubtedly treating him violently, harshly as an enemy, the only newspaper that said how much he loved Israel and noted his grandeur, was *La Libre Parole,* and that the only man who said it was Edouard Drumont. It is shameful for us that the name of Bernard-Lazare, since . . . his death, has appeared only in a hostile newspaper. . . .

The others, ours, fell silent even before his death and have remained silent since, carefully, shamefully; with perfection, with perseverance, with extraordinary success.

He was dead before he died.

It is as if they were ashamed of him. But, in reality, they were ashamed of themselves in his presence.

Charles Péguy, *Oeuvres en prose, 1909–1914* (Paris: Gallimard, 1967), 549–52 and passim.

Politicians, politics itself, felt shame in the presence of his mystical spirit.

Shortly before his death, Bernard Lazare read Dreyfus's memoir, *Cinq années de ma vie,* and told its author, "You are, perhaps, more Jewish than you think, through your incoercible hope . . . your almost fatalistic resignation." Earlier he had described Dreyfus as incarnating "not only the centuries-old suffering of this people of martyrs, but their present agonies. Through him I see Jews languishing in Russian prisons . . . Rumanian Jews who are refused the rights of man. . . . Algerian Jews, beaten and pillaged." But while Dreyfus expressed "profound sorrow at the loss of his friend, so loyal and so good," he never embraced Lazare's Jewish nationalism or Herzl's Zionism. Like the majority of assimilated Jews at the turn of the century—including Joseph Reinach, who refused to place "some sort of ethnic solidarity" above the interests of France—Dreyfus defined those movements as retrograde and divisive. His faith was private, his allegiance French. That his tragedy, through Herzl's reaction to it, helped shape the foundations of the modern Jewish state stands as one of the affair's most significant and ironic legacies.[4]

Although it seemed by 1903 that the affair was dying along with its participants, it lived on through the political, social, and religious issues it had helped crystallize, if not create. And Dreyfus's judicial case owed its survival to the coalition of socialists, moderate progressives, and anticlerical radicals (the *bloc des gauches*) that dominated the Chamber of Deputies between 1899 and 1905. Waldeck-Rousseau's successor as prime minister, Emile Combes, thought occasionally about the Dreyfus affair and obsessively about Catholics and their agents within the army. The separation of church and state had been the Radical rallying cry for decades, but Combes could now point to the lessons of the affair and, with the fervor of a lay missionary, push the Chamber toward the paradise of secularization. As a young man Combes had studied for the priesthood; as an old politician he wor-

---

[4]On Lazare and Dreyfus, see the comments by Dr. Jean-Louis Lévy, Dreyfus's grandson, in Alfred Dreyfus, *Cinq années de ma vie* (Paris: La Découverte, 1994), 245. See also Michael R. Marrus, *The Politics of Assimilation: The French Jewish Community at the Time of the Dreyfus Affair* (Oxford: Oxford University Press, 1980), 188.

shiped Voltaire. "Raised in the harem," he said of his religious education, "I know its inner secrets."[5]

The policies and practices of the Waldeck-Rousseau and Combes ministries confirmed that Dreyfusards, once on top, were not immune to their own brands of intolerance and revenge. The Catholic poet Charles Péguy excoriated his old comrades for becoming tyrants in their turn, but Péguy, always the affair's John the Baptist, preached in a wilderness. On the heels of the right-wing persecution of Jews, Protestants, and Freemasons, the enemies of the right set out to punish Catholic priests, monks, and nuns who had collaborated (the argument went) in a clerical-military plot against the republic. The accusation was partly true; the desire to draw distinctions based on evidence was almost wholly absent. After 1900 Waldeck-Rousseau moved to restrict the rights of religious congregations, with Assumptionists (an order of Catholic monks whose newspaper, *La Croix,* matched the anti-Semitic virulence of *La Libre Parole*) topping his list of targets. Taking the torch from his predecessor, Combes launched an even more sweeping assault. By 1904 nearly ten thousand religious schools had been closed, thousands of priests and nuns had chosen exile over persecution, France had severed diplomatic ties with the Vatican, and the nation was poised for the final Law of Separation.

It came in July 1905, but under a new government. Convinced that every church niche and army cranny concealed an enemy of enlightenment, Combes had enlisted the support of his minister of war and fellow anticlerical, General Louis André. Proof that Dreyfusards, though still a minority, could now be found in the sanctum sanctorum of the high command, André aimed to protect republican soldiers from their reactionary comrades. And in his quest to ferret out monarchists and nationalists, he forged a secret alliance with Masonic lodges. On thousands of slips of paper *(fiches),* the minister's spies divided French officers into two groups: those with republican credentials who deserved promotion, and those with a habit of attending Mass who deserved oblivion. The *affaire des fiches,* confirmation that the Dreyfusard pendulum had swung past the center of good sense, provided fodder for critics who had always insisted that a secret syndicate lay behind the Dreyfus affair. It triggered

---

[5]Quoted in Gordon Wright, *France in Modern Times* (New York: W.W. Norton, 1995), 250.

the collapse of the Combes ministry and marked one of the first steps toward a "nationalist revival" in France.

Before that folly, however, in 1903, Combes's parliamentary allies, led by Jean Jaurès, pushed the Dreyfus case toward another revision. Re-elected to the Chamber of Deputies the previous year, Jaurès embodied one of the affair's most important legacies. Rallying to Dreyfus as a victim of reaction, many French socialists had abandoned the dogma of nonparticipation and worked with reformist bourgeois parties. The shift had started before the affair, but Jaurès involvement in the Dreyfusard cause stood as a defining moment. In the spring of 1903 Jaurès again manifested his cooperation when he prepared a major speech on the affair and sought the support of Combes, Waldeck-Rousseau, and Brisson. (He also showed a draft to Mathieu and Alfred Dreyfus, who called it "perfect."[6]) For two days in the Chamber of Deputies, Jaurès revisited all the bogus evidence and false testimony of the affair. He parried the insults of militant nationalists, and though careful to avoid a sweeping condemnation of the military, he made it clear that the army's control over the Dreyfus case, like its threat to the republic, had been turned back with the turn of the century.

Although the cautious center and angry right defeated Jaurès's motion for an official inquest, Minister of War André promised a "personal" investigation of the affair's documents. Heralded by Dreyfusards as a "period of new gestation," the minister's inquiry stretched on until October 1903, when Combes received the long final report. It retraced the affair's familiar topics and included new evidence that additional forgeries, fabricated by Henry in 1895, had been presented to the judges at Rennes. Dreyfus, who now enjoyed a direct line to the government through Jaurès, learned of the report and of Combes's willingness to support a second revision. With the help of Henri Mornard, Dreyfus composed a formal petition to the minister of justice.

---

[6]Alfred Dreyfus, *Souvenirs et correspondance* (Paris: Grosset, 1936), 354.

ALFRED DREYFUS

Petition to the Minister of Justice

November 25, 1903

At the time of the debates that took place in the Chamber of Deputies on April 6 and 7, 1903, the deputy Jaurès established that a brazen forgery had weighed on the minds of certain judges [at Rennes]. That forgery is a document attributed to the German emperor, about which the defense had no knowledge.

On April 21, 1903, I had the honor of addressing to the minister of war . . . a formal request for an investigation of the grave errors committed to my detriment in the departments under his control. . . . In addition to the conclusive results of that investigation, revision is also justified on the following grounds. . . .

False testimony of Cernuszki: A new witness called by the prosecution at Rennes, a person named Cernuszki, claimed to have learned from an Austrian official, a Dr. Mosetig, that I was a spy in the pay of Germany. That deposition was untrue. Its falsity is confirmed by a statement from Dr. Mosetig that I have attached to my investigation request of April 21, 1903. . . .

False testimonies of Savignaud and Gribelin: Savignaud was a witness recruited by the prosecution to destroy the authority of Lieutenant Colonel Picquart, who had discovered the error committed by the judges in 1894 and the schemes directed against me.

Gribelin, the archivist [of the Statistical Section], had been called for a similar reason.

The false testimony of Savignaud was established by letters from Scheurer-Kestner to Leblois, and that of Gribelin was acknowledged by Gribelin himself.

False documents: The secret dossier used against me contained altered documents, and those who used them were aware of their falsity.

New elements: Colonel Schwartzkoppen and Colonel Panizzardi, who had been, according to the prosecution, the foreign agents to whom I had delivered secret documents, have both acknowledged that they had no relations with me. . . .

Schwartzkoppen's word of honor that there had been neither direct nor indirect contact with me was also known to the prosecution, which con-

Alfred Dreyfus, *Souvenirs et correspondance* (Paris: Grasset, 1936), 375–78.

cealed it from my judges. The minister of war holds the proof in his archives.

A letter from the prince of Münster to Joseph Reinach contains the same confirmation and, for the first time, makes it known that Colonel Schwartzkoppen had confessed to his ambassador that the spy who informed him was Esterhazy and that their contact dated from 1893. . . .

The minister of war had [during the Rennes trial] documents that . . . established that Colonel Panizzardi's informant continued relations with him after my arrest.

My conviction, so laboriously extracted from judges who expressed their doubts in the form of extenuating circumstances, is therefore the result of forgery and deception.

I request the revision of my trial, because I must have all my honor, for my children and myself, because I have never failed in any of my duties as a soldier and a Frenchman.

One month later the minister of justice, following a unanimous vote by the Revision Commission, referred the Dreyfus case to the Cour de Cassation. Anti-Dreyfusards "might still wax indignant," as one historian puts it, but in Reinach's words, "they were beating on punctured drums."[7] It took more than two years—from the preliminary sessions in March 1904 to the final deliberation of the combined chambers of the Cour de Cassation in July 1906—to hear the testimonies and review the evidence that nearly every participant knew by heart. Mercier, Gonse, Picquart, Casimir-Périer and dozens of others reappeared like a repertory company of aging actors in a melodrama that had lost its appeal. Dreyfus made no better impression than he had at Rennes, and though Mornard argued more powerfully than Demange had done in 1899, courtroom histrionics no longer mattered. The audience was too small, the outcome too evident.

And besides, the affair had been eclipsed by other conflicts in France and abroad. "It is frightening," observed one Dreyfusard. "The social revolution has begun. We sowed the wind and we're reaping the whirlwind."[8] The excesses of Combes and André had led to their political fall, and the separation of church and state had been met with protests in the Catholic strongholds of western France. At the same time, in cities and

---

[7] Quoted in Jean-Denis Bredin, *The Affair: The Case of Alfred Dreyfus,* trans. Jeffrey Mehlman (New York: George Braziller, 1986), 463–64.

[8] Ibid., 474.

industrial towns throughout the country, strikes continued to spiral, with more than one thousand recorded in 1904 alone. Georges Clemenceau, after a long career as a rebel on the left, had moved to the center of power as minister of the interior, and by the early months of 1906, with calls for a "general strike" intensifying, he had mobilized police and soldiers to suppress protests and maintain public order. The "Tiger" had become "the first cop of France."

With the nationalist right in check, if not tamed, the political center, including large numbers of Dreyfusards such as Clemenceau, looked left and found the threat of social revolution. Jean Jaurès, with all his brilliance and energy, could no longer convince the majority of socialists (or himself) that bourgeois governments stood for anything other than "monk hunting" and the protection of private property. The class struggle had gotten lost, it seemed, in the struggle for Dreyfus. In April 1905, under pressure from the socialist Second International (which condemned all forms of "ministerialism"), Jaurès rejoined his old rivals, Marxists and others, to help form France's first united socialist party, the French Section of the Workers' International. Temporary coalitions were still permitted with the center-left (and in that regard the affair left its mark), but the new revolutionary party prohibited the kind of collaboration that had brought the socialist Millerand into Waldeck-Rousseau's bourgeois fold. At the same time, while divided on domestic issues, Dreyfusards also split over foreign affairs. In 1905, when Germany threatened French interests in Morocco and war seemed imminent, socialists adhered to the internationalist policies of antipatriotism and antimilitarism, while the majority of their old allies, including Dreyfus himself, supported the army of the republic and pledged to protect the fatherland.

In the midst of that social, political, and religious whirlwind, the Dreyfus case finally came to a quiet close, as if in the eye of a storm. Nearly twelve years after the captain's arrest, the presiding justice of the Cour de Cassation took one hour to read the judgment aloud and then turned to its final paragraphs.

BALLOT-BEAUPRÉ
Annulment of the Rennes Verdict
July 12, 1906

Whereas, in the final analysis, nothing remains standing of the accusation against Dreyfus,

And that the annulment of the court-martial's verdict leaves nothing that could be qualified as a crime or misdemeanor;

Whereas by application of the final paragraph of article 445 of the Criminal Code, there should be no declaration of referral to another judicial venue;

On these grounds,

The court annuls the verdict of the court-martial of Rennes, which, on September 9, 1899, condemned Dreyfus to ten years of detention and military degradation . . . ;

Announces that it was by error and wrongfully that the condemnation was pronounced;

Records that Dreyfus renounces claim to monetary indemnity that would be granted him by virtue of article 446 of the Criminal Code;

Orders that . . . the present decision be posted in Paris and Rennes and inserted in the *Journal officiel,* as well as in fifty Parisian and provincial newspapers of Dreyfus's choice;

Authorizes Dreyfus to have it published at the expense of the Treasury and at the rates for legal insertions in fifty Parisian and provincial newspapers of his choice;

Orders that the decision be transcribed on the registers of the court-martial of Rennes and that mention be made in the margins of the annulled decision.

The decision to annul the Rennes verdict *sans renvoi* (without sending it back for a new trial) provided fuel for future generations of anti-Dreyfusards. Technically, the Cour de Cassation had no authority to acquit or convict; its charge was to "break" decisions and return them to the appropriate venue—in Dreyfus's case, to a military tribunal. The lawyer Mornard, however, anticipated the argument and stressed a fine point of law: When a verdict is annulled and no criminal charges "remain standing" against the accused, the high court may pass judgment *sans*

Joseph Reinach, *Histoire de l'affaire Dreyfus* (Paris: Fasquelle, 1929), 6:555.

renvoi. Furthermore, the Cour de Cassation may have willingly misinterpreted the law, as one scholar notes, in order to eliminate any further judicial proceedings in the affair.[9] Dreyfus still wanted to be acquitted by his fellow officers, but he knew—and the government feared—that a third court-martial could end in a third conviction. The civilian judgment stood, and Dreyfus's enemies took note. Time and again throughout the twentieth century, they would repeat that Alfred Dreyfus, in the domain of military justice, remained guilty of treason.

Through a law adopted by the Chamber of Deputies, however, the army officially rehabilitated Dreyfus, promoted him to major, and on July 20, 1906, awarded him the cross of the Knight of the Legion of Honor at the Ecole Militaire. As the ceremony unfolded, in a small courtyard only steps from the site of his degradation, Dreyfus could not push back the memories.

[9]I am grateful to Professor Benjamin F. Martin for his comments on the *sans renvoi* issue.

ALFRED DREYFUS

Painful Reverie

July 20, 1906

At 1:30 P.M. the honor guard, two mounted batteries and two squadrons of the First Armored Cavalry, lined up parallel to the three sides of the courtyard. . . .

At 1:55 P.M. the trumpets sounded. General Gillain, commandant of the First Cavalry Division, with a martial air and white mustache, walked forward. Taking long strides, he reviewed the troops. There was a heavy, impressive silence, and in that silence my mind, distracted, took flight, awakening the memories of a dozen years before, the shrieks of the crowd, the atrocious ceremony, my officer's stripes so wrongly torn away, my sword broken, its fragments scattered at my feet. . . . My heart beat to the point of breaking, blood rushed to my temples, sweat covered my brow. . . . Only through an immense effort of will could I regain control and not cry out all the anguish of my past.

Alfred Dreyfus, *Souvenirs et correspondance* (Paris: Grasset, 1936), 434–37.

The order "Trumpets and drums" wrenched me from my painful reverie and brought me back to refreshing reality. . . . General Gillain, his voice full of emotion, made the customary speech and, while fastening the badge of honor to my uniform, said quietly, "Commandant Dreyfus, I am delighted to be the one to confer on you the Legion of Honor. I know what excellent memories you have of the First Cavalry Division." He then gave me a hearty embrace, and tears came to his eyes. . . . The order "Forward march" rang out. Preceded by a flourish of trumpets, the troops marched past . . . , the officers raising their swords in salute. The brass instruments sang out high and clear on that day of joy.

The troops dispersed. Immediately I was surrounded by shouts of "Long live Dreyfus!" No, I exclaimed. "Long live the Republic; long live truth!" Hands were extended; I shook them with a nervous grip. I embraced my friends. . . . Anatole France approached and said, "I am very happy and very moved. I do not know how to do homage to the steadfastness you showed through so much suffering. It enabled us to accomplish the work of justice and reparation, and today's ceremony is its coronation. And so I shake your hand, unable to say more."

Then my son threw himself in my arms, followed by my wife, all my family. The delightful embrace of all those I love, of all those for whom I had the courage to live.

I went to find General Picquart, who attended the ceremony and who warmly shook my hand. I expressed all my gratitude. . . . But the emotions were too strong. Chest pains struck, and I suffered a momentary crisis. When I recovered, I departed in a carriage with my son. . . .

It was a glorious day of reparation for France and the Republic.

My affair was over. Lieutenant Colonel Picquart had been reinstated in the army with the rank of brigadier general, as compensation for the persecution he had suffered for having come to my defense. . . . If all those who had fought for justice, and who were still alive, had not been able to receive the same reward for the suffering they endured for truth, they found it, to be sure, in the satisfaction they felt deep within themselves and in the high regard that their sacrifices had earned from their contemporaries. And even if they seemed forgotten, fate was not unkind to them, for they struggled not only for a specific cause but contributed, in large part, to one of the most remarkable acts of rehabilitation that the world has ever witnessed, one of those acts that echoes into the distant future, because it will have marked a turning point in the history of humanity, a grand step toward an era of boundless progress for the ideas of liberty, justice, and social solidarity.

"No further passions, no further anger," wrote Joseph Reinach of the period immediately following the high court's annulment, "no more gusts

Figure 14. Postcard photograph, July 21, 1906, following the "parade of decoration." In a courtyard of the École Militaire, near the scene of his degradation, Dreyfus, second from right, wears the cross of the Knight of the Legion of Honor.

coming in from without. . . . No longer any doubt, not a single doubt as to Dreyfus's absolute innocence. No more Dreyfus affair."[10] Reinach, always a wishful thinker, may have captured the sentiments of his closest allies in the wake of 1906. But the Dreyfus affair, like the Revolution that preceded it by a century, never drew to a definitive close. Sometimes explicitly, more often indirectly, the affair and its conflicts reappeared throughout the century.

In 1908, when the government transferred Emile Zola's remains to the Panthéon, the secular repository of France's grand heroes, Louis-Anthelme Gregori, an old admirer of Edouard Drumont's, approached the invited guests and fired two shots at Alfred Dreyfus. The wound was slight, but the nationalist press treated the "courageous attack" as a "very French gesture" and as a major salvo in its ongoing revival. Swept

[10] Quoted in Bredin, *The Affair,* 479.

up in "patriotic exaltation," Gregori had aimed not at Dreyfus, he said in his defense, but at "Dreyfusism," and the jury agreed; the assailant could not be held accountable for an unpremeditated act of blind devotion.[11] From the other side came condemnations of the "odious and cowardly assault,"[12] as well as a private letter addressed to Dreyfus from one of his most renowned supporters. Sarah Bernhardt, at the height of her fame, had followed the case since the morning of Dreyfus's degradation. An assimilated Jew with the credentials, as an actor, to judge the 1895 "parade" as performance, she knew that the prisoner's protests of innocence rang true. Thirteen years later, in the aftermath of Gregori's attack, she wrote to the man she never met.

[11]See *Action Française* and *La Libre Parole,* June 5, 1908; *La Patrie,* June 6, 1908; and *Gaulois,* Sept. 12, 1908.
[12]*L'Aurore,* June 6, 1908.

SARAH BERNHARDT

Letter to Alfred Dreyfus

June 6, 1908

You have suffered again. We have cried again. But you should no longer suffer, and we should no longer cry. The flag of truth is placed in the hand of the illustrious man resting under the [Panthéon's] glorious arches. That flag will snap louder than the barking of the dog pack.

Suffer no more, our dear martyr. Look around you, close by, then farther on and farther on still, and see this crowd of people who love you and defend you against cowardice, lies, and the quest to forget. Your friend is among them.

Six years later, in the first month of the First World War, Dreyfus reentered the army just short of his fifty-fifth birthday and served with distinction, as did his son and Mathieu's son, who died in battle. References to their affair, however, met with censorship. As part of the "sacred

Alfred Dreyfus, *Souvenirs et correspondance* (Paris: Grasset, 1936), 442.

Figure 15. Film still, *L'Affaire Dreyfus,* 1899. George Méliès, a pioneering filmmaker, recreated the major events of the affair in his "realistic" eleven-reel motion picture. Here a Devil's Island official refuses to accept Dreyfus's petition.

Figure 16. Paul Muni (left) as the young Zola in a scene from the Academy Award–winning American motion picture *The Life of Emile Zola* (1938). The film, like the earlier work of Méliès, was banned in France.

union" of France (the suspension of political conflicts during the struggle for national defense), the government prohibited all motion pictures on the Dreyfus affair, including Georges Méliès's pioneering film, which had inflamed audiences when first released at the turn of the century. Memories of the army's darkest days, authorities noted, could again "trouble public order." Nor did the censorship end with the 1918 armistice; no motion picture dealing with the affair could be shown in the nation's cinemas until 1959. Citing "the possibility of riots," a series of governments also kept foreign films from entering the country, most notably the Academy Award–winning American movie *The Life of Emile*

Zola, which, as Prime Minister Edouard Daladier put it in 1938, "injured the honor of the French army."[13]

Daladier and his immediate predecessors had reason to fear the affair as art. In 1931 a French writer had adapted a German play on the Dreyfus case for the Théatre de l'Ambigu in Paris. A feeble drama soon to be forgotten, *L'Affaire Dreyfus* opened at a moment when militant nationalists were stepping up their attacks on the parliamentary republic. That corrupt system, they argued, could neither tame the early ravages of economic depression, nor turn back communism, nor keep out hordes of immigrants, many of them Orthodox Jews from Eastern and Central Europe. The Action Française, born of the Dreyfus affair and still led by Charles Maurras, now sixty-two years old, came of age with its assault on the affair's theatrical rendition. Hurling stink bombs into the theater and fighting along the streets outside, cane-wielding *Camelots du roi* (the heirs of the young baron who had attacked President Loubet) shouted, "Hang the Jews from the lampposts! Down with the Germans! Spit on Dreyfus!" It took twelve hundred police and the final closing of the play to restore order. The majority of protesters, too young to have fought in the first affair, had been raised on its memory, and the name Dreyfus had become a useful profanity in the nationalist lexicon.

But no event triggered more memories of the affair than the death of Alfred Dreyfus in 1935, at the age of seventy-five. His later years had been spent in quiet seclusion with his family in Paris, and though he outlived most of his allies and enemies, he never shed the symptoms of malaria or the specter of Devil's Island. Briefly, in the summer of 1927, his name reentered the news, in France and abroad, when a Paris-based committee, mobilized to protest the pending execution in the United States of two Italian immigrants, called on Dreyfus's "moral authority as the living symbol of injured innocence." Nicola Sacco and Bartolomeo Vanzetti, professed anarchists, had been convicted for murders connected with a holdup in a Massachusetts town. In what seemed to many observers like an American version of the Dreyfus affair, they had been condemned as much for their background as for

---

[13]Quoted in Antoine de Baecque, "L'Affaire au cinéma," in *L'Affaire Dreyfus de A à Z,* ed. Michel Drouin (Paris: Flammarion, 1994), 549.

the crime they denied committing. Dreyfus, who abhorred anarchism and saw few connections with his own affair, agreed that a "miscarriage of justice" may have taken place and warned, according to one news report, that the execution "would be the greatest moral disaster of many years, fraught with terrible consequences to American justice." But his interest in the case was "humane," not "political," and he asked to be left in peace. Years earlier, in a letter to an ally, he had summarized his place in the affair. "I was only an artillery officer," he wrote Victor Basch, "whom a tragic error prevented from pursuing his normal career. Dreyfus the symbol is not me. . . . It is you who created that Dreyfus."[14]

In the midsummer of 1935, in the days following Dreyfus's death, newspapers connected his affair to the contemporary crisis of French politics, to conflicts that pitted extreme nationalists against the new Popular Front of socialists, communists, and radicals. "Dreyfus has died," went one report on July 13, "at a moment when France seems divided again, as it had been for or against him." Léon Blum, Dreyfusard in his youth and soon to become the first socialist and first Jewish prime minister of France, responded to Dreyfus's death with seven articles published through the late summer. Inspired by "the wave of memories" that Dreyfus's passing "brought forth," Blum retraced the affair's grand struggles and lost opportunities. And with fascism on the rise, he recalled, as a warning, the timidity shown by many Jews in the face of anti-Semitism.

---

[14]*New York Times,* July 28, 1927; and *New York World,* Aug. 21, 1927. Dreyfus's letter to Basch is quoted in Stephen Wilson, *Ideology and Experience: Antisemitism in France at the Time of the Dreyfus Affair* (Rutherford, N.J.: Fairleigh Dickinson University Press, 1982), 1.

LÉON BLUM

Memories of the Affair

1935

In general Jews had accepted Dreyfus's condemnation as definitive and just. They did not speak about the affair among themselves; far from raising the subject, they avoided it. A great misfortune had fallen on Israel. They suffered it without uttering a word, and they waited for time and silence to efface the effects.

The majority of Jews even greeted the first steps of the campaign for revision with caution and suspicion. The dominant feeling was expressed by the formula, "This is something that Jews should not get mixed up in." In this complex sentiment, all the parts were not of equal quality. There was, to be sure, respect for the army, confidence in its leaders, a reluctance to consider them biased or weak, and all of it informed by patriotism, even by a timid patriotism. But there was also a sort of egoistic and fearful prudence that one might qualify in more severe terms. Jews did not want anyone to believe that they defended Dreyfus because Dreyfus was Jewish. They did not want anyone to impute their attitude to a difference or a solidarity of race. Above all, by coming to the defense of another Jew, they did not want to fuel the anti-Semitic passion that raged at that time with marked intensity. . . .

Rich Jews, middle-class Jews, Jewish functionaries were afraid of the struggle for Dreyfus just as they are afraid today of the struggle against fascism. They think only of digging themselves in and hiding. They imagined that anti-Semitic passion would be warded off by their timid neutrality. Secretly, they cursed those among them who, in coming forward, delivered them up to the old misfortune. They did not understand then, any better than they understand today, that no precaution, no pretense fooled the adversary, and that they remained victims offered up by triumphant anti-Dreyfusism or fascism. . . .

In writing these memoirs, I have no other purpose than to evoke the human cause, which was so glorious, which was able to touch, without distinction, all men. I have yielded, above all, to the desire to restore, to communicate, before it becomes completely unintelligible, the state of mind and passion that I felt, that was felt by the generations that framed my own. . . .

The "Affair" I have just recalled was won, plainly and completely won, since Dreyfus was able to serve during the [1914–18] war with his officer's stripes; since he has just died, old, at peace, and among his family and friends; since there no longer exists anywhere in the world, in any coun-

---

Léon Blum, *Souvenirs sur l'affaire* (Paris: Gallimard, 1981), 42–44, 149–53.

try, a single thinking person who can harbor a doubt about his innocence; since the history that will carry his name and his legendary adventure has already rendered its judgment. The other Affair, or rather the aftereffect of the Affair, which developed into a political battle, was fated to leave behind only a precarious and uncertain result. . . .

The other "Affair" was neither won nor lost. We had not succeeded in bringing about revolutionary change. . . . The crisis had traveled over the surface of violent and long passions; it had not shaken the country to its depths. Once the cyclone passed, France found itself almost exactly as it had always been. . . . As the tossing waves ebbed, the same ocean reappeared under the same sky; we saw the same world form again. Before or after the "Affair," before or after the war, what had fundamentally transformed in France?

Is it true, as one hears repeated often, that collective life in France obeys a singular law of stability? It is possible. For a century and a half, revolutionary changes succeeded each other in France at very short intervals, but one could claim reasonably enough that . . . they altered only the outward appearances. . . . But how could the law of stability be particular to France when the facts it claims to express are not? Great political crises have transformed England no more than they have transformed France. Even at this moment, do we not feel the worst obsessions weigh upon us daily—of living again in the Europe of 1914, of seeing political forces gather again under the same signs and according to the same devices?

Must we look, then, for an explanation in the materialist philosophy of history? If, after the "Affair" or the war, society returned silently into itself, is it because . . . social relations had not been altered, because nothing had affected the "human condition," nothing had affected work, earnings, social security, the way people housed, fed, and clothed themselves, the way wealth was acquired, exploited, and passed on? This is what must be affected, as it had been with the Revolution of 1789. Then . . . the grand movement of water, which forever transforms the surface, will arise from the depths of the great sea. Is that why historic crises like the "Affair" and the war have left fewer marks on the world than a simple crisis of industrial "overproduction"? . . . I offer these reflections, or rather these questions, to the reader because they emerge naturally from my subject, but I have no desire to linger there; even I resist pursuing them. They would bring me back to the present after a few hours far away, recalling the past, remembering the days of youth, the "time refound," the lost friends.

Blum's assessment of Jewish reactions to the Dreyfus case revealed more about the tensions of the 1930s than about the realities of the affair. With France threatened by an armed and international anti-Semitism, as well as a resurgent anti-Dreyfusard movement from within,

Blum lamented that his coreligionists had not been more resistant, more explosively active through the fin de siècle. But, in fact, significant numbers of rich and middle-class Jews had populated the Dreyfusard ranks, and if their motivation had not been "revolutionary," as Blum had wished, their commitment to the republic had been courageous and, in the end, effective. Beyond a doubt, many French Jews had shown timidity. But caution, indifference, and even ignorance of the affair marked what might well have been the majority of the French population. Furthermore, absent from Blum's "wave" of memories were the duels fought by Jewish officers against anti-Semitic journalists and the recognition that Alfred Dreyfus himself, by surviving Devil's Island and refusing to retreat after Rennes, had fought perhaps the most heroic battle of all. When Blum, with a rhetorical flourish, asked in another section of his memoirs, "If Dreyfus had not been Dreyfus, would he have been a 'Dreyfusard'? " he revealed his misunderstanding of the man.[15] When he focused on the affair as a failed opportunity in the history of revolutionary socialism, he oversimplified a complicated struggle that survived as a symbol with many facets. Still, if Blum's history of the affair was, in many ways, partial, his call for action in the face of fascism captured the same courage that he and others had displayed in the fight for Dreyfus.

Five summers later, in June 1940, the seventy-year-old Third Republic fell to a German invasion from without and collaboration from within. The government of the new French state, established in the town of Vichy, imprisoned political opponents (including Léon Blum); enacted a series of anti-Jewish laws; purged schoolbooks of references to the innocence of Captain Dreyfus; staged a festival to honor the memory of Edouard Drumont; and established a Commissariat for Jewish Affairs, to the helm of which would come Charles Mercier du Paty de Clam, descendant of Dreyfus's first interrogator. And beyond the dreams of its German masters, the new French state worked to rid the fatherland first of Jewish immigrants and then of Jewish citizens involved in the Resistance against Vichy. While Lucie Dreyfus, well into her seventies, spent those years on the run and, near the end, sheltered by Catholic nuns, her children and grandchildren spent it in the Resistance. Madeleine, the granddaughter who had been closest to Alfred Dreyfus during his twilight years, who had accompanied him to movie theaters and stamp-

[15]Léon Blum, *Souvenirs de l'affaire* (Paris: Gallimord, 1981), 34.

collecting booths near the Champs-Elysées, was denounced by French collaborators and sent by the Gestapo to her death at Auschwitz.

"What made France fall," wrote political philosopher Hannah Arendt in the depths of the Second World War, "was the fact that she had no more true Dreyfusards, no one who believed that democracy and freedom, equality and justice could any longer be defined or realized under the republic."[16] Arendt exaggerated to make a point. She was right about those members of the National Assembly who voted in 1940 to bury the republic and capitulate to Hitler, and her assessment applied to the old nationalist warriors and young fascist crusaders who, throughout the Vichy period, defined democracy as decadence and pinned every evil in France on a Judeo-Masonic conspiracy. But the Resistance to Vichy and German occupation, however limited at the outset and fractured at the end, had among its combatants "true Dreyfusards," as Charles Maurras made clear at the close of his trial in 1945. Convicted by a French court of "intelligence with the enemy," sentenced to "national degradation" and life imprisonment, the seventy-six-year-old leader of the Action Française denounced the verdict as "the revenge of Dreyfus!"[17]

Parallels should not be tightly drawn. Vichy and the fight against that regime was not the Dreyfus affair reborn. Much more was at stake, vastly more people perished, the French state of 1940–44 actively persecuted Jews, Germany did not remain aloof as it had in the 1890s, and many communist members of the Resistance, unlike most of the socialists led by Jean Jaurès, cared little about republicanism and even less about liberty. But as a symbol of civil war, of the fight waged by the citizens of a single nation over what it meant to be French, the Dreyfus affair had resonance during the Vichy epoch, just as it would have during the Algerian conflict that divided France for more than fifteen years following the Second World War. Other frames of reference, from Vichy to Vietnam, were more powerful for being more recent, but when the Algerian crisis engaged the republic's civilian government against renegade factions of its own army, not a few observers drew comparisons with the conflicts of the affair.

"France for the French!" the rallying cry made popular by Drumont's *La Libre Parole,* survived the century and reemerged during the new fin de siècle as the proud slogan of the extreme right. Jewish immigration

---

[16]Hannah Arendt, "From the Dreyfus Affair to France Today," *Jewish Social Studies* 4 (July 1942):195–240.

[17]*Le Procès de Charles Maurras* (Paris: Albin Michel, 1946), 371.

had fueled fears and shaped the politics of anti-Semitism through the 1880s and 1890s, as it did again throughout the 1930s. But in the closing years of the twentieth century, while anti-Semitism survived in France, North Africans—mostly Muslims, though race mattered more than faith—became the primary targets of the nation's new "anti-Dreyfusards." For the National Front party, as for their ideological ancestors during the Dreyfus epoch, France was again threatened by enemies within. And in the spirit of the old anti-Dreyfusard Léon Daudet, the new right championed "the closed ranks" as "our ranks."[18]

Against that backdrop of xenophobia, the affair still had power to provoke. In 1985, two years after the socialist president François Mitterrand commissioned a statue of Alfred Dreyfus, the army, defining the monument as a symbol of division and a memory of humiliation, refused to accept it for the Ecole Militaire. It remained in storage until its unveiling in a corner of the Tuileries gardens in 1988. A few days after that event, swastikas and anti-Semitic profanities were found scratched on Dreyfus's tomb in the Montparnasse cemetery. In 1994, during the centennial commemorations of Dreyfus's arrest, the head of the army's Historical Section published a summary of the affair that prompted an outcry, not only in the left-wing press and among Jewish organizations, but in the chambers of a conservative government. Colonel Paul Gaujac's account, though correct in many details, virtually ignores the crimes of the General Staff, defines the Dreyfusard campaign as a radical quest to destabilize the army, and closes with the most provocative comment of all.

[18]See Léon Daudet, "The Punishment," in Chap. 3 above.

COLONEL PAUL GAUJAC

A Theory of Innocence
January 31, 1994

On the one side, Dreyfusards recruited above all from the ranks of the left, notably from republicans dissatisfied with compulsory military service who find [in the affair] an opportunity to try to destroy the military caste. They are joined by Freemasons, radicals, and socialists (Jaurès), as well

Sirpa actualité, Jan. 31, 1994, quoted in *Le Monde,* Feb. 10, 1994.

as by the League of the Rights of Man. On the other side, the right, which tries, in the context of preparation for war with Germany, to counter the attempts to destabilize the army. Personalities such as Barrès and Maurras are backed by the champions of anti-Semitism and by Catholics. They form the League of the French Fatherland. . . .

Today three principal consequences of the affair are acknowledged:

Political consequences: the revision [of the Dreyfus case] is maintained to be a republican victory that allows for the integration of socialism into the parliamentary system. *A contrario,* it also contributes to giving new vigor to the right, which finds it own form of alliance.

Military consequences: the essential result is the dismantling of the French intelligence service and the reduction of funds for the armed forces at a time of German rearming.

Consequences for the Jewish community: given the importance of the affair in developing the ideas of Theodor Herzl, and of drawing attention to them, it is considered as the starting point of the Zionist movement.

Today Dreyfus's innocence is the thesis generally accepted by historians. To the political affair was also grafted an affair of counterespionage directed against German intelligence, and still, to this day, no one is prepared to state if Dreyfus had been a conscious or unconscious victim.

Minister of Defense François Léotard, reacting with "black fury" at the army's attempt "to unearth an old civil war," quickly removed Colonel Gaujac from his post. A short time later the government announced its "complete" and official support of a new film on the Dreyfus affair, including permission to use the courtyard of the Ecole Militaire and soldiers of the Republican Guard. On September 7, 1995, a special screening of that motion picture, sponsored by France's Central Jewish Consistory, drew an invited audience of nearly two thousand to Paris's Hotel de Ville. It also drew the new chief of the army's Historical Section, General Jean-Louis Morrut, in full dress uniform and on an official mission to shatter a century of silence. "The army's position is clear," the general announced. "Dreyfus was innocent," the victim of "a military conspiracy, in part based on a fraudulent document, which led to the conviction and deportation of an innocent man."[19]

As one observer noted, the army "said what needed to be said." And yet, during the same period, rallies organized by the National Front offered copies of a recent book with a title drawn from the General Staff's secret dossier. André Figueras's *Ce canaille de Dreyfus* (That Scoundrel

---

[19]*Libération,* Sept. 12, 1995.

Dreyfus) portrays the captain guilty as charged and defines the affair as a massive affront to the fatherland.

January 1998 marked yet another centennial, the anniversary of Zola's "J'Accuse," one of the most famous manifestos of the modern era.[20] France's conservative president, Jacques Chirac, like his socialist predecessor, François Mitterrand, understood that the affair's legacies lived on and that two ideas of France were encoded in its memory. Celebrating the novelist's courage and reaffirming the captain's innocence, Chirac addressed a public letter to the descendants of the Zola and Dreyfus families.

[20]On the centenary of "J'Accuse," see *Les Cahiers naturalistes* 72 (1998).

JACQUES CHIRAC, PRESIDENT OF THE REPUBLIC

Letter on the Centenary of "J'Accuse"

January 1998

Precisely one century ago, France experienced a grave and profound crisis. The Dreyfus Affair, like the blade of a plow, tore French society apart; it separated families and divided the country into two enemy camps that confronted each other with extraordinary violence. Because Captain Dreyfus must at all costs remain guilty, the trials that succeeded each other were only pitiful mascarades. After his officer's stripes were ripped away and his sword broken, Dreyfus paid dearly on Devil's Island for the treacherous schemes hidden away in some office.

Despite the tenacity of Captain Dreyfus's family, the affair had to be disposed of. A dismal task, unworthy of our country and our history, a colossal judicial error, and a shameful surrender of the State's principles. But a man rose up against the lie, the baseness, and the cowardice. Shocked at the injustice against Captain Dreyfus, whose only crime was to be Jewish, Emile Zola launched his famous cry "J'Accuse." Published on January 13, 1898, in *L'Aurore,* that text struck like lightning and, in a few hours, changed the destiny of the Affair. Truth was on the march.

On that day Emile Zola addressed himself to the President of the Republic. Today we celebrate the centenary of that letter, which has entered into History. Today I would like to tell the Zola and Dreyfus families how

Jacques Chirac, "Letter on the Centenary of 'J'Accuse,' " January 1998, Dreyfus family private collection.

grateful France is to their ancestors. With admirable courage, they devoted themselves to the values of liberty, dignity, and justice.

Let us never forget that the man who was rehabilitated to shouts of "Long live Dreyfus!" responded in a strong voice, "No, long live France!" Despite the humiliation, the exile, the suffering, the blows to his body and soul and dignity, Captain Dreyfus knew how to forgive. Magnificent forgiveness, magnificent response: the love of the Fatherland against intolerance and hatred.

Let us never forget the courage of a great writer who, taking every risk, putting his tranquillity, his fame, even his life in peril, dared to pick up his pen and place his talent in the service of truth. Emile Zola, a literary and moral figure of high eminence, understood that it was his responsibility to shed light, that it was his duty to speak when others remained silent. In the line of Voltaire, he embodies the finest intellectual tradition.

Captain Dreyfus's tragedy took place a century ago. However, after so many years, it speaks to our hearts in a powerful way. Zola's text rests in our collective memory as "a moment in the conscience of humanity."

A half-century after Vichy, we know that sinister forces, intolerance, injustice, can creep into the state's highest level. But we also know that at moments of truth, France—grand, strong, unified, and vigilant—knows how to find its way again, and for the better. Without a doubt, that is what Emile Zola and Alfred Dreyfus are saying to us across the years. Because they had faith in our common values, the values of the Nation and the Republic, and because they loved the country so deeply, those two exceptional men were able to reconcile France with herself.

Let us never forget this magisterial lesson of love and unity.

In the 1990s a French poll revealed that nearly 70 percent of the population considered "the lessons of the Dreyfus affair still of present interest." With France engaged "in a constant state of spiritual civil war," added one of the most acute critics of the twentieth century, "the Dreyfus case is by no means over yet."[21]

Centuries turn, and Zola's "Fifth Act" plays on.

---

[21]George Steiner, "Totem or Taboo," *Salmagundi* 89–90 (Fall 1990–Winter 1991): 385–98. For the results of the French poll, see Marc Knobel, "En cette année 1994 . . . L'affaire Dreyfus," *Les Cahiers naturalistes* 69 (1995): 302.

Chronology of Events
Related to the Dreyfus Affair
(1859–1998)

1859
Alfred Dreyfus born in Mulhouse, in the eastern French province of Alsace.

1870
Franco-Prussian War and defeat of the Second French Empire.

Third Republic proclaimed in France.

1871
Treaty of Frankfurt ends the Franco-Prussian War.

Paris Commune.

1889
General Georges Boulanger, former minister of war, elected to the Chamber of Deputies.

1892
Edouard Drumont's newspaper *La Libre Parole* launches attacks on Jews in the army.

1894
September   Military memorandum (bordereau) reaches the Statistical Section of the French General Staff.

October 15   Captain Alfred Dreyfus arrested.

October 31–November 1   Newspapers *Le Soir* and *La Libre Parole* reveal Dreyfus's name as the traitor.

December 19–22   Court-martial held in closed session.

December 22   Dreyfus convicted by unanimous vote.

1895
January 5   Military degradation of Dreyfus at the Ecole Militaire.

January 17   Félix Faure elected president of the republic.

February   First meeting of Mathieu Dreyfus and Bernard Lazare.

April 14   Dreyfus imprisoned on Devil's Island.

July 1   Lieutenant Colonel Georges Picquart named chief of the Statistical Section.

1896

March   Picquart discovers a telegram *(petit bleu)* implicating a French officer in treason.

August   Picquart concludes that Commandant Ferdinand Walsin-Esterhazy wrote the bordereau.

September   Mathieu Dreyfus, hoping to respark interest in the case, arranges a false report of his brother's escape from Devil's Island.

September 15   Newspaper *L'Eclair* reveals the existence of a secret dossier during Dreyfus's 1894 court-martial.

September 18   Lucie Dreyfus petitions the Chamber of Deputies, demanding a review of her husband's case.

November   The Army General Staff transfers Picquart to eastern France, then to North Africa.

November 2   Commandant Hubert Henry's forged letter, naming Dreyfus as the traitor, arrives at the War Ministry.

November 6   Bernard Lazare publishes, in Brussels, *Une Erreur judiciaire: La Verité sur l'affaire Dreyfus* (A Judicial Error: The Truth about the Dreyfus Case).

November 10   Newspaper *Le Matin* publishes facsimile of the bordereau.

1897

February   Reorganization of the Antisemitic League of France.

June   Picquart confides to Louis Leblois, a lawyer, his knowledge of Dreyfus's innocence and Esterhazy's guilt.

July 13   Leblois divulges Picquart's information to Auguste Scheurer-Kestner, vice president of the Senate.

October 19   "Espérance" letter warns Commandant Esterhazy of the investigation.

October 29–November 5   Esterhazy's letters to the president of the republic.

November 16   Mathieu Dreyfus denounces Esterhazy in an open letter to the minister of war.

November 25   Emile Zola publishes "M. Scheurer-Kestner" in *Le Figaro*.

November 28   Publication of Esterhazy's "Uhlan" letter in *Le Figaro*.

1898

January 10–11   Esterhazy's court-martial and acquittal.

January 13   Newspaper *L'Aurore* publishes Emile Zola's "J'Accuse: Letter to the President of the Republic."

January 13   Picquart arrested and held in Mont Valérien Fortress, released and discharged from the army in February.

January–February   Anti-Semitic riots in France and Algeria.

February 7–23   Zola tried and found guilty of libel.

June 4   First general assembly of the pro-Dreyfus League of the Rights of Man.

July 7   Minister of War Cavaignac, convinced of Dreyfus's guilt, presents evidence, including the Henry forgery, to the Chamber of Deputies.

July 13   Picquart arrested for divulging military secrets; held in Santé Prison.

July 18–19   Zola, reconvicted by the Versailles court, flees to England.

August 13   Henry's forgery discovered by Captain Cuignet, attaché to Minister Cavaignac.

August 27   Esterhazy cashiered by the army for "habitual misconduct."

August 30   Henry arrested and imprisoned at Mont Valérien.

August 31   Henry commits suicide; Army Chief of Staff General Raoul de Boisdeffre resigns.

September 1   Esterhazy flees to Belgium, then England.

September 3   Lucie Dreyfus petitions for an appeal of the 1894 judgment.

December 1898–January 1899   *La Libre Parole* calls for contributions to support Colonel Henry's widow (the "Henry Monument").

December 31   Foundation of the anti-Dreyfus League of the French Fatherland.

1899

February 16–18   Death of President Félix Faure and election of Emile Loubet as president of the republic.

February 23   Members of the League of Patriots and other anti-Dreyfus organizations fail in their attempt to stage a coup on the day of Félix Faure's funeral.

June 3   Court sets aside Dreyfus's 1894 verdict and orders a new court-martial to be held in Rennes.

June 5   Emile Zola returns to France from England.

June 9   Dreyfus, after more than four years on Devil's Island, leaves for France on the cruiser *Sfax*.

June 13   Picquart released from prison; all charges dismissed.

July 18   *Le Matin* reports that Esterhazy has admitted writing the bordereau, but under orders of Colonel Jean Sandherr, chief of the Statistical Section in 1894.

August 7–September 9   Court-martial in Rennes; Dreyfus reconvicted with "extenuating circumstances."

September 19   Dreyfus accepts presidential pardon; Auguste Scheurer-Kestner dies.

Georges Méliès's eleven-reel motion picture *L'Affaire Dreyfus* is released and then banned by the government.

1900
April 15   Paris World's Fair opens.

December 27   Passage of Amnesty Law, covering all suits and prosecutions related to the Dreyfus affair.

1901
Publication of Dreyfus's memoirs, *Cinq années de ma vie* (Five Years of My Life), and the first volume of Joseph Reinach's *Histoire de l'affaire Dreyfus.*

1902
April–May   National elections lead to victory of the *bloc des gauches,* a coalition of parties of the left and center-left that had supported Dreyfus.

October 5   Emile Zola's funeral.

1903
September 2   Death of Bernard Lazare.

November 25   Dreyfus petitions for a retrial.

1904
March 5   Cour de Cassation orders review of the Rennes verdict.

1905
July   Parliament passes law separating church and state.

1906
July 12   Cour de Cassation annuls the Rennes verdict and orders Dreyfus's rehabilitation.

July 20   Dreyfus, promoted to major, receives the cross of the Knight of the Legion of Honor in a ceremony at the Ecole Militaire.

October   General Georges Picquart is named minister of war.

1907
Dreyfus retires from the army.

1908
June 4   During the ceremony marking the transfer of Emile Zola's ashes to the Panthéon, Dreyfus is shot and wounded by journalist Louis-Anthelme Gregori.

1914–1918
With the outbreak of war, Dreyfus returns to military service; promoted to lieutenant colonel, he is assigned to the defense of Paris.

1923
Esterhazy dies in England.

1930
October 22   Mathieu Dreyfus, principal organizer of his brother's affair, dies in Paris.

1931
February   Riots surround performances of *L'Affaire Dreyfus* at a Paris theater.

1935
July 11   Alfred Dreyfus dies in Paris.

Publication of Léon Blum's *Souvenirs sur l'affaire* (Memories of the Affair).

1938
French government bans the Academy Award–winning American film *The Life of Emile Zola.*

1945
January 27   Following the liberation of France, Charles Maurras, leader of the neo-royalist, anti-Dreyfusard Action Française is convicted of "intelligence with the enemy"; he calls the verdict "the revenge of Dreyfus."

December 14   Lucie Dreyfus dies in Paris.

1985
Statue of Alfred Dreyfus commissioned by President François Mitterrand and sculpted by Louis Mitelberg.

1994
On the centennial of Dreyfus's arrest, Colonel Paul Gaujac, head of the army's Historical Section, calls Dreyfus's innocence a "thesis generally accepted by historians"; the minister of defense removes Gaujac from his post.

1998
On the centennial of Emile Zola's "J'Accuse" President Jacques Chirac reconfirms Dreyfus's innocence and describes the affair as a part of the timeless struggle between the forces of intolerance and truth.

List of Principal Characters

Maurice Barrès. Novelist, journalist, nationalist politician, anti-Dreyfusard. Leading member of the League of the French Fatherland; reporter for *Le Journal* at Dreyfus's second court-martial.

General Raoul François Charles Le Mouton de Boisdeffre. Army chief of staff 1893–1898. Testified against Dreyfus; warned that the scandal weakened France and threatened war with Germany. Resigned following Colonel Henry's suicide in 1898.

Georges Clemenceau. Journalist, politician, Dreyfusard. Political editor of the newspaper *L'Aurore;* chose the title "J'Accuse" for Zola's open letter to the president of the republic. Argued against the presidential pardon of 1899 and for Dreyfus's full exoneration; condemned the Amnesty Law of 1900.

Edgar Demange. Renowned criminal attorney in charge of Captain Dreyfus's 1894 court-martial defense. Represented Mathieu Dreyfus at the Esterhazy court-martial in 1898. Served with Fernand Labori as co-counsel for the defense at Rennes in 1899.

Captain Alfred Dreyfus. Son of a prosperous textile manufacturer in Alsace, graduate of the Ecole Polytechnique and Ecole Supérieure de Guerre, assigned to the Army General Staff. Arrested in October 1894, accused of high treason, court-martialed in closed session, degraded, and deported to Devil's Island. Retried in 1899, reconvicted with "extenuating circumstances," and pardoned by the president of the republic. Rehabilitated and reinstated in the army in 1906; awarded the cross of the Knight of the Legion of Honor.

Lucie Dreyfus. Wife of Alfred Dreyfus, mother of two children, legal guardian of her husband's interests after the 1894 arrest. Worked closely with defense counsel. Petitioned the Chamber of Deputies in 1896; two years later successfully petitioned the Cour de Cassation for her husband's retrial.

Mathieu Dreyfus. Brother of Alfred Dreyfus, textile manufacturer, principal organizer of the Dreyfusard campaign. Recruited Edgar Demange,

Bernard Lazare, and other allies; issued the first public denunciation of Esterhazy; devoted five years and the family's fortune to securing his brother's release and defending the Dreyfus name.

Edouard Drumont. The most influential anti-Semitic writer of the epoch. Author of the best-selling *La France Juive* (Jewish France), director of the newspaper *La Libre Parole* (Free Speech). Condemned the presence of Jews in the army; emerged as a powerful anti-Dreyfusard leader.

Commandant Armand Mercier du Paty de Clam. Officer in charge of Dreyfus's arrest and prison interrogation. Investigated the captain's family and allies; helped compile the "secret dossier"; intrigued with Colonel Henry to protect Esterhazy.

Commandant Ferdinand Walsin-Esterhazy. French infantry officer, spy for the German attaché in Paris. Protected by members of the General Staff; court-martialed in 1898 and acquitted. Fled to England following Henry's suicide. Later insisted he had written the bordereau as a double agent under orders of the French army's Statistical Section.

Félix Faure. Sixth president of the Third Republic (1895–99). Opposed revision of the Dreyfus case. Died in office; funeral became setting for failed coup by anti-Dreyfusards.

Gyp (Sibylle-Gabrielle Marie-Antoinette de Riqueti de Mirabeau, Comtesse de Martel de Janville). Novelist, journalist, anti-Dreyfusard. Self-described professional anti-Semite; reported on the Zola trial; published attacks on Dreyfus's defenders in *La Libre Parole* and other militant nationalist newspapers.

Commandant Hubert-Joseph Henry. Officer in the army's Statistical Section; later promoted to head of that intelligence office. Co-conspirator in the plot to frame Dreyfus; forged documents for the "secret dossier." Arrested in 1898; committed suicide in prison. Praised by extreme nationalists and anti-Semites as a hero and martyr.

Jean Jaurès. Leading socialist in the Chamber of Deputies, historian, journalist, active Dreyfusard after 1898. Advocated socialist participation in the parliamentary republic until 1904, when, turning against ministerialism, he embraced socialist unity.

Bernard Lazare. Anarchist writer, author of *Antisemitism: Its History and Causes* (1894), early Dreyfusard, Jewish nationalist. Published first pamphlet in defense of Dreyfus, *A Judicial Error,* in 1896. Helped recruit key Dreyfusard allies.

General Auguste Mercier. Minister of war responsible for Dreyfus's arrest. Testified at every major trial; refused to open the "secret dossier" on grounds of national security. Replaced as minister of war in 1896; later elected to the French Senate.

Charles Péguy. Poet, journalist, Dreyfusard. Recruited to the Dreyfus campaign by Lucien Herr, socialist librarian of the Ecole Normale Supérieure. Signed first protest petitions of intellectuals in January 1898. Fierce critic of political opportunism on all sides; defined the essence of the affair as a spiritual quest for justice and truth.

Lieutenant Colonel Georges Picquart. With Emile Zola, the most popular Dreyfusard hero. Promoted to chief of the Statistical Section in 1895; discovered evidence of Esterhazy's treason. Clashed with General Staff colleagues; arrested in 1898, imprisoned; dismissed from the army. Reinstated in 1906 and promoted to general.

Joseph Reinach. Centrist (Opportunist) politician, journalist, historian, early Dreyfusard. Disciple of Léon Gambetta, one of the founders of the Third Republic in 1870–71. Primary target of anti-Semites throughout the 1880s and 1890s. Author of the seven-volume *Histoire de l'affaire Dreyfus* (1901–11).

Auguste Scheurer-Kestner. Vice president of the French Senate, Dreyfusard. Informed by Georges Picquart's lawyer of Dreyfus's innocence and Esterhazy's guilt in 1897. Subject of vicious press attacks by militant nationalists. Helped enlist Emile Zola in the Dreyfus campaign. Died on the day of Dreyfus's presidential pardon in 1899.

Maximilien von Schwartzkoppen. German military attaché in Paris, in charge of espionage operations. Worked closely with Italian attaché Colonel Alessandro Panizzardi. Employed Esterhazy as a spy in 1894.

Séverine (Caroline Rémy). Social activist, journalist, Dreyfusard. Director of the progressive newspaper *Le Cri du peuple,* then on the staff of *La Fronde,* France's first feminist daily. Reported on the Zola trial and the second Dreyfus court-martial at Rennes.

Emile Zola. Renowned novelist and, after 1897, committed Dreyfusard. Published "J'Accuse," an open letter to the president of the republic, on January 13, 1898. Galvanized public opinion; helped turn the judicial case into a national and international affair. Convicted of libel; fled to England; returned to France in 1899.

Selected Bibliography

BIBLIOGRAPHIES

Busi, Frederick. "A Bibliographical Overview of the Dreyfus Affair." *Jewish Social Studies* 40 (1978).
Drouin, Michel, ed. *L'Affaire Dreyfus de A à Z.* Paris: Flammarion, 1994.
Lipschutz, Léon. *Une Bibliographie dreyfusienne: Essai de bibliographie thématique et analytique de l'affaire Dreyfus.* Paris: Fasquelle, 1970.

PRIMARY SOURCES

Barrès, Maurice. *Scènes et doctrines du nationalisme.* Paris: Félix Juven, 1902.
Blum, Léon. *Souvenirs sur l'affaire.* 1935. Reprint, Paris: Gallimard, 1981.
Dreyfus, Alfred. *Carnets: 1899–1907.* Edited by Philippe Oriol. Paris: Calmann-Lévy, 1998.
———. *Cinq années de ma vie.* 1901. Reprint, Paris: La Découverte, 1994.
———. *Five Years of My Life.* New York: Peebles Press, 1977.
———. *Lettres d'un innocent.* Paris: Stock, 1898.
———. *Souvenirs et correspondance.* Paris: Grasset, 1936.
Dreyfus, Mathieu. *L'Affaire telle que je l'ai vécue.* Paris: Grasset, 1978.
Drumont, Edouard. *La France Juive: Essai d'histoire contemporaine.* 2 vols. Paris: Marpon et Flammarion, 1886.
Esterhazy, Ferdinand. *Les Dessous de l'affaire Dreyfus.* Paris: Fayard, 1898.
Grand-Carteret, John. *L'Affaire Dreyfus et l'image.* Paris: Flammarion, n.d. [1898?].
Halévy, Daniel. *Regards sur l'affaire Dreyfus.* Paris: De Fallois, 1994.
Jaurès, Jean. *Les Preuves: l'affaire Dreyfus.* Paris: La Petite République, 1898.
Jean-Bernard (J. B. Passerieu). *Le Procès de Rennes: Impression d'un spectateur.* Paris: Alphonse Lemerre, 1900.
Labori, Marguerite-Fernand. *Labori: Ses notes, sa vie.* Paris: Attinger, 1947.
Lazare, Bernard. *Une Erreur judiciaire: La Verité sur l'affaire Dreyfus.* Brussels: Vouve Monnom, 1896. (New edition with graphologists' reports, *Une Erreur judiciaire: l'affaire Dreyfus.* Paris: Stock, 1897.)

Paléologue, Maurice. *My Secret Diary of the Dreyfus Case.* Translated by Eric Mosbacher. London: Secker and Warburg, 1957.

Péguy, Charles. *Oeuvres en prose, 1909–1914.* Paris: Gallimard, 1967.

Pressensé, Francis de. *Un Héros. Le lieutenant-colonel Picquart.* Paris: Stock, 1898.

Proust, Marcel. *In Search of Lost Time.* Translated by C. K. Scott Moncrieff and Terence Kilmartin. Revised by D. J. Enright. London: Chatto and Windus, 1992.

———. *Jean Santeuil.* Paris: Gallimard, 1971.

Quillard, Pierre. *Le Monument Henry: Listes des souscripteurs classées méthodiquement et selon l'ordre alphabétique.* Paris: Stock, 1899.

Reinach, Joseph. *Histoire de l'affaire Dreyfus.* 7 vols. Paris: La Revue Blanche, 1901–11.

Repertoire de l'affaire Dreyfus: Dates et documents, 1894–1898. Paris: n.p., 1898.

Scheurer-Kestner, Auguste. *Mémoires d'un senateur dreyfusard.* Strasbourg: Beub et Reumaux, 1988.

Schwartzkoppen, Maximilien von. *Les Carnets de Schwartzkoppen: La Verité sur Dreyfus.* Paris: Rieder, 1930.

Séverine (Caroline Rémy). *Vers la lumière: Impressions vécues.* Paris: Stock, 1900.

Sorel, Georges. *La Révolution dreyfusienne.* Paris: M. Rivière, 1909.

Steevens, G. W. *The Tragedy of Dreyfus.* New York: Harper and Bros., 1899.

Zola, Emile. *The Dreyfus Affair: "J'Accuse" and Other Writings.* Edited by Alain Pagès. Translated by Eleanor Levieux. New Haven: Yale University Press, 1996.

———. *L'Affaire Dreyfus: La Verité en marche.* 1901. Reprint, Paris: Garnier-Flammarion, 1969.

SECONDARY SOURCES

Arendt, Hannah. "From the Dreyfus Affair to France Today." *Jewish Social Studies* 4 (July 1942).

———. *The Origins of Totalitarianism.* New York: Harvest, 1973.

Barrows, Susanna. *Distorting Mirrors: Visions of the Crowd in Late Nineteenth Century France.* New Haven: Yale University Press, 1981.

Baumont, Maurice. *Aux Sources de l'affaire: l'affaire Dreyfus d'après les Archives diplomatiques.* Paris: Productions de Paris, 1959.

Birnbaum, Pierre. *L'Affaire Dreyfus: La République en péril.* Paris: Gallimard, 1994.

Birnbaum, Pierre, ed. *La France de l'affaire Dreyfus.* Paris: Gallimard, 1994.

Bottomore, Stephen. "Dreyfus and Documentary." *Sight and Sound* 53, no. 4 (1984).

Boussel, Patrice. *L'Affaire Dreyfus et la presse.* Paris: Armand Colin, 1960.

Bredin, Jean Denis. *The Affair: The Case of Alfred Dreyfus.* Translated by Jeffrey Mehlman. New York: George Braziller, 1986.
———. *Bernard Lazare: De l'anarchiste au prophète.* Paris: De Fallois, 1992.
Brown, Frederick. *Zola: A Life.* New York: Farrar, Straus, & Giroux, 1995.
Burns, Michael. *Dreyfus: A Family Affair, 1789–1945.* New York: Harper-Collins, 1991.
———. *Rural Society and French Politics: Boulangism and the Dreyfus Affair, 1886–1900.* Princeton: Princeton University Press, 1984.
Busi, Frederick. *The Pope of Antisemitism: The Career and Legacy of Edouard-Adolphe Drumont.* New York: University Press of America, 1986.
Byrnes, Robert. *Antisemitism in Modern France.* New Brunswick, N.J.: Rutgers University Press, 1950.
Cahm, Eric. *The Dreyfus Affair in French Society and Politics.* London: Longman, 1997.
Chapman, Guy. *The Dreyfus Case: A Reassessment.* Westport, Conn.: Greenwood, 1979.
Charles, Christophe. *Naissance des intellectuels, 1880–1926.* Paris: Minuit, 1990.
Denis, Michel, Michel Lagrée, and Jean-Yves Veillard. *L'Affaire Dreyfus et l'opinion publique en France et à l'étranger.* Rennes: Presses Universitaires de Rennes, 1995.
Drouin, Michel, ed. *L'Affaire Dreyfus de A à Z.* Paris: Flammarion, 1994.
Duclert, Vincent. *L'Affaire Dreyfus.* Paris: La Découverte, 1994.
Feldman, Egal. *The Dreyfus Affair and the American Conscience.* Detroit: Wayne State University Press, 1981.
Fitch, Nancy. "Mass Culture, Mass Parliamentary Politics, and Modern Anti-Semitism: The Dreyfus Affair in Rural France." *American Historical Review* 97, no. 1 (February 1992).
Goldberg, Harvey. *The Life of Jean Jaurès.* Madison: University of Wisconsin Press, 1962.
Griffiths, Richard. *The Use of Abuse: The Polemics on the Dreyfus Affair and Its Aftermath.* New York: Berg, 1991.
Hyman, Paula. *From Dreyfus to Vichy: The Remaking of French Jewry.* New York: Columbia University Press, 1979.
Johnson, Douglas. *France and the Dreyfus Affair.* London: Blandford, 1966.
Kayser, Jacques. *L'Affaire Dreyfus.* Paris: Gallimard, 1946.
Kleeblatt, Norman L., ed. *The Dreyfus Affair: Art, Truth and Justice.* Berkeley: University of California Press, 1987.
Larkin, Maurice. *Church and State after the Dreyfus Affair.* New York: Harper and Row, 1974.
Lindemann, Albert S. *The Jew Accused: Three Anti-Semitic Affairs. Beilis, Frank, 1894–1915.* Cambridge: Cambridge Univers' 1991.

Lombarès, Michel de. *L'Affaire Dreyfus*. Paris: Lavauzelle, 1985.

Malino, Frances and Wasserstein, Bernard, eds. *The Jews in Modern France*. Hanover, N.H.: University Press of New England, 1985.

Marrus, Michael R. " 'En Famille': The Dreyfus Affair and Its Myths." *French Politics and Society* 12 (1994).

———. *The Politics of Assimilation: The French Jewish Community at the Time of the Dreyfus Affair*. Oxford: Oxford University Press, 1980.

Martin, Benjamin F. *Crime and Criminal Justice under the Third Republic: The Shame of Marianne*. Baton Rouge: Louisiana State University Press, 1990.

Miquel, P. *L'Affaire Dreyfus*. Paris: PUF, 1961.

Mitchell, Allan. "The Xenophobic Style: French Counterespionage and the Emergence of the Dreyfus Affair." *Journal of Modern History* 52 (1980).

Pagès, Alain. *Emile Zola: Un intellectuel dans l'affaire Dreyfus*. Paris: Seguier, 1991.

Peter, Jean-Pierre. "Dimensions de l'affaire Dreyfus." *Annales: Economies, Sociétés, Civilisations* 16 (November–December 1961).

Rémond, René. *The Right Wing in France from 1815 to de Gaulle*. Translated by James M. Laux. Philadelphia: University of Pennsylvania Press, 1965.

Silverman, Willa Z. *The Notorious Life of Gyp: Right-Wing Anarchist in Fin-de-Siècle France*. New York: Oxford University Press, 1995.

Snyder, Louis L. *The Dreyfus Case: A Documentary History*. New Brunswick, N.J.: Rutgers University Press, 1973.

Sorlin, Pierre. *Waldeck-Rousseau*. Paris: Armand Colin, 1966.

Sternhell, Zeev. *La Droite révolutionnaire, 1885–1914: Les Origines françaises du fascisme*. Paris: Seuil, 1978.

Thomas, Marcel. *Esterhazy, ou l'envers de l'affaire Dreyfus*. Paris: Vernal et Philippe Lebaud, 1989.

———. *L'Affaire sans Dreyfus*. Paris: Fayard, 1961.

Weber, Eugen. *Action Française: Royalism and Reaction in Twentieth Century France*. Stanford: Stanford University Press, 1962.

———. *France, Fin de Siècle*. Cambridge, Mass.: Belknap, 1986.

———. *The Nationalist Revival in France, 1905–1914*. Berkeley: University of California Press, 1959.

Wilson, Nelly. *Bernard Lazare: Antisemitism and the Problem of Jewish Identity in Late Nineteenth Century France*. Cambridge: Cambridge University Press, 1978.

Wilson, Stephen. *Ideology and Experience: Antisemitism in France at the Time of the Dreyfus Affair*. Rutherford, N.J.: Fairleigh Dickinson University Press, 1982.

Index